Tales from the
OLD INLAND WATERWAYS

BROTHERS

Tales from the
OLD INLAND WATERWAYS

EUAN CORRIE

For present-day managers of inland waterways; in the hope that they might remember that the knowledge and experience of those who preceded them is at least as valuable as modern methods and computerised databases

Page 1: A pair of ex-Grand Union Canal Carrying Co narrowboats, now part of the nationalised British Waterways fleet, head southwards from Braunston Tunnel in the late 1950s (Author's collection)

Page 2: A Trent Ketch of the type that monopolised the upriver trade before the construction of the large locks described by George Trevethick

Page 3: The Grand Union Canal Carrying Co's layby at Bull's Bridge Depot, near Southall in Middlesex, in the 1940s. The long line of narrowboats tied stern on to the canal wall are awaiting orders for loading in the London area whilst their crews catch up on domestic chores and routine maintenance. Behind the camera was a complex of offices, workshops, stores, drydocks and slipways, where even the heaviest repair work was carried out
(British Waterways Archives, Gloucester)

Page 5: Ernie Poole leading his horse through Lymm on the Bridgwater Canal, while at the same time holding the nose bowl for the midday feed. The boat, which can just be seen approaching the bridge, is Trixie. *This photograph was taken on 14 September 1932, and the original print from which this copy was produced unfortunately gives the impression of having been in somebody's pocket ever since!* (Jack Poole)

Author's note: Subsequent to the first edition of this book, George Wood died (February 1998), artist Edward Paget-Tomlinson died (November 2003) and Harry Bentley has also died.

Jacket illustrations: (front cover) Much of what is remembered as best about the carrying narrowboats of Britain's canals was preserved right up to the end of long-distance carrying by the Willow Wren company as seen here. *Tern* and *Snipe* are resplendent in traditional 'roses and castles' paintwork with polished brass and scrubbed white ropework. On the morning of 6 July 1959 Mr & Mrs Bill Wilson were waiting at Cassio Bridge, Watford, to deliver coal from Warwickshire to Dickinsons' paper mills at Croxley (Leslie Reason)
(back cover) A pair of Grand Union Canal Co boats in Sandiacre Bottom Lock on the Derby Canal. Ralph Mould (on the motor boat gunwale) was with Dick Boswell (steering) and Bill Rogers (on the lockside) trying to force a passage up the virtually derelict, if legally navigable, canal from its junction with the Erewash Canal below this unworkable lock (*Leslie Hales*)

A DAVID & CHARLES BOOK
David & Charles is a subsidiary of F+W (UK) Ltd.,
an F+W Publications Inc. company

First published in the UK in 1998
Reprinted 2005
First paperback edition 2005

A catalogue record for this book is available from the British Library.

ISBN 0 7153 0542 5 hardback
ISBN 07153 2294 X paperback

Maps and plans by Richard Dean (www.cartographics.co.uk)
Portraits by John Paley
All other artworks by Edward Paget-Tomlinson

Typeset by ABM Typographics Ltd, Hull
Printed in United Kingdom by Butler & Tanner Ltd
for David & Charles
Brunel House Newton Abbot Devon

CONTENTS

INTRODUCTION

Inland waterway transport has been important to the inhabitants of the British Isles since before the Romans built their Fossdyke Navigation and improved the river Witham to serve their settlement at Lincoln. In the Middle Ages, material for cathedrals was often brought to the site by water although there is evidence to suggest that this mode of transport was well known to the builders of Stonehenge. However, the first 'modern' canals were principally schemes to improve the navigation of rivers, such as the Exeter Ship Canal which parallels the Exe estuary, in Devon. The first wholly artificial navigation in this country, independent of any river's course, was built by the Duke of Bridgewater; the first section was opened in 1761.

Part of the duke's education had involved a tour of Europe to absorb some of the continent's culture. One of the most notable wonders he visited was the Canal du Midi, in France, which had been opened in 1681 to provide a link between the Atlantic and the Mediterranean, and it seems likely that this great work of civil engineering made a permanent impression upon the young duke. Returning to England, he devoted the rest of his life to the management and improvement of his various estates; amongst these was land at Worsley a few miles from the small town of Manchester. It included small coalpits, but their product was only sold locally since transport costs ruled out much use in Manchester or further afield. However, the duke conceived the idea of a canal to carry his coal to the growing population of Manchester. His brother-in-law, Lord Gower, had engaged an ill-educated millwright, James Brindley, who came from Pennine Derbyshire, to survey part of what was later to become the Trent & Mersey Canal. Brindley has been described as a 'schemer' and it is not clear how much of the credit for the subsequent construction of the duke's canal should be apportioned to him as opposed to the duke's agent John Gilbert. Certainly Brindley spent much time at Worsley Hall in the early 1760s. It had been intended to construct a canal to Salford on the river Irwell's west bank, and cart coal over the river to the larger town of Manchester. It seems likely that Brindley first suggested diverting the canal into Manchester itself, rather than the more easily accessed Salford. It also seems that John Gilbert tackled many of the engineering problems, including making the resulting aqueduct over the river Irwell watertight when it threatened to collapse. The canal was opened through to Manchester in 1763.

The Bridgewater Canal was an immediate success, halving the price of coal to Manchester's poor, as well as its industries, overnight, and plans were already in hand for the canal's extension through Cheshire to the Mersey near Runcorn which would give access to the estuary and so to the port of Liverpool. Brindley was already collaborating with the potter Josiah Wedgwood and others in projecting the canal from the Mersey to the river Trent, and was soon to be involved in more projects throughout the country than he could possibly undertake. He died before the majority were complete at only fifty-five years of age as a result of overwork compounded by a chill caught whilst surveying. He had meanwhile suggested a grand cross scheme of waterways to link the Mersey, Severn, Trent and Thames.

Few, however, had Brindley's breadth of vision. Whilst the waterways with which he was

(Above) A posed view of Fellows Morton & Clayton's Stafford *at Brentford in 1924 with members of the Ward family. It seems likely that this is the local canal boat inspector checking up on the condition and cleanliness of the cabin. It is not so likely that all those present lived in the one cabin which would have been registered for occupation by a maximum of two adults and two children. Notice the usual, everyday clothing of the boat people; white aprons did not long remain pristine walking behind the horse or loading and unloading dirty cargoes and handed down cast-offs were the order for children, except for the more often photographed Sunday best* (Boat Museum – Ware collection)

(Above left) Jim Preston waits at the Dutton entrance to Preston Brook Tunnel with his W. H. Cowburn & Cowpar motor boat Swan *in the late 1930s. He was returning from Courtaulds' man-made fibres plant at Coventry to Trafford Park for another load of the chemical raw materials which were at the time considered too dangerous for road or rail transport* (Mary Gibby)

involved were generally built to accommodate what became known as narrowboats, which were intended to pass from end to end of the country, most waterways were devised for purely local purposes. As a result locks and bridges were generally built to accommodate the craft already in use on the nearest estuary or river navigation. Thus even to this day, broad canals radiate from the Thames, Mersey and Humber but they are interconnected by narrow canals which accommodate boats of only 7ft beam. This situation reaches heights of incomprehensible confusion in the north where local Mersey barges (known as 'flats') up to 74ft by 14ft 6in can enter the Bridgewater or Leeds & Liverpool canals from the Mersey, can pass into the Rochdale Canal at Manchester, but then cannot pass out of it into the Ashton and Huddersfield Narrow canals which are narrow-beamed. Crossing the Pennines these flats could reach the Huddersfield Broad Canal which is wide enough for them, but whose locks are only 57ft long, matching the Humber barge (or 'keel'). An alternative trans-Pennine route appears on the map as the Leeds & Liverpool Canal, but whereas this accommodates the long boats at its western extremity, these cannot pass through the 62ft locks beyond Wigan. At Leeds this canal discharges into the Aire & Calder Navigation whose locks have been, by stages, lengthened to over 450ft and can accommodate 650 ton barges!

The system gradually expanded until there were over 4,250 miles of non-tidal inland navigation on the British mainland. Roughly three-quarters of this mileage remains available to pleasure craft, and enthusiasts have restoration schemes in hand for a high proportion of the remainder, although some of these are very long term.

The canal companies never realised the advantages of co-operation in matters of gauge, through freight rates, tolls and so on, as the railways did from earliest days. As a result these

The confined but practical layout of a narrowboat cabin looking astern from the bed

primarily local undertakings remained so for their almost 200-year commercial history. As a consequence, most of the characters who appear in these pages also remain firmly local in their outlook, unlike the pleasure-boat crews who have, in recent years, taken their places.

Living on the Waterways

Canal companies provided accommodation for their key staff from the earliest days. Lock keepers were often expected to attend to traffic or water control at almost any hour of the day or night and so had to be on hand. Toll keepers and ostlers, like wharfingers, worked within yards of their homes. The canal inspector often had a substantial house at the entrance to his principal maintenance yard and could be called upon at any moment to deal with an emergency. In recent years this long-established system has broken down: nationalised canal administrators have raised rents so as to remove the 'perk' of cheap accommodation, with the result that staff have moved away from the interruptions and lack of privacy inseparable from living on the job. Now only a few overgrown remains of gardens mark the site of remote lengthsmen's cottages, and more convenient houses provide desirable residences for commuters from distant towns.

At first boat crews only lived aboard their craft on longer journeys, but railway competition encouraged economical living on their own or their employers' boats. However, once the long-distance carrying trades disappeared from our smaller canals, unemployment for these hard-working individuals also threatened homelessness.

Of those whose stories appear in this volume only the Hornes still live in canal company

The more spacious arrangement of a keel cabin looking aft from the hold as though the bulkhead was missing

Much of boat people's time was spent outside their small cabins either steering, loading and unloading or looking after the boats. Even many domestic chores were more conveniently performed on the bank. Gladys Horne caught Mrs Sam Brooks doing the washing in the 'oiling up' [fuelling] length at Bull's Bridge depot (Gladys Horne)

accommodation; at the same time, none can forget their time on the water. A surprising proportion of waterway people return to the canal bank to walk the dog, or they supervise passing traffic from the living-room window or garden hedge. I called on most of those who appear here in these waterless houses where photographs of boats, and even paintings of maintenance workshops, decorate the walls alongside horse brasses and lace-edged 'hanging up plates'. Only Violet Mould was uncertain about my intrusion into her home: 'I don't like it in this flat' she insisted, staring at the floor. I thought it would be a bit cold for a day out to visit my boat in early winter, but I was wrong: 'Ooh, that'd be all right, I'm not doing anything Saturday,' she smiled broadly.

Many of the boats trading on the inland waterways of England and Wales up until the 1960s or 1970s were used more or less as full-time dwellings. The exceptions were – and some still are – used on short-haul traffics where journey times were shorter than a working day so that boat crews could return to a home on the land each night. Competition from the railways encouraged economies to the extent that long-distance narrowboat men began to live afloat, as their colleagues working coastal and tidal water craft had long been accustomed to do. Some started to take their wives and families aboard as crew, and eventually, particularly with the rapid increase in road transport competition after World War I, most of their canalside cottages were given up.

This floating population had begun to attract the attention of Victorian reformers in the second half of the nineteenth century, especially that of George Smith, of Coalville, in Leicestershire. He campaigned hard for legislation to regulate what he saw as immoral and insanitary living conditions on the narrowboats. Eventually the Canal Boats Act was passed in 1877: this decreed that inland craft not registered as sea-going merchant ships, must have a certain cubic cabin space available for each occupant, and must be registered with the local authority in whose area the boat was intended to operate, for the purposes of its inspection and the education of any children.

New craft were inspected and registered with local authorities under this act, and their registration place and number painted on the outside. Because of the need to measure the internal size of a cabin, many of the initial inspections were carried out at the boatbuilder's yard, with the result that many boats registered at Uxbridge in Middlesex, for example, spent most of their time trading in Cheshire and Staffordshire. As a result, despite the provision of attendance record cards, there was little really effective control over the continuity of the boat children's schooling.

Subsequently, any local authority canal boat inspector could make a spot check that the cabin remained up to standard. Those whom I have met that were involved with these routine inspections from either side, recall that the system was applied very variably, depending upon the interest of the local authority sanitary inspector responsible. For example, boat people were careful to put extra children on a childless relative's boat when going to Manchester in the 1960s. The inspector at Macclesfield in the previous decade happily accepted any excuse for the state of the cabin and its occupants. In some towns inspectors were simply never seen.

The cabin of a Humber keel or Mersey sailing flat was generally spacious because of the 14 or 15ft beam of the vessel and depth of its hull. Narrowboat cabins almost invariably followed a standard layout and were built to the minimum specification of the act. It is not clear whether the plan really changed very much with the coming of the Canal Boats Acts.

Both horse-drawn and motorised narrowboats are arranged so that they are as easy to work for long hours in all weathers as possible. The cabins are placed at the extreme after-end of the boat, so that the whole of its 70ft length is easily watched through narrow bridges and into and out of locks which allow only an inch or two to spare on either side. The stern doors open from a flat counter deck on the motor, or a small well at the stern of the butty. Inside these doors is a substantial wooden step, or footboard, on which the steerer stands; thus the doors can be closed behind him to keep the snow out when travelling on a winter's night. In this position he has at his left foot a coal stove. It seems unlikely that any boatman ever *bought* the coal for this necessity, since if he didn't have 25 tons, or more, of it just beyond the cabin, he had full hams, cartons of HP sauce, bars of soap, sugar, tins of groceries, Guinness or some other ready currency! There was at least a 50:50 chance that the boat at the next mooring outside the pub that night would be loaded with house coal.

Many boatmen owned their own small, cast-iron cooking range. These were miniature versions of the ones built into many house kitchens until the advent of the gas cooker. These small ranges were soon installed in the cabin, with a chimney fitted up at the boatyard, when moving aboard a new boat. Some of the big carrying companies such as Fellows Morton & Clayton or the Grand Union Canal Carrying Co provided a bottle stove instead of a range, which gave warmth but had no oven or hot plate on which to cook a full meal.

Descending from the footboard, the intermediate step was formed on the front edge of a box used to store the immediate coal supply. Reaching the floor it is obvious that a butty, or horse-boat cabin is more spacious than that on a motor-driven vessel. In the latter, the engine controls are carried from the engine room, between the cabin and hold, under the cabin roof and the propeller shaft reaches the stern beneath the floor. The absence of these in the unpowered boats means that the floor is set lower and one's head is less liable to damage in the absence of the inevitable boatman's hat!

In any case, there is not usually enough headroom for the average adult to stand straight, so the instant reaction of anyone entering a narrowboat cabin is to sit down; this is usually accomplished to the right of the entrance where there is a side bed. This is really a bench seat formed by the top of a locker. As a bed its limitation is usually the fact that it is less than 5ft long. Seated, and facing the range, the table cupboard becomes obvious. This cupboard extends from floor to ceiling immediately forward of the range. The upper part of this has a door hinged at its bottom edge, say about 3ft above floor level. This falling door opens to form the dining table and reveal the crockery cupboard. Most food is actually stored outside in a cupboard astern of the well deck on the butty or beneath the counter deck on a motor; these two remain cooler than the cabin because of the proximity of the water outside the hull. Below the drop door of the table cupboard a broad, narrow drawer accommodates cutlery, and there is usually a further large cupboard at floor level.

Forward again from the table cupboard and the end of the side bed is the cross bed, occupying the remaining space against the engine room or hold bulkhead. Here the boatman was often born, and here he usually expected to die. It is likely to be about 3ft 6in wide, and the occupants lie across the boat. Their feet extend to the left-hand side of the hull into 'the bed 'ole'; during the day the bedding was often rolled up into this large cupboard. The central section of the bed is then seen to form another cupboard door which can be folded up to conceal the bedding. This reveals larger drawers beneath both the head and foot of the bed, although these were unfortunately regularly cold and damp, being below the boat's waterline. There is also usually a linen and clothes cupboard above the foot of the bed. With the bed thus folded away, it was possible to use the 'back door' to reach either the motor boat's engine room or the hold of a horse-drawn or butty boat. Many motor boats built for the Grand Union Canal Carrying Company in the 1930s had a solid steel bulkhead here to make the engine room fire-proof, but on a horse-drawn boat, useful extra space and ventilation could be obtained if the door was not blocked by the cargo. Indeed there was ample space for a child's swing to hang from the cross beams in the hold, and for many similar games.

Despite sanitary inspections of the boats, 'sanitation' was unknown! A bucket might be positioned next to the engine in motor boats, many of which had well carpeted and gleaming engine rooms! However, there were no shore facilities for emptying these buckets until well into the pleasure-boating age! The enlightenment of the 1960s brought about narrow boats designed with a small compartment between the cabin and hold for a chemical toilet, but this was promptly condemned by the local authority inspectors since the chemical closet had to be carried out through the cabin for emptying when the boat was loaded!

Fresh water was stored in cans carried on the roof, invariably near the chimney where they would be kept a little warm in frosty weather. They were often positioned with the mop resting on their handles, so as to aid the problem of passing a horse-boat towing line over these obstructions when boats passed one another. A large, saucepan-like hand bowl served as a sink, and often a bath. A few families had galvanised 'tin' baths which could serve for serious ablutions before the warmth of the range, or could be taken onto a convenient loading wharf or towpath with a fire beneath them for wash day.

One of the most striking features of the majority of long-distance carrying narrowboats was the bright traditional 'roses and castles' style of decoration, very fully described in Tony Lewery's *Flowers Afloat*. Decoration often surrounded the boat owner's name on the cabin side. Within, the table cupboard door and often the bed flap were adorned with a landscape scene complete with a fairytale castle, and any available space could feature bunches of roses and other decorations. All the woodwork inside would otherwise be grained using scratch combs in a technique often referred to as 'scumbling', and beadings and shelf edges would be picked out in contrasting colours. Over these the boat woman would hang a display of crochet work, all kept immaculately white despite the constant loading of coal. Ornaments were best kept flat in such a limited space; the favourites were undoubtedly 'hanging up', or 'lace' places with their ornate pierced edges, each carrying an illustration of a holiday resort or flowers. Handles, hinges and drying rails over the range were invariably of gleaming brass.

Many owners of preserved working boats attempt to maintain these traditions, so they can still be seen occasionally around the canals, for example at the Ellesmere Port Boat Museum's Easter weekend gathering of working craft.

*

In the late twentieth century canal holidays are sold as happy and carefree outings on sunny summer days to those who have never seen a boat before. I have heard boatyard staff tell the hirer of a luxury narrowboat over 60ft long and weighing in excess of 10 tons that 'it's only like driving a car': nothing could be further from the truth.

The great advantage of water transport has always been the absence of friction between the boat and its watery road: once moving, a boat is difficult to stop, whether it is of 30, or 30,000 tons. The pilot of the 30,000 tonner plans 10 or more miles ahead, using wind and engine power to reduce his vessel's speed to a snail's pace, when anchors or outsized steel mooring cables can be used. The craft featured in this book were stopped with ropes and lines sometimes made of cotton and only $^{1}/_{2}$in thick. Considerable skill is required to handle these boats and their lines effectively so that no damage occurs to the numerous lock gates or swing bridges along the way, or to the boat itself. In the event of any mishap causing a rope to break when straining around a bollard to bring even 25 or 30 tons of narrowboat and cargo to a stop, any human limb between boat and wall or finger between rope and bollard will be lost. Loading and unloading these craft with heavy packages of steel or machinery, and moving them in docks amongst outsized barges and ships only increased the risks.

Every boatman or woman I have ever talked to has some memory of a close friend or relation killed on or around the boats. So, if it was such a dangerous occupation, how did anyone survive for me to talk to? Because of the comparative isolation of the boating community from the outside world, a high proportion of boat crews followed their parents' vocation. Children brought up on a narrowboat, for example, would be on the move as soon as their mother was fit enough to stand at the tiller after giving birth. By the time they could sit up they would be wrapped up warmly and placed on the sliding hatch to the cabin immediately under mother's eye. There they could not escape seeing the tiller pushed to and fro as the long hull was guided round the many twists and turns. They would see the extension pipe of the chimney taken down to pass under any low bridges.

As the boat entered each lock, mother would jump off, running up the nearby steps to shut the gates and draw paddles to admit water to the chamber. Here was the opportunity

Young members of a boatman's family soon learned to walk long distances each day and brave the great outdoors. Not many of the horses required driving but almost all needed to be kept aware of a presence on the path behind to keep them moving well. That was occasionally achieved by hanging an old boot on a string from the towing line so that it would drop and clatter on the path if the horse should slow down and the line sag!

to crawl across the roof and fall between the lock wall and the rising hull into the turbulent water as the lock filled – unless secured by reins, or more likely an old length of mooring line, to a towing stud or to the ring which secures the chimney's safety chain to the roof. Some were fastened to the drinking water can which habitually stood by the chimney, but the strongest proved able to push this overboard so that it dragged them to the bottom of the canal. Other parents had a ring screwed into the wooden coaming of the small well-deck outside a horse-boat's cabin doors, to which a toddler could be secured to take the air whilst mother worked in the cabin or at the range.

Those left in the cabin soon learnt not to touch the cast ironwork of the range which inflicted nasty burns even if the pan handles were out of reach. Any of these accidents could be provoked by a bump in a lock chamber or a narrow bridge hole.

Once able to run about the boats and locks, the possibilities were multiplied to an extent which would horrify today's 'health & safety'-conscious society. One strong ten-year-old decided he could get the top paddle of a lock near Chester drawn up whilst his dad was still shutting the bottom gate behind the boats. Running along the top of the tanks of his 'oil boat', he stepped onto the fore-cabin roof, and putting a foot on the top of the chimney pipe there, reached up for the coping stones of the lockside to pull himself up. Unfortunately, just as his sister started water running into the lock from the paddle on the far side, the chimney pipe bent and he fell into the lock chamber and was carried beneath the fore-ends of their two boats by the rushing water. Perhaps thanks to the presence of mind of his sister in shutting off the water almost before he went under, he was brought out on the end of a boat shaft more or less alive and was able to tell me the tale forty years later! He certainly remembered his father re-enforcing the lesson learnt!

Boat people were generally rescued from deeper water by use of a hooked boat shaft or rope. Few learnt to swim. Bill Gibbins of Leighton Buzzard told me how his dad fastened a rope round him and threw him over the stern of their moving horse boat, shouting at him to splash until he caught up with the boat. When Bill was exhausted, or half-drowned, his brother took his place until both were judged to have some chance of saving themselves in the event of falling in. However, the main hazard remains to this day the possibility of falling in in front of a moving boat which cannot be stopped before it crushes the person against a lock, bridge, or dock wall. Boat people will only attempt to board or leave the forward part of a boat in rare circumstances, because it has been drummed into them from their first memory that if they fall in from the stern they may be able to climb out again after the boat has passed. Neither will you see them pit their own strength against a moving boat as the inexperienced inevitably do. If a boat cannot be stopped with a rope or engine the only recourse is to a fender, not an arm or leg.

And, of course, all their difficulties were compounded by bad weather conditions – snow, ice and gales, or floods – like those described by Violet Mould, which holiday makers rarely experience. However, if you are paid only for delivering your cargo, and not for the length of time you manage to spin the job out, you naturally press on until conditions become totally impossible, with attendant increase in the risks taken.

In the same way, health often came second to keeping the boats moving and the income flowing. Additionally there was the worry for employees of larger fleets that they were not entitled to live on the boats if they did not carry the owner's cargoes with them. Therefore anybody becoming physically incapable of boating was also liable to become homeless. If Harry Bentley's father had asked a doctor to attend to his injured leg he ran the risk of being told that he must not continue his extremely physical employment until fully healed. Therefore he would have to come off the boats, and if his wife and children could not work them without his assistance, all ran the risk of homelessness.

There were a few trusted doctors and nurses around the canal system whom the boat people would visit. The best known example was Sister Mary Ward who lived in a canalside cottage at Stoke Bruerne in Northamptonshire, on the Grand Union Canal. A qualified nurse, she understood the boat people well and they, in turn, trusted her not to insist

The Grand Union Canal Carrying Company provided a school room on an old barge at its Bull's Bridge Depot. Although this picture was posed at the dedication ceremony at Paddington it illustrates the likely range of ages in the single class. Nonetheless much good work could be achieved by providing the facility on familiar ground handy for the parents to recover children when the boats were suddenly ordered away for loading. In later years maintenance was saved by lifting the Elsdale *from the canal onto the bank alongside the depot buildings* (BW Archives, Gloucester)

on hospitalisation where it could be avoided. It was common for a crew to aim to tie up outside her front door as shortly as possible before the expected arrival of a new baby; and for Sister Mary to perform the midwife's role in the cramped confines of the back cabin. It was also by no means unknown for Sister Mary to instruct the all-powerful owner of a pair of narrowboats that the craft and their cargo would be delayed for medical reasons and that it was impossible for the crew to be taken off. In return for such assistance Sister Mary seems rarely to have been paid full consulting fees, but to have been showered with gifts and ornaments as well as the undying love and respect of her boating community.

Crews working on the bigger barges such as Humber keels, described by George Trevethick, rarely encountered such problems. Being all-male crews they more usually had a house in a convenient canalside village where children could attend school for a few years, and their way of life was more acceptable to the local doctor.

Few children brought up on narrowboats had the opportunity to attend school because their home was always on the move, since the parents were only paid when they delivered each cargo. A few charitable organisations and canal companies attempted to resolve this problem. There were hostels, where children could live during school term time, at Brentford and Birmingham, for example. The Canal Boats Acts required local authority schools to take boat children into their classes whenever their craft were tied up in their area. This was only partly satisfactory since there might be breaks of several weeks, or months, between each few days' attendance. The boat children tended to be pushed to the back of classes which often consisted of regular attenders much younger, and yet more educationally advanced, than they were. Many boat children tell of being ridiculed by the townsfolk, and when the problem came to blows the boat lads were invariably in trouble for the ease with which they silenced the opposition!

Perhaps the most satisfactory school was that set up by the Grand Union Canal Co on board the old barge *Elsdale* at their Bull's Bridge depot in Southall, Middlesex. Many craft collected at the depot to await loading orders at Brentford, or in the London Docks, and the children were in familiar surroundings where they could be easily recalled when their parents received orders to move off. The full-time teacher specialised in coping with the variable abilities of the ever-changing class. When the barge's hull became difficult to maintain it was lifted onto the bank and gave several years' further service.

Nonetheless one of the reasons for so many crews leaving employment on the boats from the 1940s onwards was parental concern that uneducated children would not be able to find work if the carrying trades continued their obvious decline. On the other hand several canal carriers maintained that the continuing departure of their crews made it impossible for them to operate their fleets effectively enough to obtain new contracts.

*

There has always been a very strict etiquette amongst the boating community in general, which still applies today. For example, if you go visiting you stand in a position where you cannot see into the cabin doors, you knock on the cabin side, and then you wait for an answer. You *never* step onto anyone else's boat uninvited. If you are tied up breasted together (*ie* alongside one another) and you want to get from your boat on the outside onto the tow path you walk at least to the hold area, if not to the foredeck, before giving warning, perhaps by shouting 'May I cross?', before stepping lightly over the other boat(s).

GEORGE TREVETHICK

Towage Contractor and Marine Engineer

Keadby is a small community grouped around the junction of the Stainforth & Keadby Canal with the river Trent. The Trent here is a broad, sweeping estuary of fierce tides and deceptively shallow sand and gravel bars. The canal enters from a lock between wharves where ships call from the Rhine and all parts of the European coast. The view to the right, upriver from the lock, is bounded by Keadby railway bridge, a lifting bridge which was fixed in the 1930s thus preventing larger ships from continuing upstream towards Gainsborough, Newark and Nottingham.

The canal entrance was busy until the 1960s with barges arriving on the tide from Hull to travel up the canal to the Sheffield & South Yorkshire Navigation. These were met by craft leaving the lock to take the tide down the Humber with cargoes such as Yorkshire steel and coal. Much of this canal route was modernised and enlarged in the 1980s, but too late to prevent road transport taking over most of this trade. George Trevethick arrived at Keadby down the broad river from Nottingham on a small tug, and has never returned!

I first met George Trevethick on the towpath of the canal above Keadby Lock with a request for some assistance from the marine engineering business there. The obviously senior member of staff had a bright watch chain and mischievous twinkle in his eye, and he directed me to the obviously younger man in overalls, commenting 'I'm only the lad here, you'd better ask the boss!' Once 'the boss' had returned to important concerns in the depths of a Lister engine, 'the lad' dealt in leisurely fashion with the bill, and conversation turned to memories of steam tugs and commercial craft which made it obvious that George's memory stretched back long before the boss could have been born.

A few hundred yards southwards from the entrance lock, along the bank of the Trent, is an estate of houses which has extended the old canal-side village. The neat garden of one of these includes a garage workshop where small-scale engineering is all-important. At the workshop door I renewed acquaintance with George Trevethick, and we went to sit in his garden in summer sunshine; nearby there was a small vertical boiler on a bench.

'Well, I should have been doing that if you hadn't been here. I make 'em, you know. I've always made 'em. I suppose that's where my son, Richard, gets his engineering from. He runs the business now. I don't know where *I* got it from, my dad, I should think. My brother's three years younger and he isn't the same. With me being the oldest, and from when I was about ten, when I was off from school, I'd get up and get off to work with my dad and help him down the yard. My brother being that bit younger never did, and I think he missed out, you know. He finished up as a machinist in a toolroom, but he never went down to Granddad's yard like I did... We lived at Burton Joyce, and I used to go after school. It was only about 2d on the train, but sometimes I went on the back step of my dad's bike. Well, I used to go and clean all the sawdust out of the bottom of the boat they were working on – and of course, the next night it was as bad again. I used to get mad!

'I used to go collecting horse muck, too. There was loads of horses on the roads in them days pulling carts, there weren't no lorries much. We collected it for making the challico.' I asked George what this was used for, and he explained that the horse dung was mixed with gas tar and pitch, and horse hair added, to make a waterproofing sealant to pack between the timbers of a wooden boat.

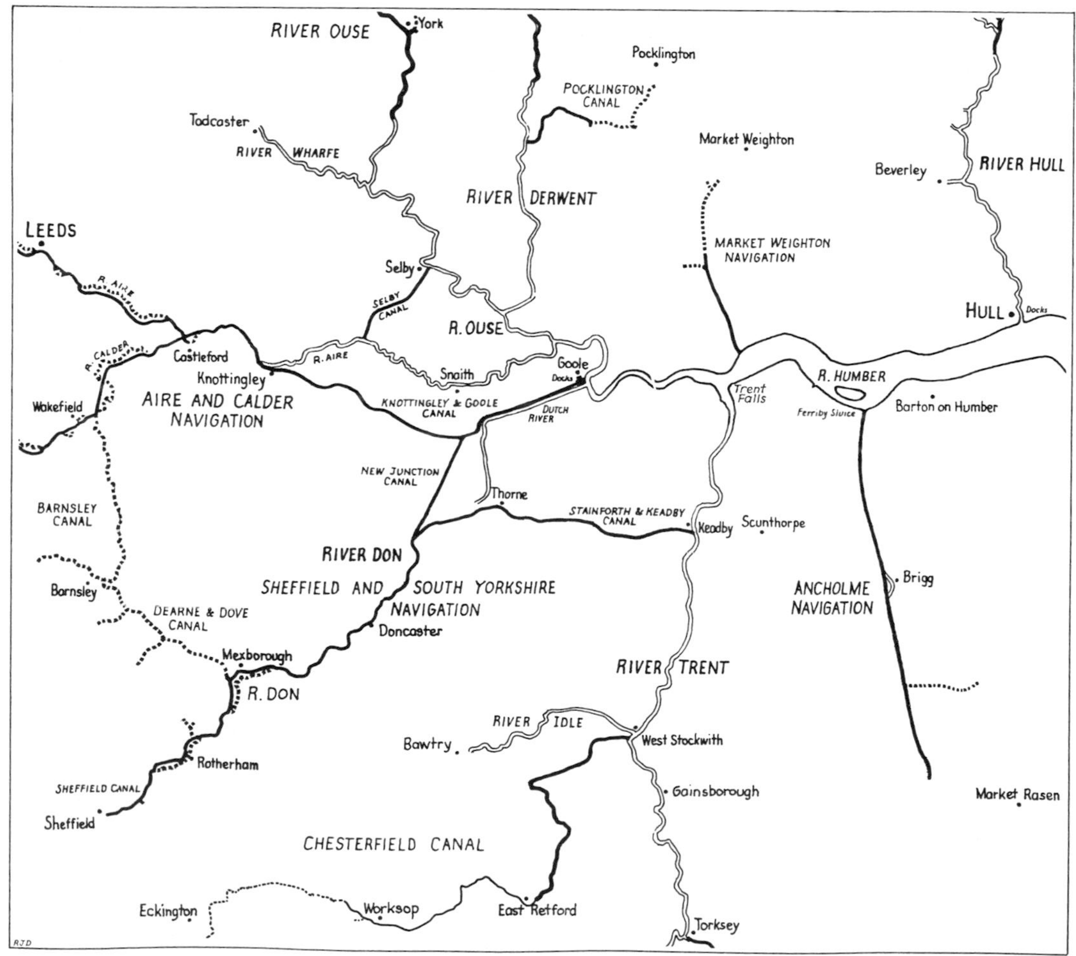

The North Eastern Waterways System

George Trevethick's grandfather's boatyard at Gainsborough. The newly repaired ketch would be launched at the height of one of the year's highest tides. The extensive production of masts and spars is evident (Lincolnshire Library Service)

'Me granddad was the first in the family with a boatyard; it was at Gainsborough. It was only a little bit of a tin pot boatyard like, just below Gainsborough bridge on the town side. He used to build Trent ketches, and they made a lot of masts and spars for the sailing barges as well. That's where my granddad started, though I don't know if *his* dad was a boat builder. He moved to the yard at Lenton in Nottingham in 1913, but I couldn't tell you why. All I know is that my dad once said that they moved on a barge, loaded all their gear and furniture on, and it was brought up by a horse.

'At first, after school I used to have to walk down to the yard and chop sticks. I did them by the thousand, into a heap as big as my shed is now! All the scrap wood used to be bundled. Me dad had a bundling machine and it was bundled up with wire and sold to the shops.

'It was whilst he was there that my dad had some little launches, the sort with a canopy on and a fringe round it. They carried about twelve people or a few more. He did trips from Castle Lock on a Sunday up to Trent Lock, and I used to have to go along and play a gramophone. Of course, we were up against Witty's at Trent Bridge on the river, and they had steamers, and a bloke on board with a concertina, and me with a gramophone was really the poor relation! We used to go up to Trent Lock where there were two pubs – still are, I think – one on the riverside and one on the lockside where the Erewash Canal comes out. My mother used to go too, although she never liked water at all.

'Between the two pubs there was a little bit of a dyke that came out into the Trent, and there was a bridge over it, just made of three planks, and I can remember falling in there, as though it was yesterday! It was dry, but it was all black sludge! I can see my mother now, she didn't go

in pubs or nowt, like, but she went in the pub then and got a newspaper, and cleaned me down with it. I can see that now – but that's the only thing I can remember about going up there.

'Whilst my father was at that yard a man called Frank Rayner came down to see him; he was the engineer for the Trent Navigation Company, and asked my dad if he wanted a job "for them boats". It was to tow the Trent pans because they were going to start building big locks; and he accepted. They also had a steam tug of Bob Teal's, *Forest King* or *Alan-a-Dale*, and they used to bring the pans up to Stoke Lock with that, and then we used to tow them with our little launches up to Trent Concrete's works – and that was the start of a job which went on for many years. That would have been in 1925 or 1926. We went to live at Burton Joyce because it was handier there; you could tie the boats up at night to the telegraph poles all down the river's bank.

From the *Nottingham Journal* 24th July 1929

The scheme for making the river navigable to Hull at all seasons of the year with an efficient waterway six feet deep (reports the Trent Navigation Committee) is now completed.

Increasing Trade

Dredging Work Which Pays For Itself

The work of dredging was completed on 27th February last, states the committee.

"In a period of about 6½ years no fewer than 1,439,323 tons of material have been dredged from the river bed. Of this total 577,360 tons consisted of gravel, sold to Trent Concrete Ltd."

For some years to come it will be necessary to retain two dredgers to keep the channel clear from silting. It is expected that the sale of the gravel will cover the cost of this work.

Petrol Distribution

A report to be presented to the city council next Monday [29th July 1929] states: "One of the first fruits of your committee's work has been establishment of a new industry on the banks of the river in connection with the distribution in this area of petrol, and as this is an all year round traffic a steadily increasing revenue can be anticipated from this source.

In the first months of your committees control of the river in 1927, 48 tons of petrol was carried. In May 1929 the amount had increased to 5,536 tons, and there are still two further companies negotiating for sites to establish depots."

In July 1928 the City Council authorised the committee to construct a river wall, and in March last a warehouse at Trent Lane Wharf and this work is now proceeding satisfactorily. The original length of 570 feet of wall is now nearing completion and the foundation piles for the warehouse have all been driven.

An Idea of the Cost

When the essential works are completed it is confidently anticipated that they will not only be self supporting, but will add materially to the attraction of the waterway for transport purposes and increase the corporation's revenue from tolls. Some idea of the cost of the river improvement scheme may be gathered from the following:

Holme Lock	£54,129
Stoke Lock	£98,767
Hazelford Lock	£70,778
Gunthorpe Lock	£60,456
Deepening Old Holme Lock	£2,338
Dredging river	£204,132
General charges	£19,771
Total	£510,371

(Above) Where the towpath of the Trent tideway changed sides, stone-built ramps were provided. The keel could be brought alongside these and the horse was then walked onto the foredeck and was ferried across to the other path
(Left) The construction of one of the large new concrete Trent locks in the late 1920s

'As a little lad I can remember Stoke Lock being built, then Gunthorpe, and Hazelford Lock. They did them one by one, dredging all the gravel out of the river, the surplus going to this concrete works at Colwick; there must have been fifty or sixty of them Trent pans on it. There are still a few knocking about. They were steel, built by Watson's at Gainsborough, and they had a crew of two with a little cabin aft.

'My dad told me that before they did those locks there was no lock between Newark and Nottingham at all, and only about 2ft depth of water. The idea of building them was to guarantee 7ft from Hull to Nottingham, because they wanted to make Nottingham an inland port. It was a very big scheme, and it worked. We weren't allowed to go down to the Trent alone as youngsters, though of course we did; you couldn't be there half an hour before there was something coming up or going down – it was simply a stream of boats. The United Towing Company at Hull even built special tugs for the Trent: *Motorman* was the first, then *Waterman*, then *Hillman*. The Trent Navigation Company had boats built to tow others, as well; there was *Tyne*, *Yare*, *Stort*, loads of them, and often named after rivers. It was all tied up with Nottingham Corporation, and of course that was big business men. One was Mr Barlock of Barlock Typewriters, and so there was *Barlock*, and *Barlet*, which was the little typewriter. They was the same as the *Tyne* and the *Yare*.

A flotilla of pleasure craft approach the head of the newly completed Hazelford Lock on 25 June 1926. In the leading boat Neville Chamberlain prepares to cut the white ribbon. Unfortunately none of these craft can be identified as belonging to the Trevethicks (Nottinghamshire Libraries)

'Before that scheme and the new locks, me dad used to tell me that it took 'em a week sometimes to come from Newark to Nottingham. The keels from Hull and so on used to go to Gainsborough, lighten a bit into the warehouses, and then they'd go to Newark. Otherwise they could put some into ketches at Gainsborough, and those'd carry it on to Nottingham. Some of the keels could go to Newark, well lightened, but they wouldn't go above Newark, and they used to pull them ketches up with horses.'

George asked me if I'd seen the sloping stone landings by the river; I said that I had, and he went on to explain what they were for:

'As you went up the river there were pairs of them on opposite sides of the river – they weren't straight across, one would be a bit upstream of the other. Well, they used to pull the ketch up alongside one on the side where the horse was, and put what was called a "stow-er" down the offside: that was like a big pole, almost a tree trunk, with a forked iron spike on the end. They'd lash it to a timber-head and that would hold the boat alongside, and then they could walk the horse aboard, onto the forepart of the barge. Then they would let go and shove her over, and she'd drift down and over to the other side. They'd hold her against the landing at the other side and walk the horse ashore there, and then they'd pull up that side; but pulling from the other side would give the horse a rest, and eased his shoulders. There were no ferries except at Hazelford and Stoke, but there was the toll bridge at Gunthorpe.

'So it was a revolution, building those new locks, and a fantastic tonnage went up to Nottingham after that was done, even during the war. But now there isn't a thing, is there? I do think it was a damn good idea using the surplus labour, instead of paying them dole. They bought, I think it was three, dredgers from Holland, and of course as a lad I thought it was wonderful.

'Another thing which does stick in my mind as well was that those little boats of me dad's would be only 28 or 30ft, and they had something like a 10-horse Petter or an old Brook Marine engine in or summat like that. I could operate them, and thought I was a clever little devil, you know! – though I could only stop it and start it, that was all! On a Friday we used to leave Burton Joyce and run up to Meadow Lane for 9 o'clock and pick the pay clerks up, two chaps from the Shire Hall. They used to pay all the people working on that improvement scheme. As I got older, twelve or thirteen year old, I used to have a day off school to go and do that – you wouldn't be allowed today, would you? They used to come aboard with a Gladstone bag, which always amazes me today when you're talking of money. They came into the little cuddy on that boat, just a three-sided shelter, you know. And they had like a knife-box with little sections in and they put all these wage packets in them. So you used to go off downriver and you used to pay Holme Lock keeper, then go down and

The Trent Navigation Company's steam tug Little John *towing craft upriver. This illustration is from the cover of* Nottingham's Highway to the Sea, *the brochure prepared for the opening ceremony for the new locks which George Trevethick remembers being built. It gives a clear impression of the way the tug was designed, with its boiler effectively on deck to minimise the vessel's draft for work on the unimproved river* (Nottinghamshire Libraries)

After living at Thorne, George Trevethick took a house in one of the side streets opening onto this road alongside the Trent at Keadby. The river was a scene of constant activity, as seen here, with United Towing steam tugs plying to and from Hull with keels, Thames and even Dutch sailing barges calling to load coal (Lincolnshire Library Service)

round up at Trent Concrete and pay the lighters that was laid at that wharf. Of course, as you went down the river, any that were towing up you'd round up and pay them as they were going along. Then there'd be the dredger crew; there were two dredgers working. Later, of course, as work progressed downstream you had to go down to Gunthorpe and then Hazelford. And there was all that money in that little bag. I remember sometimes they'd give me me dad's money. I think it was somewhere around £12 or something. That was for two or three boats and towing the barges with a bloke on them and all that. You can't believe it now.

'When that work finished me dad had nothing to do. But there were plenty of barges going up there then, and the men on them said, "Why don't you take your boats down to Donkey Dyke?' – they called it Donkey Dyke up here, the Sheffield & South Yorkshire Navigation, though Doncaster Dyke it was really. You see, it was all horses up here, except when they could sail a bit. That's why Dad came down here.

'Me mum and dad lived in a house at Thorne. I was down here at Keadby most of the time on the tug. I was on the biggest tug, not big by today's standards, but it was about a 70- or 80-horse diesel, with an Elwe engine, a Swedish semi-diesel. I would say we worked in this canal more than we were running down to Hull, although I've known us running to Hull for three months at a time. But there was enough work for us to stay in the canal. I used to think it were horrible, like, because it's a lot better out there. They were real agony trips up to Doncaster, so slow! Although it was different in them days, you know. You wouldn't think now that two 7ft draft boats could pass with ease then. We came here in about 1931, and that work went on until about halfway through 1958, I suppose. Before we came it was horses. There had been one or two steam tugs in here, but it didn't work with the steamers being more expensive. But disregarding them we came, and the horse marines didn't like it very much. You see, even on a Saturday night like tonight, there could be as many as a dozen horse marines waiting for the barges to come up on the tide and the chance of a job. If the barges couldn't sail up the canal they'd hire a marine and his horse to take 'em, and so we were doing them out of a job. I used to like it when we'd about four on, but I know as once we'd up to fifteen. That was a proper agony trip! I should say the average was four or five. But, of course, that was four or five marines we'd done out of a job. But me being only a young lad, and just looking after the engine, I got on with them all right. There was never any bother, like they would make today; they'd probably knife you today! But then, we got on as mates and they accepted the competition.

'I can remember the first time we came in here there was a Doncaster miller. They were the worst to tow. They'd only got one steel keel and the other four were wood, and they used to be loaded to a good 7ft. You could get through to Doncaster with that, but you'd only want 6ft or 6ft 6in at the most to go to Sheffield. The horse marines didn't like the millers because they pulled hell out of the horses, like, so they didn't mind losing them. I always remember we were laid here and the skipper off one came walking round, and he said "If that 'effing' thing can pull me out of the lock, you've got yoursen a bloody job. But that thing won't pull me out 'cause motor engines aren't no good at all!" Of course we hung on to him and yanked him straight out and took three of 'em up that first trip!

'We only took any of 'em to Doncaster, and they went with the horses above there, thank heaven! I was fed up by the time we'd got to Doncaster. You imagine getting to a lock with six on the tug and there was three came down with horses on or sailing, in between that. It wasn't just that you had to wait while he got through the lock. Your one as you'd got pulled into the lock tail, with the tug, ready for going up when the tug cleared, had to be pushed out of the way by hand to let him come down. When the downgater had cleared, you'd to pull your barge into the lock. Then you'd to keep the tug and barges clear at the lock head if anything was to get in to go down. You could be at a lock for two hours. Bramwith was lengthened as we came here, about 1932 it was finished.

'The cost to the boats was the same as for a horse. It was 12s from Keadby here to Thorne, 12s from Thorne to Doncaster. And so on Mexborough, Rotherham; 12s a stage, in other words. Then 8s light, but 15s for one of those Doncaster millers. I think if we took twenty quid a week we'd covered our costs. We were quicker than a horse. But there was enough work for both us and the horses, you see, some days there weren't enough horses and so the barges had to wait here for one to come down. If we got four to take to Thorne it was only £2 sommat, but you'd had a good day, like! Fuel was 3d [1.25p] a gallon. When I finished I was on thirty bob [£1.50] a week. I know United Towing offered me a job on one of their river tugs. They carried two engineers on them. I'd have loved to have gone, but I stayed with my dad. I would have got 31s with United. In other words I wasn't far off the going rate. So the wage bill wasn't a lot if the tug were earning £5 or £6 a day, like.'

I wondered how that compared with other local jobs, and George said that he thought it compared well with the railway men in his wife's family but that the hours tended to be longer. Railway men in general had worked a basic eight-hour day (although generally rostered as a forty-hour fortnight) since 1921.

'The river Don comes in and out of the navigation further up, you know. It used to flood badly in the old days – it would come up overnight, but it could stay up for weeks and weeks. Like the Trent, they've made it better now.

The lengthening work at Bramwith Lock, on the Sheffield & South Yorkshire Navigation, above Thorne, was almost complete when this view of the Trevethick tug Sulzer *was taken in 1932* (BW Archives, Gloucester)

Tide time at Keadby. The keels in the foreground have been brought upstream by steam tugs and are awaiting their turn to enter the lock giving access to the Sheffield & South Yorkshire Navigation just out of sight to the left. The substantial towing lines used in the estuary are being laid down on the hatch covers and lighter lines for canal work prepared. The skipper of the fourth vessel out from the wharf where the cameraman stood is stowing the sail which has been used to assist the tug on the voyage or at least in 'rounding up' into the tidal flow on arrival off the lock entrance. At the wharf in the left background a Thames sailing barge awaits her next coal cargo back down the coast and three steam tugs are assembling their tows of keels for the return to Hull. Beyond them a towing barge makes its way upstream with at least one empty and another loaded keel. On the lockside horse marines would be waiting to contract with the keel skippers to tow them to Doncaster or beyond in competition with the new technology of the Tevethicks' diesel tugs (Lincolnshire Library Service)

Trevethicks' tug Sulzer *towing the keel* Danum *to the Mill at Doncaster*

When it was like that the canal company would get us to go top side of Doncaster Lock, up to Mexborough Bottom Lock. They paid for it, to keep the traffic going and get revenue coming in. You see, top side of Doncaster there was no proper bank for the horses to walk on so they couldn't've pulled them in any case. There were times when we could only take one, though mostly we took two. Many a time we went to Rotherham as well doing that. But only once have I been to Tinsley [at the bottom of the canal into Sheffield].

'After the floods had gone it used to leave a bar across Sprotbrough Lock and Conisbrough Lock. Top side of the lock, it was, where you come out of the river into the cut. When the river went down you could see the mud. There was always a steam bucket dredger here, it lived here at Keadby, with some mud flats. It dredged here almost all the while; that's why it's bunged up now, because the dredger's never here any longer. We used to have to tow that for the canal company – we used to have to go all night. If we came down with a load of barges, like, at seven o'clock at night, it'd be "Here you are, you've to tow that and take it up to Sprotbrough". We did that, and of course we used to go to Hull quite a lot. We didn't go down there looking for work, we went because somebody sent us. One was Bisby from Thorne. He had a little steam keel, she was a lovely little thing, *Swift*. Well, he once got it on the piles where the Trent meets the Ouse, known as "wall end", that is, Trent End; he got it on there, right inside the piles on the biggest tide there was, and it was there for three months until it could float off again. He got me dad to hire him the tug and I went as engineer and the mate went with it as well; we were out there for three months towing his boats,

boats, you see. We went from time to time and tried to pull it off, and other powered boats did too, and eventually, one day, one did and the tide was high enough and off he came.

'He were a market boat, that *Swift*. He used to leave Hull on a Wednesday. You could put a parcel on him in Humber Dock on a Wednesday and he'd come up here with it. He'd stop here, at Keadby, with a bag of corn for this farm and two bags for that, and so on; he'd be maybe three or four hours discharging. He had a steam derrick on board so he could put cargo straight onto the old farm carts. Then he'd have maybe the odd one for Crowle but not much. Then there'd be a load for Thorne and then a bit for Doncaster. And he used to tow a keel, *Lavinia*, which used to take all Darley's beer to Hull from Thorne. There wasn't Boothferry Bridge then, remember, so you couldn't get by road like you can now. He'd tow that *Lavinia* up from Hull full of all the empty barrels and leave it at Thorne and carry on to Doncaster. Then he'd come back on Friday night or Saturday morning and lay at Thorne. While he'd been up there Darley's had unloaded all the empties and reloaded this *Lavinia* with full barrels. On Monday morning he used to go back down to Hull to start picking up again and come back. There used to be a lot of market boats, up the Trent as well. It was quicker than the post is today to put a parcel on them.

'Anyway, me dad's tug showed 'em what a diesel engine could do. Then of course, I think it'd be about 1936, Listers came out with that little 21-horse, the JP2. They put one in a keel, *Evangeline*, for almost nothing – well, at cost – just to show what it could do. And it would work wonders – it could tear the arse off a bus, to tell the truth! So then they went like wildfire. The canal company put six or eight or ten into Bleasdale's boats for nothing. They had a plate on, saying "This is the property of the Sheffield & South Yorkshire Canal Co". Because of course Bleasdale's were a very big barge company, all their boats were called something *'cliffe*. Of course it was good for the canal company because it brought them revenue because the boats were getting two trips a fortnight instead of one a month so they were getting more tolls. Eventually those engines killed us off, but that's how it goes on.'

George obtained a job advertised in *The Motor Boat*, reconditioning pleasure craft engines in Brentford, Middlesex, despite the owner's reservations about his youth. 'But then the war started, and of course his work just vanished. So I came home and he says, "I'll let you know when to come back, because I'm in for some big contracts from the government and things like that."

'But whilst I was at home, Harker's [the tanker barge operators based at Knottingley] wanted me dad's tug to tow for them up to Leeds; so of course I went on that. But that finished quite early, in the first six months of the war, so I was out of work again. You see, they'd packed up doing petrol from Saltend, just below Hull there, because it was that risky in the war bringing tankers through the channel. You were lucky if one in ten could get through and reach Saltend. Harker's were still emptying the tanks there, but that would come to an end.

'So I came away from Harker's, at Knottingley, and went straight into Dunston's, at Thorne, because I knew them all there. You see, we used to tow their new craft away from there as they finished them, and the boss said "Yes, start at dinner time!" The manager, old Bill Robinson, he says "I can't give you fitters' rates, you may be a good bloke with a diesel engine on a tug, but that doesn't mean to say you're any good on installation. So," he says, "I'll give you improvers' rates." That was £2 19s 6d a week or something. So I said, "Fair enough," like. "Start at dinner, come a month, and we'll see how it goes," he says. Anyhow,

I'd been there a week and he come in and says, "Ah, you'll be all right, you can have fitters' rates." And I was there all through the war.

'I learnt some stuff there, I really did; we worked bloody hard. We were living at Thorne, of course. There was a period when we were building some tugs and I was lining the engines up to the stern tubes. We went in on the Monday morning and worked all Monday, all Monday night, all day Tuesday, go home on Tuesday night, back at half-past seven next morning, Wednesday, work all day till tea-time (just a normal day), then back Thursday morning and work all day, all night Thursday night and all day Friday till five o'clock. Saturday you knocked off at half-past four and Sunday the same, at half-past four. We did that for months, and eventually I finished up knackered!

'All the fitters that did the installation of those engines went on trials with them. You'd burn about seven ton of coal a day, like. They were a three fire-hole boiler. We finished up in Hull about three o'clock in the morning with this particular one, and it was my turn to fire and I could never fire. I was one that made damned hard work of firing and a lot of black smoke, but no steam, you know. We had this old van – well, in fact it was a Rolls Royce shooting brake but they used it for a van. And Mr Dunston had come with us, he used to, on some of them trials; he was a good boss, old Dunston. "Right lads," he said, "we're off home now." I said, "I couldn't walk to that bloody car if there were a million pound in it!" He said, "Well, surely you're not after getting a free night." Because you were on pay all the

One of the Admiralty's new Dunston-built TID tugs on trial at Hull – black smoke by George Trevethick, perhaps

time. I said no. "All right," he said, "you can stop on board but come home in the morning. You'll not get paid for it." So I went home next morning, and when I went in, he told me to call at the doctor's at Thorne.

'I'd been gobbling Rennies for weeks because I'd been getting pains, and so I went into the doctor's. I knew him because he was the yard doctor as well. Those were the days when you could call in the doctor's, and if he was in he'd see you right away, not like it is today. "What's wrong with you, then?" I said, "Indigestion's bloody killing me." He says "Get stripped off, then!" I says, "No I've only got indigestion…" And he says, "I *said*, get stripped off!" So I did. At the time me dad was in bed with a bad heart. The doctor says, "When did you have rheumatic fever?" I said, "I've never had it." "Was you invalided out of the forces?" I said, "I've never been in." Because you couldn't escape from Dunston's yard, like; we'd tried, many a time! So then he said, "You've just done too much, you've tired your bloody heart out! Go and get alongside your dad and stay there for a twelve-month." Anyway, after six months he took bad and another doctor come, and I went to see him and said, "I've come to get signed off." He signed me off, but he said, "I think you'll take half days." So I was on half days for about three months.

'I enjoyed it at Dunston's. But through the war, in times when we weren't working all those hours, although we still used to work long hours, the boat chaps used to come down our house, down Chapel Lane, and say "Can you come and have a look at our engine?" Which I used to do. Well, when the war finished they started to say, "Why don't you pack up Dunston's and come and look after us? There's plenty of us to keep you going." But while I was happy at Dunston's I didn't want to stop; I didn't want to leave. I used to bike it during the war because they stopped me petrol. But then I thought, well, if I went on my own, it would cut all that biking out, especially in winter. So I went and saw Dunston; and I'm not bragging here, like, but he says "I don't want to lose you, there's a job here for life for you. There's plenty I want to get rid of before you." We were still building stuff for the Japanese war which was being scrapped as soon as it got there, you know how it happened. But then he says "After this lot, we might have nothing to do. And even if we do, all you can hope is to become foreman. You've got to wait for Jack to die." Jack Oxley that was, who was the foreman. Lovely chap. "Then," he says, "it's between you and Bill, and Bill's been here the longest, so I shall give it to Bill. So, then, you've got to wait for your bloody mate to die." I always remember that. He did do, eventually, many years ago, but he was a good chap. So I came and set up here, at Keadby.'

The canal heads away from the Trent above its entrance lock at Keadby in a dead-straight line, almost due west. Beyond the road swing-bridge at the head of the lock and a canalside pub were oil storage tanks and cottages. It was on the site of the small oil depot that George set up his workshop, within yards of where he had awaited tide time with the tug before the war.

'There was no boatyard here when I came. When I got going I used to have four blokes with me, and at times I was regularly there at eleven o'clock at night. I mean, we'd got fifty-eight regular barges. We were continually converting them and putting engines in, in the early years like, because there were plenty still sailing after the war. Basically, we'd always one engine with a little bit of trouble, and another one we'd got stripped down with the crank out and that. You see, engines needed more maintenance in those days, you know, grinding the crank and all that. Another one we'd be installing a new engine. There'd be

A less hectic post-war day at Dunston's shipyard at Thorne, by which time George Trevethick had set up Keadby Marine at the canal's entrance lock (Author's collection)

others passing to and from the tide that would want fuelling up and so on. But they were grand to work for, if you see what I mean. If one came down the canal late for an early tide and fuelled himself from our tank he'd perhaps leave a note saying how much he'd had. On the way back next time he'd be in and pay for the diesel oil. We never had any bother getting paid.

'It's a sacrilege killing all them; it must be vested interests as has done it. You think about it, an empty barge is about 30 or 31 ton of steel. Today, in about six or seven minutes, I could untie it from this side of the canal and have it tied at yon side, 30 yards across, without you helping me. It could have 100 ton in it and I should only be about five minutes longer, if that. How else can one man shift 100 ton? So it's not the boat and it's not the water that's wrong. When they started putting these 21-horse Listers in, it was nothing for a barge leaving Hull this morning to get up to Mexborough or above there today. He'd got 90 ton with 21 horse. There's three lorry loads there, and that lorry's got a 200- or 300-horse engine in it gobbling fuel, and I doubt whether he'd do three runs in a day. The only thing is, they've shifted that mill from the side of the canal to ten mile inland, and so've made sure it can't come right through by boat. So the lorry man says, "I shall charge you five bob a ton to shift it from the barge to the mill, and six bob a ton to fetch it all the way from Hull." So you let him fetch it from Hull, don't you?

'Now it's all pleasure boats, and you get all sorts on them. There are some that come down this canal and get here, and they say, "Isn't it lovely, boating? We're going to Torksey. Which way do we go here?" And they're going out there, into the Trent tideway. It's nearly the biggest rise and fall of tide in the country and it's over a mile wide a little way down there. But off they go, not knowing what they might find!

'Many years ago when we started to get a few pleasure boats on the canal, we'd a chap come here on a Friday for some help. Now, you know Kelvin engines – they're a double-sided cone clutch, and when they had a hand lever it was a great big cast-iron lever which goes round the tail-shaft. It has a sleeve round the shaft, and it pulls the tail shaft in for ahead and shoves it back for astern. Well, on them if she's ticking over a bit too much and you're not really holding that lever, it can drag the propeller forward until it touches the clutch. Then it starts to stick a bit and the prop starts to turn. And if it's a bit fast there's enough push on that prop that it will push that lever out of your hand. With that lever – typical Kelvin, like, of heavy cast-iron, it goes *clonk*!

'Well, on them cone clutches there's very, very minute grooves in the surface. They're not machined in, they were made smooth, but with the constant slipping as you put the gear in they wear that little bit. And so as it goes in, like, it goes one too many, and of course when it goes right in like that, can you hell as like pull it out again! You *cannot* pull it out of gear. If ever you look at a Kelvin instruction book it says, if ever it does that, get someone to pull on the lever and "strike the coupling [in the shaft] sharply with a 7lb-hammer" and of course it will come out.

'So, it was in the old days when we were real busy, and we'd packed up about half-past nine on this Friday night and decided we'd have a pint that night. Well, we were there

The Stainforth & Keadby Canal viewed from Keadby Lock. The lock has gates pointing both ways allowing craft to descend to the Trent in normal circumstances or rise up from the canal into the river at times of very high tides. These gates are worked by a profusion of winches around the lock walls some of which are visible here. The sailing keel Process *leaving the lock for the canal is passing through the former wooden road swing bridge which has now been replaced by a large powered structure. The furthermost buildings by the towpath in the left background mark the present position of the Trevethicks' marine engineering business, near which the white funnel of their tug* Sulzer *is visible* (Lincolnshire Library Service)

washing our hands and messing about when this bloke comes down the canal bank. He said, "Do you know anything about marine engines?" Well, he maybe thought we was a garage or something! "Aye, I know a bit, like, what's your trouble?" He said, "I've got an engine there, it's stuck in head gear. We're off out in t'morning." I said, "Well, what sort of engine is it?" And I thought, "I bet it's a Kelvin." He says, "Err, err, I don't know;" this was in the days when everybody was converting old ships' lifeboats, double-ended lifeboats, and putting orange-box tops on them! I says, "Is it like so, and has it got a big flywheel and a tray under the flywheel?" "Yeah, yeah." "Has it got a big lever to pull it into gear?" "Yeah, yeah." I said, "You want that big hammer in the corner, mate." Well, he laid into me, ooh! Trying to take the piss and all this. I said, "Look, I'm not trying to take the mick, we want to be going for a pint. You want that big hammer." Anyway, he simmered down and he went to try what I'd told him. He was back two minutes later: "You were right," he says, "thanks a lot, you were right." He didn't say how sorry he was for disturbing us, or doubting what I'd said, or owt like that, of course! It was his first time on a boat – but do you know, he went out of here, up to Torksey and through there, Lincoln, Boston and out into the Wash and to Yarmouth, and he didn't have nothing. Yet you'll get an experienced bloke, and he'll go and drop a clanger out there.

'I've seen some lovely escapades, but I do think the way it's going now with insurances and everything, it'll not be long before you've to pass a driving test. Boating was the only thing you could do where you didn't have to ask anybody. As I say, you could go and buy the *Queen Mary* if you wanted and bugger off across the Atlantic! Nobody could stop you. But once you get regulations...

'You know, when I was on the tugs you were looked down on – water gypsies, the scum of the earth. Now, if you haven't got a boat, you're nobody! When I was courting my missus, all her family were railway engine drivers, but when I first met her aunty there was a hell of a barny. "You don't want to go with one of them there boatmen," and all that.

'I enjoyed it, and I'd do it all again... but in them conditions, not today! I liked it as it was. You were like a snail, you'd got your shell with you, your little house. I loved my little cabin. I loved me engine and I loved the life. It depended on tides and that, but if you could get to the pictures of a night because the tides were right, *you lived*! It were lovely. And fish and chips after! Ooh! I mean, I never had a drink, like, until I'd been at Dunston's a couple of years I should think. I've nothing agin it like, but, well, you couldn't afford it, for one thing. Now it's all different, all your life's different. I've never made any money, I've done no end of work for nowt, like. But I'm not pleading poverty. If I've done your job and you couldn't pay me, I would still be thrilled to bits because I've solved your problem. I've been happy, that's the thing. I've never been for a holiday in me life, always been to work. There's lots of things I would like, but there's nothing I want. You see what I mean, you want when you're hungry and you can't afford bread. But I'm happy chucking coal on my little boiler and messing about with those engines I've made. You don't come in with owt and you can't take it out with you.'

HARRY & SARAH BENTLEY

Potteries Boating

The Trent & Mersey Canal was originally promoted as the Grand Trunk and as the name implies, was intended as a long-distance transport artery. An act was obtained in May 1766 and the whole line was finished by 1777. Lord Gower was a leading promoter, and with his assistance his brother-in-law, the Duke of Bridgewater, was able to influence the scheme. The Trent & Mersey joined the duke's canal at Preston Brook, so gaining access to Manchester but also enabling the latter to control the route to the river Mersey via its Runcorn Locks. In 1847 the Trent & Mersey was taken over by the North Staffordshire Railway which worked much of the canal energetically. An electric tug was introduced to haul boats through Harecastle Tunnel whilst steamers were provided at Barnton, Saltersford and Preston Brook on the canal's northern section.

Amongst the canal's most famous promoters had been the potter Josiah Wedgwood, who built his new works alongside it at Etruria. One of its most important sources of traffic from opening until the 1960s was pottery materials uphill from the Mersey to the Stoke-on-Trent area, and finished ware down for export. This was either routed via transhipment at Anderton where the canal ran close above the river Weaver, or through to the Bridgewater Canal's Runcorn Docks. In 1875 a lift capable of passing barges of 14ft beam between the two waterways was opened at Anderton, and narrowboats began to trade down the Weaver to Weston Point Docks. It was this traffic which occupied the canal's two largest carriers, and the families of Harry and Sarah Bentley.

Like so many people who have worked on canal boats, they are not able to separate themselves completely from the water, and after over thirty years 'on the land' they still live in a house backing on to the Macclesfield Canal.

'I don't know how I came to be a boatman – I was just always reared as one! My father was well educated, though I'm not sure about his parents. I was born in a house at

Middlewich. Dad was boating while my mum was laid up; she stayed with my aunty, then she just took me back on the boats and we were away.

'Some of my earliest memories are of going up this Congleton canal [the Macclesfield Canal] a lot. We used to go right through to Ashton-under-Lyne, taking beer, of all things – from Joules brewery at Stone that was.

'There was seven of us when I was with my parents, and we had two boats then. They say that boatmen were cruel to children, but I'd ask you to consider why one boatman might have two boats and only two grown-ups? It was because either he had two boats, or he gave up his children because they couldn't fit in so many to sleep in that little cabin. It's not like today: there used to be sanitary inspectors all along the canal, Potteries, Runcorn, Manchester, and they'd come on your boat any old time asking "How many children have you got, how old are they?" You see, there's only a set number of sleeping places in a boat, and if you had one too many or the wrong mix [regulations prevented two children over twelve years of age of the opposite sex sharing the same cabin] they'd say "you can't do this". Not to you, but to your boss: so you'd get back to the depot and you'd be told you were wanted in the office; and there it'd be, "You've got to do something, Jack, you've too many children on that boat. Are you going to give your children up, or are you going to have another boat?"

'There was three before me – well, four, but one sister was drowned going up Lawton, near Red Bull. There was a bad lock where if you drew the centre paddles going uphill the water could splash into the hatches of the boat. We was working up there in the dark one

An Anderton Co boat loading pottery materials at Weston Point

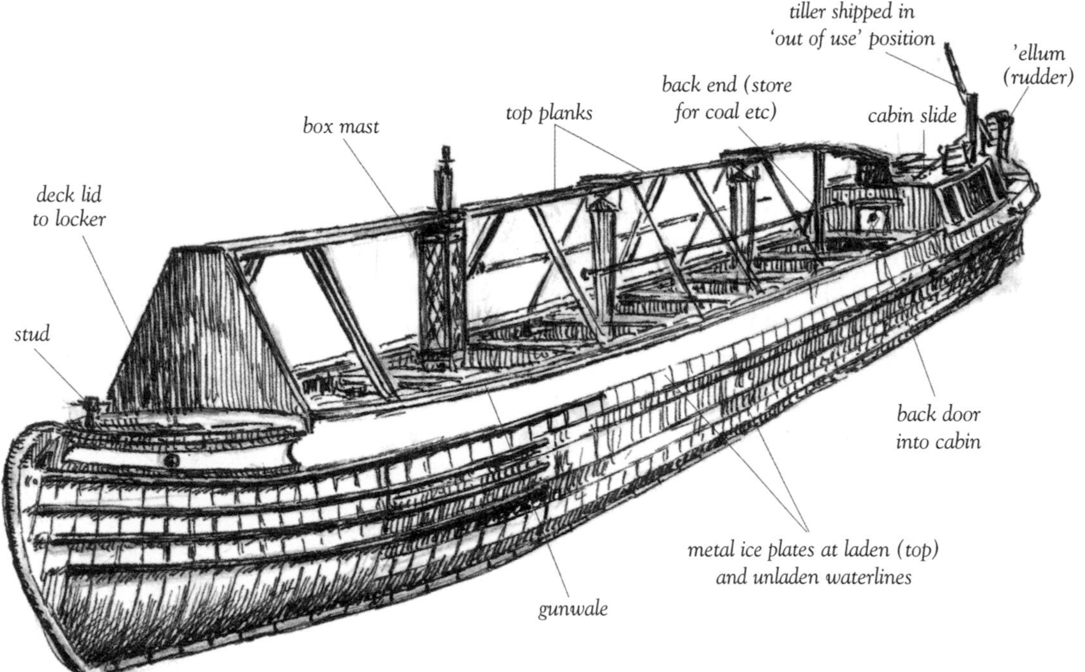

A wooden horse-drawn Anderton Company narrowboat. These craft were more rounded in section than many narrowboats which made them easier to pull into and out of the many locks on the northern Trent & Mersey Canal. On the other hand, they were liable to roll when loaded with pottery crates up to the top planks. They were strongly built at the fore end to resist the constant contact with lock cills going uphill

day and she didn't like this water coming in, so she must have got off and fell down the steps at the tail of the lock. The water would be moving with the boat working. She was always afraid of that lock, and with me being younger I couldn't stop her getting off. All as I remember was her being laid on the cabin top and taking her up to Lawton Bridge after my parents had got her out.

'Strangely enough, after Sarah and I was married we had a boat sunk at that lock, a little coal boat and the bottom was very thin. It had hit a stone and we just managed to get it up that lock before it went. Looking back on it, if I'd had me wits about me I could have saved it because it's a very short pound between the locks there, and I could have run that dry and let it settle on the bottom, and left it there until the load was taken out; though if the bottom there wasn't level it could have broken the boat in two, doing that.

'One sister was sent to live with my aunty, wife of the tug man at Preston Brook. She ended up being a district nurse, trained at Liverpool hospital, and did very well. Now, there was every intention that I would be put away with another aunt; I got as far as being bathed by her, on what was to have been my last night with me mum, but I protested and wouldn't stop with them. I suppose I'd have been about five then, and I expect if I'd stopped that one night I would have stayed, and you'd not be here talking to me now. I would have had an education then, too. My father was very well educated, but all he did was to learn me how to write my name. But he would read to us, and people would come to him and ask how to spell this or that.

'It was all a case of whether you wanted to put your children away or not. Nowadays people don't bother a lot, they just let them go to a boarding school if they can pay for it. But it didn't work like that with boat people, so me dad went into two boats. For a start they couldn't afford it. When me brother was old enough he took one of them, and we worked together, and it was hard work. I would have seen the boat work from before I knew what was happening round me, sitting on the cabin top watching. Bored stiff most of the time! As far as children was concerned, enjoyment didn't happen until you were tied up; then you might play with other children if there was enough daylight, but it was long hours with nothing to do.

'I don't remember working as a youngster. I remember playing about trying to steer and that sort of thing. But I'd be well over fifteen when I had to do a job seriously, and all it was at that time was steering a boat. I weren't allowed to get off it, or to shut gates, or to draw paddles, and they wouldn't give me a windlass. Until one day, at Sideway Colliery, we were waiting to load; the coal came by a conveyor under the railway to a spout over the boat. My father was sat on the boat side about three foot off the bankside, and when the conveyor started up, Dad jumped off the boat – and fell down. He'd throwed his knee out of place and I had to load that boat then, by his instructions. I'd never done it before, though I'd watched it being done and played about all the while – "Get off...leave that alone...keep out the way", you know, always in trouble – but this time it was the other way about.

'Then I worked the horse up the five locks at Stoke while Dad did the steering – and I made a great job of it and my father was that proud! He never did see a doctor with that knee, and he was for ever more crippled with it and limped on it. I don't know why, but he just wouldn't go to a doctor. He just worked on and said "It'll go better" – but you could see it was twisted out. I can't understand why he wouldn't go, unless it was that he didn't want to be fast in hospital; he'd have been in for some time. Anyway, that was the first time that I had to work.

'I didn't do a lot until we started to have a motor boat, and then I had to take the engine over because me dad didn't know the first thing about engines, he'd oil 'em up but no more. Of the two main carriers, the Mersey Weaver & Ship Canal Carrying Co didn't have any motor boats until the last war started; then they built four, and bought one in, with a 12-horse Petter engine. But the Anderton Company had several and had had them quite a long time, perhaps from the thirties or even the twenties. Fellows Morton & Clayton had them of course, but you never saw much of those up Cheshire Locks and round our way. There was a fellow, who the Mersey Weavers and the Anderton Company both used, a mechanic. He used to take you down for one day, say as far as Middlewich, and learn you about these engines – and then you was on your own.

'It was a 12-horse Petter engine in that boat, the *Empire*. After that we had an 18-horse Gardner, a twin cylinder, in one of the boats the Mersey Weaver Company built themselves. That was a very quiet engine, like they had in buses at that time; you could talk or anything with that going. The Anderton Company had one Petter but all the rest was Bolinders, 9- and 15- and one 20-horse which had a gearbox.

'After that I got married. We was going out for four years before that!

'I was with my old company, the Mersey Weavers, then and we had a horse boat after we got married, but I was fed up with horses. The company that Sarah had come from had motor boats, so I went to my boss and asked if we would be able to get a motor, but he said he couldn't see it happening; so we left, didn't we. We went working for Sarah's company, the Anderton Company, and the boss said we should have a motor boat within six months. And it was less than that actually, wasn't it?'

A Mersey Weaver & Ship Canal Carrying Co horse boat sets out upstream from Dutton Lock on the river Weaver. The extra long horse line can just be made out trailing in the water and the boatman is becoming concerned that it is about to sweep the camera away since the photographer stood between the horse and the river's edge! (Edward Paget-Tomlinson collection)

Sarah nodded in agreement: 'Harry didn't want the horse all the time. I liked the horses, but the motor was more convenient – you didn't have to stop at the stables when you had a motor, you could stop anywhere. The Anderton Company boats was better, too; they had more repairs done than the Mersey Weavers did – some of the Mersey Weavers leaked into the cabins, but Anderton Company paid a lot of attention to their boats.' Harry took up the tale again:

'The Mersey Weavers provided the boat, and you paid so much a week for the horse; they provided the lines and the feed for it as well. And they was the comfortablest bosses! They would come on the boat and have a cup of tea and a smoke. The Anderton Company they would shout to you "Hey, Bentley . . ." in that sort of tone, always the boss. One had a dickey bow and a fancy shirt and wore a bowler hat and carried a walking stick.

'You couldn't leave one company for the other without quite an inquest: "Why is he leaving you, is he any good?" "No." "Right, well, he can't come here!" Or, "Yes, he's got plenty to say, but he's a good worker." We never had any trouble, but I have known of people who were refused. One of the things about boating then was that if somebody left who was higher up than you, you knew what boat you'd be having – if you wanted it, that is. Now you can't tell, with all the redundancies. But none of them did as much as they could have for you – their aim was to get as much cargo in the boat as they could and get it back for another cargo as quick as possible. But you see, they really could have made the cabins a little bit bigger without losing cargo weight, and then they could have put dynamos on the engine so that you could have had electric lighting – we had an oil lamp in the cabin, that's all. And they could have done more for the children, worked something out for them, how to get them to school and also keep them in the family. Had they done that, you couldn't have said anything against them.

'I think they had to keep that system of paying you when you got back, or some people would have been six weeks on a trip, sneaking here and there a bit at a time. It was only like piecework in the factories. If you'd two boats and had to pay two people to work along with you, the captain had to pay them two out of his money.

'We never looked back then, as far as boating was concerned, I think because I was always honest with them. If I said we'd get down to the dock for a certain time we'd do our best to get there, and when we got there we'd do our best to make sure we got a load straight back again. A lot of people didn't like us for that reason. We always did well, not only with the company but at the loading and unloading places as well, because we joked and laughed with them, and weren't awkward with them. There was a lot of awkward people about then, boat people. They had a reason for it, a lot of the time.

'We didn't get on very well with townspeople, just the odd ones. They would throw things as we went past, and all sorts of things were said to us. We couldn't do anything about it. That was the part we didn't like.

'Our regular run was from Stoke-on-Trent to Runcorn or Manchester, nowhere else – the Trent & Mersey Canal, that's all. That was the Anderton Company mostly; they had a monopoly on the potters' materials to Stoke-on-Trent, and Mersey Weavers was more in the general goods line, carrying anything. We don't know anything about other parts of the country on the canals, although basically, the way they worked was pretty well the same.

'We had no house, so we didn't aim to tie up there like one or two did that had a house. The main place you made for was your depot, which for us was Longport, when we were

Mersey Weaver horse boat Margaret *discharging pottery materials at Harrisons' works at Joyners Square in Hanley, on the Caldon branch of the Trent & Mersey Canal. The works processed raw materials for supply to the pottery manufacturers. Cargoes were shovelled out by men from the works into large wooden wheelbarrows standing on the towpath; the plywood sheets lying by the boat served to stop loss of cargo into the canal* (Fred Birden)

with Mersey Weavers. A trip for us was to load either coal or earthenware, in the big old-fashioned cane crates – not metal ones as they have now. Tea pots was in massive barrels, because they were bulk, and not a weighty cargo. Well, you took them down to Runcorn, and they were offloaded into a warehouse. After a time they did away with the warehouse and then you went to Weston Point and they went straight off your boat onto a barge to carry them to Liverpool. Some went into big barges which went up the Manchester Ship Canal to get to a ship at Manchester. But mostly Mersey Weavers took coal down to Seddon's salt works at Middlewich. Then after you'd unloaded at Middlewich you'd go on down empty either to Runcorn or Weston Point and pick a load up there, mostly of potters' materials, pebbles, stone or the white clay, everything they wanted. You'd take that up to the pot banks which were mostly on the canalside at Joyners Square, and then you'd load earthenware there and set off all over again doing the same thing again!

'If you started on a Monday morning, you'd be about three days until you were back again. You could unload and reload again in the one day, and you might get on your way on that Monday. But there's a tunnel at Kidsgrove [Harecastle Tunnel] which you couldn't go through on your own, you had to go by tug. Eventually there were so many motor boats that the tug finished and you went through on your own power, like you would now. But in those days you'd be lucky if you could get your load out and another on, *and* get through that tunnel the same night. If you did get through, to Kidsgrove, you'd stay there the night and then you could get down to Middlewich or Preston Brook the next day. The day after that you'd be able to get down to the dock, which would make it lunchtime Wednesday.

'So you could only do one round trip a week, unless you worked nights, which some did. But you didn't get that sleep back – it was done for your own benefit. You didn't get paid till you got back to base, and no matter how long it took you, even a fortnight, you'd only get paid for that one journey. Sometimes, but not very often, you'd get paid tonnage for having more weight on the boat; I don't remember if it made a difference going down empty.'

Sarah intervened quickly: 'Oh, yes it did, you lost a lot on that. You'd get paid empty boat money, so there was some, but not as much as having a cargo.' Harry resumed, re-living all the comings and goings of the trade he had known so well:

'It would be about £3 for a return trip to Runcorn, before the war, so it really paid you to have a load both ways. You could draw a sub before you started, but that was taken off your week's money for that trip. They wasn't giving you anything. If you went to Manchester, which you did in the company I was brought up in, you'd get a little bit of mileage as well because it was a good way all round the Bridgewater Canal. Well, it'd be a bob or two [5p–10p] then, not a pound or two. Then if you did a trip in a short time you'd get a bonus. But all this meant a lot of hard work in long hours. You see, when you were working the boats you didn't get a lot of pleasure! Also if you were working at weekends you got no extra money for weekend work.

'On occasion we've gone down to Runcorn or Weston Point and missed loading because it's been raining on a Saturday morning, and they wouldn't work in the rain so you didn't load – especially Weston Point where it was out in the open loading conditions. Then you'd be there all weekend, and that was something we *didn't* want. Had you been loaded on Saturday morning, you'd have been up to the tunnel on Sunday night, waiting to go through with the first tug on Monday, and you'd have your money on Monday morning – but if you missed loading on Saturday you'd still be down in the dock loading on that

Anderton Co boats climbing the paired Cheshire Locks towards Harecastle Tunnel on the Trent & Mersey Canal

Monday morning. And *we* always had to stand the loss – you didn't get paid for lying down there all weekend, you only got paid when you got back, no matter how long it took you. Nowadays if a transport worker is held up he'll be paid waiting time.

'It was all go – there was no stopping for meals! You worked as long as daylight hours would allow, and sometimes in the dark. I didn't much care for working in the dark, especially in the locks. But every minute counted, when you think it was only three mile an hour. It was all done to time, and a boatman would know if he was losing time anywhere. Nor was it as comfortable as what folks think when they're doing their holiday boating now – for instance, when it comes on to rain, they stop – well, you didn't stop then! Scenery meant nothing to us in those days: it's like a lorry driver on the motorway now – he'll not be enjoying the driving, he only wants to reach the other end and get delivered. That's how it was with us.

'There was many things you had to take care of, especially with the horses; you couldn't neglect the horse. The company would buy you a horse but then you would pay for it at so much a week, a shilling was it? So if something happened to that horse you'd be at a loss and you'd to take care of it. Sometimes the horses weren't good enough. For instance, one as was too tall would be no use because there's only so much height for the horse through the bridges, especially somewhere like Marston where the ground was sinking with the salt mining. A Shire horse wouldn't go through there. We had a big one once and it was very difficult getting through bridges; you'd have to swing on its head at times to keep its head down. Lots of folks think that a boat horse was ill used, but it wasn't. A boatman knew what the horse was capable of doing, and anything more than that he would slow down. You wouldn't let it eat grass. You might think that's cruel, but it wasn't, because a boat horse was used to the hay and oats or corn and whatever they mixed for it, and anything other than that would make it ill because it was always used to that.

'The company would only fix you up with a horse that you wanted; if you said to a boss "it's no good" there'd be no arguments. We had a horse when I wasn't very old, "Trigger" – Roy Rogers' horse was identical! I really wanted that horse, I could see myself on his back as a cowboy! But he wouldn't pull a boat. Now, every horse had to be tested, and some just wouldn't pull; the moment the weight went into that collar they'd just stop. Another time you'd get a horse and take it two or three mile and back with a loaded boat and it'd be fine and you'd have it. Then you'd to pay for it, and there was quite a few people that did – in other words, the horse lasted long enough to be paid for. But some would go lame and some would go lazy; they could act like a mule and refuse to do anything, so they had to go. I don't know where they got these horses from, gypsies perhaps.'

Sarah adds: 'Some was army horses, they had numbers on their ears and their necks.' Harry continues:

'Sarah used to look after them all, she used to work them. They had two horses. Her dad had two boats so she had to look after one – and she made a better job than her dad, he was a bit rough; she'd've taken hers to bed with her if she could!

'When we came to Harecastle Tunnel the tug would take the boat through and it was mostly the children that took the horse over the path over the top – if there was grown-ups around, that is. You wouldn't be allowed to take a horse over on your own if you was less than about fifteen. But if there were other boats and there was grown-ups about, you'd be allowed, because they would watch you and the horse over; otherwise the captain would go over himself with the horse and let the children go under. The boat didn't need steering through the tunnel because the tug was on a wire rope; the rope lay in the bottom of the tunnel and the tug pulled it up and over a sort of winch on board to haul itself along.

'That tug always towed a boat behind it, a special one with a full flat deck all along it, weighted down at the same level as the tug, and that was a floating office. There was two people, the tug driver and the conductor, if you like to call him that, whose job was to take the tickets. You had to pay for a ticket, at Etruria, at the top lock, or if you were coming up, at Anderton, at the toll offices. I think it was a shilling; you got the money back from your depot. That conductor's job was to take those tickets and see the last boat in the tunnel; then he'd walk along the towpath into the tunnel. Now that towpath was broken and

(Top) A ticket for a boat to use the electric Harecastle Tunnel tug southwards from the Kidsgrove or Harecastle entrance to Chatterley on its way to the Potteries. (Bottom) A similar ticket for towage northbound from Dutton through Preston Brook Tunnel towards the Bridgewater Canal. Both are standard Edmondson pasteboard tickets of the type once familiar to all railway passengers as befitting the LMS railway management of the Trent & Mersey Canal. They were issued at the Toll Office close to the top of the Anderton Lift where boats would have their cargoes gauged to check the tonnage carried (BW Archives, Gloucester)

Trent & Mersey steam tunnel tug No 3 almost always worked in Preston Brook Tunnel. It is seen here emerging from the Dutton Portal

partly fallen in, so he had a limited amount of time to get to his boat – and he had to be quick on a Monday morning going up from Kidsgrove because there could be as many as twenty-one boats on then, behind the tug. Also, there's a sharp turn into the tunnel at the Kidsgrove end and he sometimes had to work there to pull the boats into line so they went in easily behind the tug.

'The wire rope that stretched all the way through was anchored at the Kidsgrove end on a massive square post, and all that tug was doing was winching itself through the tunnel. The rope went on board and round big massive wheels, about four or five times, and there was a big electric motor which was fed off the electric poles. That rope must have been about an inch thick, though sometimes it would stretch out a bit; if it got slack it would slip round the wheels and so they used to take the tension up at Chatterley end. And sometimes it would break, and then they would slacken it off from the end and splice it in the tunnel; you can splice a wire rope without anything showing, by putting all the ends inside. There used to be breakdowns, and sometimes a power cut. Normally it used to take the best part of an hour to pull through.

'I think that wire rope was the reason there was a limit on the number of boats: if you think about it, there could be twenty-one boats with twenty tons on each, and each would be a good five tons itself, so there's over five hundred ton dragging behind the tug. I think they were afraid of it breaking if they had any more. But the tug always went the same speed, whether there was one or twenty boats on. There have been boats left behind on a

The unusual bluff stern and horse-boat-style helm of this Jonathon Horsefield motor boat Richard *is clear in this portrait of Harry and Sarah Bentley waiting, with a cargo of coal, at the northern approach to the Barton Swing Aqueduct for a ship to pass through on the Manchester Ship Canal. They were travelling the length of the Bridgewater Canal from Marsland Green to Runcorn* (Harry Bentley collection)

Monday. When the tug came out, they went as far as they could, but that would get only five or six out and then you had to get the horse lines on and pull the rest out. The motor boats had to be pulled by him as well, and they'd to put their engines out going through.'

Sarah adds, 'You kept your cooking range in, but you didn't do so much stoking coal on it because it was better for yourself.'

Harry continues, re-living the events he talks about as if they were yesterday: 'Of course the Barnton and Saltersford tugs were steam, and there the boats had to be steered through. There were three steamers, one at Preston Brook, one at Barnton and a spare one. The worst was the one at Preston Brook because the tug had to get up steam going through, so they had to put coal on the fire. Those tunnels had vents in them, but on a calm, damp day it wouldn't clear and sometimes the wind would be going the same way as you so the smoke would keep with you. We were OK, but the blokes that worked those tugs was yellow with always being in it! My uncle worked on one of those, but he died before I was old enough to see him; they said he was yellow.

'When you got to the other end of the one at Preston Brook, you were on the Manchester Ship Canal part; they owned the Bridgewater Canal and that was different altogether, deep and fairly clean.

'Our last boat job was on the Bridgewater, on the Horsefield boats from Runcorn to Manchester collieries. We had three and a half years on that, and it was the best boat job we ever had, with no locks and good money. It was two boats, and we'd a butty of course – but they was very ugly! Big, and the cabins were very high but a lot shorter. We didn't like 'em at all, but it was a better job because there was no locks and you only had to steer the butty boat loaded, you didn't have to steer it empty. You took it up short on what we call cross-straps and Sarah could do the housework, cabin-work if you like.'

The stern of a Horsefield motor boat seen from the fore-end of its butty which is under tow on cross-straps

Sarah observes: 'They wasn't very comfy, the cabins, because there wasn't enough room in them. They were high, and you could stand up in them easily, and they were wide, but not very long.' Harry continues, remembering every detail of those days:

'You got paid by tonnage there – it was two bob [10p] a ton then. It was from Marsley Green [Marsland Green on the Bridgewater Canal's Leigh branch], Boothstown occasionally,

Harry Bentley steers the motor boat Richard *towards Runcorn Gas Works towing butty* Winifred *steered by Sarah whilst young Colin sits on the cabin top enjoying the attention of the photographer* (Harry Bentley collection)

and we carried washed slack from Boothstown to the tanneries at Runcorn. From Marsley Green it was washed beans for the gasworks at Runcorn; six loads a week it was there, they had the most coal. There were no locks on that, but it was a very dreary journey. Like I say, it wasn't a working holiday! If you loaded at Marsley Green of a morning you could probably make Runcorn for about eight o'clock that night. Unload next morning, back up again that afternoon and load on the third morning again. You'd be faster running empty on the way back of course, you see. But it could be midnight before you were tied up some days. What used to happen was that there would be two pair of boats of one company and two pair of another company – Waddingtons of Bolton, I think that was. With Horsefield's you'd have three trips one week and two the next.

'The two trips would make you about £12, and the three about £15. It was good money because you'd got no house rent, no fuel to buy, no lighting. To be quite honest we don't know what we did with that money. We didn't have holidays or anything like that. We can't say with all honesty what we did with £15 a week and nothing to pay out, that was a very good wage in the 1950s. The average wage on the shore then, with piecework, was about £12. The difference was that it was £12 or £15 a week, even if there was fifteen people working on the boats – we only got the one settlement. [Peter Semmens, in *Engineman Extraordinary*, his biography of railway locomotive driver Bill Hoole, records that Bill had been paid £23 0s 2d for a week driving the *Capitals Limited* in 1950. This involved footplate work halfway from London to Edinburgh before swapping with the Scottish crew and travelling the rest of the way as a passenger. He lodged overnight before driving his section of the route southbound the next day. His wage was adjusted to allow for the three nights away from home and the mileage covered, making it one of the highest paid footplate jobs in Britain at the time. Bill's basic rate for a week's driving without adjustments was £7 1s 0d that year.]

'We did have a lot of time to ourselves on that as well. When you'd done your three trip

The approach to Runcorn Top Lock photographed about 1930, before the Bentleys started to work down the locks regularly. Canal flats line the towpath on the right opposite narrowboats, including two loaded with glass carboys of chemicals destined for Littleborough on the, since closed, Rochdale Canal. A Patriot class locomotive accelerates a southbound train from Liverpool away from the Runcorn High Level Railway Bridge over the Manchester Ship Canal and river Mersey. The left- and right-hand arches of Waterloo Bridge, just in front of the railway span, lead to the twin flights of locks by which the Bridgewater Canal reached Runcorn Docks and the Ship Canal. The centre opening, which is occupied by two Bridgewater Canal 'Little Packet' steam tugs, gives access to a drydock (Harry Bentley collection)

week, you'd load on a Friday morning and get down to Runcorn on a Friday night, and if you were early enough you'd be able to go to the pictures. Then you'd come up to the wharf and unload on a Saturday morning, and then you wouldn't have to load again until Tuesday morning. So you could have all that long weekend. So what we used to do was go up on the Sunday and have all the Monday up at Leigh, handy for the shops or pictures, and then load Tuesday. Unload Wednesday, load Thursday and unload on Friday which would be your two trips. Sometimes you'd get two weeks of three trips one after the other, if there was a breakdown with one of the other boats. We did as much as three trips a week for three weeks once and made a lot of money!

'You see we never liked to tie up at the end of a trip knowing that the next move was to get back ready for loading. So when we'd finished emptying at the gas works and got settled up we'd start off straight back towards Marsley Green. That way we could be handy for loading in our turn. If we wanted the shops or pictures we could go through to Leigh and tie up there for a weekend, if we had the chance. You wouldn't lay at the loading tip – that'd be like picnicking on the hard shoulder of a motorway in today's terms! From the bridge at Leigh, by the shops, was only half an hour's run to be at the loading place on Monday morning.

The Bentleys on a wet Sunday in December 1956 making for Runcorn, near Preston Brook. On the motor boat Richard, *Harry has a specially constructed rain shelter of canvas over a wooden frame but on butty* Winifred *Sarah didn't get a proper rain shelter. 'That's how he used to treat me– he got his!'* (Edward Paget-Tomlinson)

'I liked that run, but it didn't keep going long after we left, the trade was all going to road waggons. This happened on the railway as well. We would have stopped on there, except that my son, Colin, was getting up to ten year old and had never been to school, and we thought "something's got to be done". So we had to sacrifice that. I gave up £15 a week to come and earn £7 – that's with house rent to pay and all. I went working at Twyfords sanitary ware place at Alsager, and I was seventeen years there.

'I did miss the water for a while after I'd come off. I'd have gone back again if I could have gone on a day-to-day job where I could have left Sarah at home and gone back to the house at night. Sarah didn't mind leaving, but I did because I didn't know how I was going to go on. But I soon realised that I knew a lot more than most of the blokes I were working with – though I couldn't go anywhere or get up the line any because I weren't educated. That's what I was thinking about my son, so he started as a ten-year-old, at school. He went down to Alsager school, and you can imagine it was difficult for him; but he's ended up in a good job.

'We was all right on the Runcorn job. We was among friends, and we'd never had many among boat people, you know – not even your fellow boatmen, they weren't friends. You see, one was always trying to get past the other one, and you were only friends when you wasn't moving. The moment you started to move on your trip it was everyone for himself; and if anyone could get past you they'd go, whether you were moving or at night. Because if you could get in front of that next boat you'd have a load in a day before him, so you'd get back quicker and get paid quicker. The companies you worked for knew this was going on, but they wouldn't lift one finger to stop it because it was to their advantage to get the boats back quick.'

TOM KELLY

Ship Canal Tug Skipper

Schemes for a Manchester ship canal had been suggested by the commercial leaders of the city for a century before the start of work at the end of the 1880s. The plan adopted was for a ship canal with five locks rising from the Mersey estuary at Eastham.

The Manchester Ship Canal is a minimum of 26ft deep over a width of at least 120ft. There were three locks side by side at Eastham; the other locks were duplicated and allowed ships up to 600 x 45ft to reach Manchester. The canal cut across the entrance to the Shropshire Union Canal at Ellesmere Port, with traffic from the latter passing down to Eastham to gain access to the Mersey. Craft from the river Weaver and Bridgewater Canal could cross the ship canal to reach the Mersey estuary by way of side locks. The uppermost access to the river was through Walton Lock near Warrington. Navigation continued on the estuary above Eastham under the control of the Upper Mersey Navigation Commissioners who maintained the river channels and associated markers as far as Warrington.

The canal was sufficiently complete to receive its first through traffic on 1 January 1894, and Queen Victoria performed the official opening ceremony on 21 May. Traffic was slow to build up, but docks, wharves and other facilities gradually grew up along the whole 36 miles, which became a linear port.

Typical of the canal's heyday was the maintenance of an immaculate vintage steam tug solely for the use of directors and important clients as well as occasional staff outings. In later years the skipper of this fine vessel, the *Daniel Adamson*, was Tom Kelly. Tom now lives quietly with his wife Dot in Runcorn, when they are not cruising smaller canals on their narrowboat. Their Runcorn home is situated in a quiet square of senior citizens' dwellings, almost within sight of the Manchester Ship Canal. Tom is a small, slightly built man, always smiling and ready to provide hospitality and help to others. He is unfailingly alive to Dot's

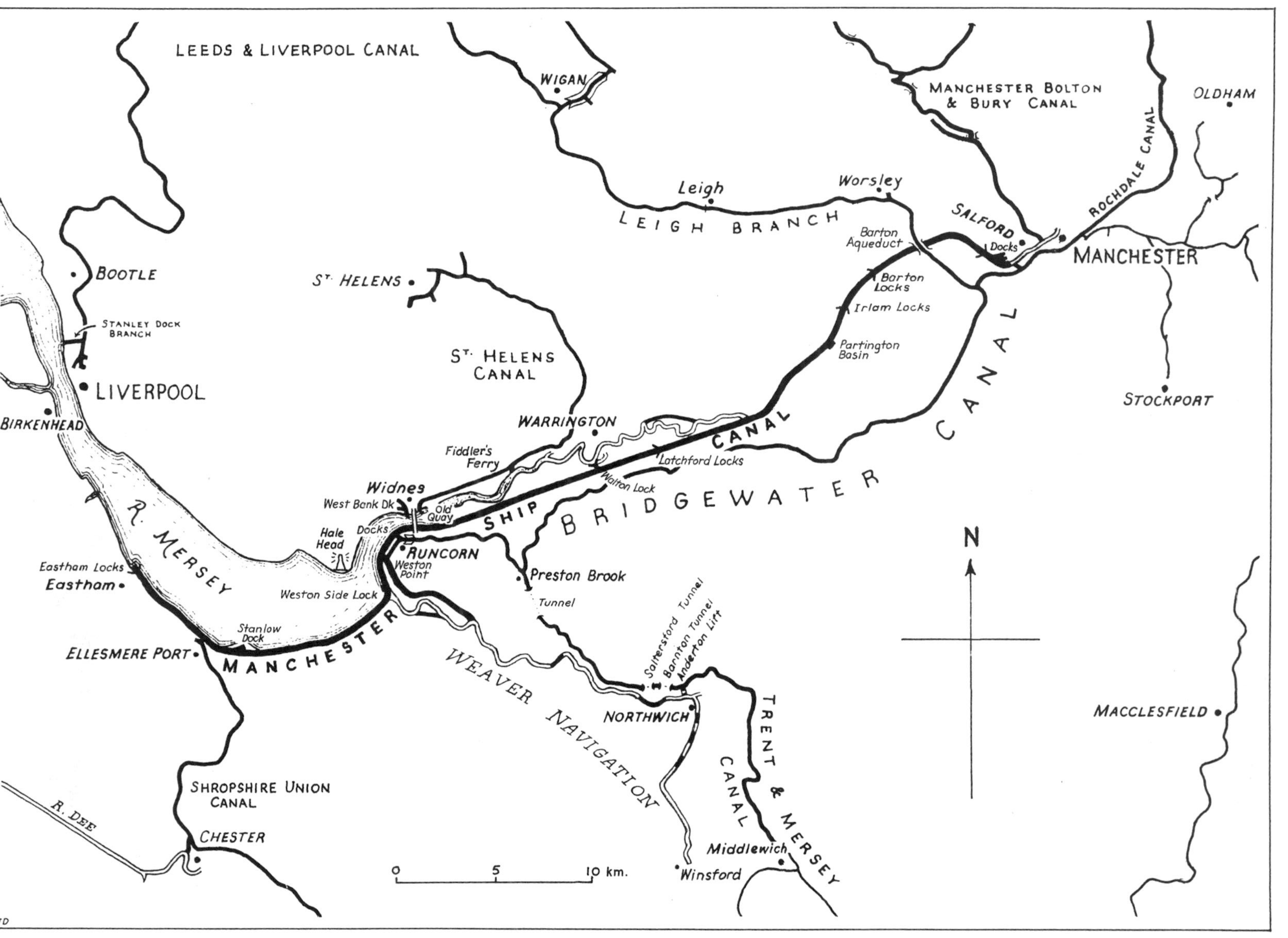

The north-west waterways system

needs and will do everything he can to prevent her activities becoming restricted by her failing eyesight. We talked in their shady front room, Tom busying himself with teacups and sandwiches amidst the memories. He has spent almost all his life in Runcorn. 'We lived in Balfour Street, not far from here. That's where I started work from, there. I had a brother and six sisters. My brother used to be a blacksmith at the Ship Canal yard at Old Quay making all the chains and things like that but he's gone to live in Canada, now.'

Tom has spent a lifetime on the Ship Canal: 'I started at the age of eight! My dad was on the tugs. We never had a summer holiday going abroad and all that, like the kids do now, you know. So I used to spend all the holidays on the tugs going up and down the Ship Canal. That's how it got into my blood. I used to think I was the bees' knees when we passed all the other school kids and I was on this tug waving to them! All the folk on the Transporter Bridge [between Runcorn and Widnes] would be waving down to us, too. I'd be away from home for about a fortnight like that. When we had to come home for a change of clothing and everything, well, my dad would bring us on the train or bus from wherever we were, Salford or wherever.

'When I left school at fourteen [in 1937], I was too young to go on the tugs so I went and worked for the Upper Mersey Navigation for a while, doing the buoys in the river. There was quite a bit of traffic up the river estuary then, despite the Ship Canal being busy, too.

'You see, a lot of the coasters used to come up that bit of river to get into Runcorn so as to save the dues on the Ship Canal – with being in the river it was free of any tolls, that

A ship stemming the tide to enter Old Quay Side Lock stern first from the Mersey estuary

Jessie Wallwork *attending to one of the Upper Mersey Navigation Commission buoys*

bit. Yes, that was a tricky job. You see, they'd to come up the old river channel through the railway bridge at Runcorn. Then they had to swing round – that was awkward, with a 30ft tide behind you – but, by doing that, they were facing down into the flood tide. Then they'd drop backwards, working their engines ahead to steady them, and let the tide take them into the lock. Of course there were lock gatemen there, then, to take the line off them; they'd be in the lock stern first, you see, which gave them better control of the vessel and their speed. They could easily back out into the Ship Canal then, in the still water, and get away across to Runcorn, or Weston Point Docks or wherever they were for.

'There would be plenty going above that to Warrington and so on, such as Bishop's Wharf Carrying Co. There was pulp going up to those paper mills along Chester Road in Warrington, too. We only used to go right up there in a launch because it went shallower and shallower, and you could only do that on certain tides. Lower down we used an old steam trawler, the *Jessie Wallwork* – it was always painted battleship grey, with the boss being ex-Navy! It had a big cat-head, you know, a roller with a winch, to handle the anchor chains over the bow. Then there was a derrick which you could use to get the buoys onto the deck to bring them back into dock. When we'd to bring one in we'd steam alongside it first and the mate or somebody would jump down onto the buoy, they had handrails round to hold onto; then we'd give him a line and he'd put that over it and pull a chain round which would drop down under the buoy, round its anchor chain. When we'd got a bight round it like that we could start heaving up on the winch to pull it in; we'd have to go astern to pull at it as well as using the winch. Once we'd got it to release from the mud we could bring it on deck, or tow it to its proper position without bringing it on board and just let go of it again. If we were just moving it we'd often simply let it float alongside. If you didn't keep putting them right there would be ships running aground with relying on the buoys to navigate the channels.

'We used to work the day tides only. Sometimes we'd start at six, but never much earlier because you couldn't work in the dark. If we weren't sailing, the hours were half eight in the morning till half four at night. We didn't stay on board overnight or anything, it was just a daytime job, that. We were based at Weston Point Docks so we used to cross the Ship Canal and go out of Weston Mersey Side Lock into the river. If we were out too long to get back in there on the same tide, we'd go down to Eastham and come back up the Manchester Ship Canal. If we weren't dealing with the buoys down there we used to go out through Old Quay Lock, at Runcorn, on the little launch. We used to go up as far as Fiddler's Ferry, where you get into the St Helen's Canal, doing the narrow channel there. From there we used to go on up into Warrington, to Walton Lock, and come into the Ship Canal through that, and home down the Ship Canal that way. But we were only ever a few hours in the river.

'There was quite a good variety of jobs we used to do. It was mostly laying the moorings and keeping the buoys in order. We used to bring some of the buoys back to the yard for repairs or to be painted up and so on. We used to make new concrete castings for mooring them to – they weighed about 6cwt or something like that, you know; just like a big lump of concrete to fasten the mooring chains to.

'When our vessel was laid up in Weston Point the skipper used to go round and survey

Painting one of the Mersey estuary navigation marks from the Preston *which carried out the same duties as the* Jessie Wallwork *on which Tom Kelly later worked* (The Boat Museum, Ellesmere Port)

Extract from the log book of the Upper Mersey Navigation Commissioners covering the activities of the *Jessie Wallwork* and their launch which is in the archives of Merseyside Maritime Museum.

'1st February 1940:
Steamer [*Jessie Wallwork*] out [into the Mersey] via Eastham. Placed W3 boat-buoy off Dungeon Point boat-buoy as this was considered to be the more dangerous position. Also regulated D4, which had dragged to a position off Hale Head lighthouse. Soundings again carried out in the Hale Head area and food and coal landed at the lighthouse. Steamer returned to base via Eastham.'

'2nd February 1940:
Duties carried out at base making moorings, etc, the stock of which had become exhausted through losses due to the ice which had formed on the river during the very cold spell of weather during the previous Neap Tides and the last Spring Tides. Survey party down river with motor launch via Old Quay Lock. Attended Pickering's, Decoy and North Dungeon beacons. Attended UMNC No 2. Survey carried out Eastham to Runcorn. Dungeon Point Beacon observed to be lying on its side at low water having been forced over by ice in river. Motor launch returned to base via Old Quay Lock.'

Jessie Wallwork *delivering coal to Hale Head Lighthouse*

the channel. He'd get on top of Hale Head Lighthouse, or up on Runcorn Hill, and get all the bearings of the markers and buoys. Then we'd go out in the river and one of the deck-hands would get a lead line and check the depths and positions of all the channels. Then we'd get hold of the mooring chains of the buoys and lift them with the winch, carry them to where they were wanted and drop the weight down again.

'They'd be all right then till the big spring tides would shift them again; they could drift for miles at times and get lost, you know. They had numbers painted on them, and the sands and everything could shift and take them well away. Some were lost for years!

'On a Saturday morning, if we weren't black-leading the stove on the boat or something like that, we had to go with a two-gallon can of oil on a bike with one of the men. We'd go along the foreshore, round Hale Head Lighthouse, and along there, filling the lamps in the navigation markers and so on. Other times we had to go up in a bosun's chair and white-wash Hale Head Lighthouse itself.'

As was the case for most of his friends who were not involved with shipping coming and going to catch the tides, Tom's weekend began early on Saturday afternoon. Wherever one went in Runcorn the sight and sounds of the Mersey estuary and Manchester Ship Canal were close at hand, however.

'One of the other things we used to do was to take coal to the lighthouse there. We'd come up to the lighthouse on a flood tide, but a small one, and swing the *Jessie Wallwork*, head down, into the flow of the tide. Then we'd lower the lifeboat down with the davits.

We'd fill it with eight or ten bags of coal and then row it over to the lighthouse, and the lighthouse keeper would take them off us; there was a keeper on there all the time in them days. Then it was back for another ten bags. When the Upper Mersey Commission finished, that lighthouse was sold in 1958 and a Dutchman bought it. I believe he's still living in it.

'I was in that job for about three years or so, but it was only a small wage; I was only getting about 13s a week, or something like that, so I went to Coopers carrying sand. We heard they wanted men and it was about £4 to £5 a week, which was a small fortune to us! They carried a lot of sand, for ballast for ships, during the war.

'I was on one called *Elizabeth Cooper* which got sunk in the canal a few years after I left it. One of our friends, who used to go pleasure boating with us on the Bridgewater Canal, was drowned in that – he got his nephew out from below deck as it sank, but he couldn't swim off to save himself, then. It hit the *Mancunian* – it had an electric-driven steering gear and it failed. If you tried to steer it too quick it would stall the motor on it. It was a new idea but it was before its time, and it had never been perfected; many a time we had to whip it into manual gear very quickly. There was a great big wheel to steer with then, and it was very heavy if she was loaded with sand. The rudder on it was like a barn door, you know! If we was running light, without a cargo, we used to always keep it in hand gear. She was quite easy to steer like that, light, but you couldn't steer it like that when she was loaded because she'd have about six hundred ton in and she'd be down to the deck. If it did fail like that it took two of you to turn the wheel, one either side of it.

'A lot of the cargoes were for ballast, but it also went to builders' merchants. We used to run down into the middle of the Mersey and they had the hoppers there, the *William Cooper* and *John Henry Cooper*, which dredged the material from the river bed. Abels and the Mersey Docks & Harbour Board dredged out there too, but the tide kept carrying more sand and gravel in all the time. We used to go alongside them and they had a grab or a sucker, depending on what material you'd to load: if it was fine sand you went for, they'd put the big pipe from the sucker into your hold and it would come in like a slurry. You'd to get a

The dredger William Cooper *which was usually stationed out in the Mersey estuary loading the company's barges with sand for transport to Garston or up the Manchester Ship Canal* (Merseyside Maritime Museum)

pole and keep sounding it till you felt the sand building up from the bottom. Then you'd to get the deck pumps on and keep pumping the water off it until you had a full load of sand, rather than water. We took it right up the length of the Ship Canal into Pomona Docks.

'The accommodation was that poor. There was a room for the skipper, and one for the engineer and mate, but all I had was one of those drop-down chairs, by the stove; it was a really rough job, that. There were only the four of us, and I was deckhand, cabin lad come everything, me, cooking and helping down the engine room and all. With there being only one engineer, when he wanted a spell I used to go down and work the engine controls. We were working all the time on that, with the tides. Sometimes I'd get home on a Friday night and then I'd sleep all weekend, I would; with only being about sixteen or seventeen at the time, and all the hours we worked, that was. It'd be late Saturday afternoon before I'd come to, like. My parents made me come off it because of those hours. Billy Cooper he kept his men at it, he was a bit greedy with it.

'I went on the Ship Canal tugs when I was eighteen. That was in the war, 1941. That almost doubled my wages, but you never knew when you would get home off the tugs; in fact the Ship Canal wouldn't employ anyone on the tugs before they were eighteen because of the hours.

'I started on a paddle tug as a relief, you know, when somebody was off. Then I had a week or two on the *Eccles*, another paddler; then I went on a head tug, a screw tug, *Bison*, as a relief lad. But the other lad was sacked in the meantime for some reason, and I was fortunate enough to get his job; I was there for a few years. They used to call you "number one" or "number two" lad. As "number one" you were more or less a cabin boy, scrubbing the cabin and trimming the lamps and so on. You had to learn as you went along, to splice ropes and things like that, though you did get a trick on the wheel now and then – just on straight lengths, like from Latchford to Runcorn, you know. That's how you learnt steering with steam steering gear and all that.

'We worked day and night on those, and it was very difficult in the war because there was the blackout, of course. There were all kinds of accidents during the war because your navigation lights weren't allowed to show properly; the red and green lights had a sort of perforated tin guard round them. There was one particular time going through Ince Cutting, you know, that high rock cutting. It was so black that a coaster met us and we were abreast of each other before we realised there was anything there.

'That's one of the paddle tugs working at the stern of Manchester Progress *almost into Irlam Locks. See how the tug's going astern to slow the ship down'* (Tom Kelly collection)

'It was all stern tug work with those paddle tugs on the ships. We had to hold them back and guide them round the bends. The stern tug had to take the way off them, because loaded ships would travel on for quite a distance before they could be slowed down, you know. So they'd be working the ship's engine astern and the paddle tugs would be working the paddles backwards. For instance, to go in Latchford Lock, you could start pulling astern on the stern tug about three-quarters of a mile

The Pacific Enterprise *(furthest from the camera) on passage down the Manchester Ship Canal passes* Sculptor *inward bound just below Barton Locks. The head tug of the outward bound ship is gradually leading her towards the centre of the canal whilst at the stern the paddle tug is working her engines astern and pulling towards the other ship in order to prevent the* Pacific Enterprise'*s stern pivoting out onto the canal bank. The Harrison Liner* Sculptor *obviously arrived before the* Pacific Enterprise *was ready to clear the large lock, which can just be seen at the right of the picture. Her tugs therefore brought her up to the tail of the small lock to allow the outward ship plenty of room to clear. The stern tug on* Sculptor *has been turned to tow the ship backwards and obtain room for the head tug to get her lined up with the large, further, lock chamber* (The Boat Museum/MSC Co)

away, to get the headway off a ship before you arrived there; a ship with a draft of about 26ft would want quite a lot of stopping. However, with the paddlers you could hold it in any position for as long as you wanted. If you were meeting another ship you could swing your stern over against the bank, put your rudder over so as it wasn't damaged and you could hold your ship dead still whilst the other ship passed.

'The ship would be under its own steam, and they'd take a Ship Canal pilot and helmsman aboard; they had the head tug ready to keep the ship in line. They'd take a run, you see, the ships, if they got too near the shallow water by the bank. If the ship smelt the bank it would sheer off towards it, so the pilot would give the head tug a signal. Say they wanted him to pull off the starboard bow, they'd give one long blast and three short ones on the ship's whistle. The tug would answer, and he'd steer over, and put on full speed to correct the course. At the same time the stern tug would be pulling in the opposite direction to square the ship up and then he'd carry on again.

'If the ship wanted slowing down, the pilot would blow three, and the paddler would be pulling astern until he decided they'd got enough way off it. Then it was four short to stop

SCHEDULE OF SIGNALS

I. SOUND SIGNALS

Number of Blasts	Meaning of Signal
1. **One Prolonged** (When inward bound)	To call attention generally, e.g. when i. Approaching another vessel; ii. Approaching or passing a lock; iii. Approaching a swing bridge which is required to be opened; iv. Approaching a bend; or v. At intervals of not more than two minutes when navigating in or near an area of restricted visibility.
One Prolonged and one Short (When outward bound)	
2. **One Prolonged and Two Short**	(To stern tug) – "Pull on port quarter".
3. **One Prolonged and Three Short**	(To stern tug) – "Pull on starboard quarter".
4. **One Very Short (½ second duration)**	(To forward tug when getting under way) – "Ready, go ahead". (To stern tug) – "Cancel last signal".
5. **Three short**	(To stern tug) – "Pull astern".
6. **Four short**	*(a)* (To tugs) – "Hold ship in position". *(b)* "Am holding ship in position".
7. **One Prolonged, One Short and One Prolonged**	(To stern tug) – "Am about to pass another vessel".
8. **Four Short and One Prolonged**	"Vessel temporarily out of control".
9. **One Prolonged, Two Short and One Prolonged**	"About to swing".
10. **One Very Long of not less than 8 seconds duration**	"Have completed swing".
11. **Three Polonged and Three Short**	"Attendance of boatman is required".

The following signals shall be given by means of MOUTH WHISTLE:–

Number of Blasts	Meaning of Signal
12. **One Polonged and Two Short**	(To forward tug) – "Pull on port bow".
13. **One Polonged and Three Short**	(To forward tug) – "Pull on starboard bow".
14. **One short**	(To forward tug) – "Cancel last signal".

and wait whilst we met another ship coming, and we'd answer with four short blasts. There was all different codes on the whistle for different manoeuvres: one long and three short to pull on the starboard bow, one long and two short for the port bow; then one long for stop; three for astern. If it wasn't too windy or anything you might go right through without too much bother. If we could see that the ship was swinging or anything we'd get in position ready, but you couldn't pull without the pilot's orders – if anything went wrong like that you'd end up blaming each other, you didn't do anything without orders.

'When they started with ship-to-shore radios and the walkie-talkies the pilot could just give verbal orders then. That did away with a lot of the noise at night-time, and the people in those houses on the Latchford length started asking "Why are the tugs so quiet at night? We never hear them unless they are blowing for the swing-bridge, now." We got those radios about 1970, or something like that.

'The tugs wouldn't go in the locks with the bigger ships like the Manchester Liners. The *Carchester* was the biggest one that used to come up; it used to fetch grain to Manchester. With those, as soon as you got the ship's bow in the lock entrance, the head tug would trip the towing lines off the hook and back away, and he'd go into the smaller lock alongside. Then when the ship was settled in the lock, the stern tug would let go, and go in the small lock with the head tug. It was a lengthy job, this was. Then the two locks would be filled up together. When the ship and tugs were level, the head tug would go out first onto the lead-in jetty at the head of the ship's lock, make his tow ropes fast, and then the ship would start to sail out. As it left the lock the paddle tug could sail up behind and make his ropes fast. You had to pick that up underway. One of the ship's crew would throw a heaving line down, and we'd fasten our towing line on, and the ship's crew would heave that up.

'We had a set rope made up to the right length with eyes in either end, but sometimes the ship's crew wanted to use their own ropes, and that was hard work because they were often old sisal lines, wet through, and they were very hard to make fast round your bollards just right. We used a hemp rope with a wire towing rope fixed onto it through a galvanised thimble; with that it was just a matter of them heaving the rope up and dropping the big eye in its end over a bollard. At the locks all they'd to do was lift the eye off the bollard and drop it overboard, and we'd heave it in. We used two, crossed over between the ship and the tug: that made it like an articulated lorry, and we could pull or push on the ship then. If the ship was travelling light and we wanted to steer with that tug we could see as soon as the ship's rudder went over. Say it went over to

Hemp rope spliced to a towing wire

A stern tug pushing on the crossed towing lines thus tightening the rope to the starboard quarter to manoeuvre the ship's stern to port

starboard, the rudder, we could go over the opposite way and go ahead round his stern quarter and push on the outside rope; that would help him to counteract any swing. And when we see'd him start to straighten his rudder up, we'd ease off our engine.

'The hardest thing to tow was the ore carriers. When you looked down in their holds you'd think there was hardly any cargo in them, but all the weight was down in the bottom and when they started to run about they seemed to want an awful lot of stopping – the tug could be pulling off the bow for five or ten minutes before they won and got the ship moving towards the middle again. If you were with one of those and you were to meet another ship you'd have to tie up and wait, because it was too dangerous to meet on the move, what with the displacement of water: you'd pull the vessels to each other and there would be an accident. So the traffic control would order one of the ships to tie up, and which one it was would just depend who was nearest to a tying-up place.

'That was easier once we had those ship-to-shore radios because they could tell you what traffic was moving and when we could expect to meet it at any given point. Say if we were coming to Old Quay and he was coming past Bridgewater Docks; we'd have to pull in at Old Quay and let him get round the bend and pass. The tug men used to have to jump off and make the ship fast, you know.

'With a ship like that you'd generally get to Manchester in a good day. But sometimes with being in fog, we've been as long as a week. Then again the traffic was so heavy in the

An ideal angle of view to appreciate the work of the two screw tugs handling the Manchester Explorer, *one of Manchester Liners' vessels, in the Manchester Ship Canal. On a straight section such as here the ship is moved by her own engines with the tugs simply using enough power to keep the towing lines taut. They come into their own when manoeuvring the ship or meeting other craft when they would be required to provide steerage by pulling to one side or the other at bow or stern* (The Boat Museum/Stewart Bale)

canal in those days you wouldn't often get a straight passage right through. You'd be tying up at the lay-bys waiting for ships coming the other way, and then you'd have to tie up on the dolphins above or below the locks waiting for one to come out, and wait till you got clearance from either traffic control or the lock master.

'There was always something interesting going on. Sometimes when you got to Manchester you could be there a fortnight. You'd have to move ships about from one berth to another, or move the floating grain elevators to the ships, and all sorts of jobs like that. Whatever tugs were handy they'd be used – when you got to Manchester there could be about six or eight tugs there. They'd work all the movements out and then you'd all be given your orders for the next day, or the night as the case may be; you could be there all week. Then there might be a ship to Eastham and you'd be off with that. The next one might be from Eastham to the oil dock at Stanlow, and you could be working between Eastham and Stanlow for a week after that. I was married by then – it's Dot's and my fifty-fifth anniversary this year.'

Dot recalled that she'd fancied Tom for a good many years as he used to come to visit one of his pals in her street, and he always had a cheeky remark or a whistle for her. And he was a dashing figure in his Sea Cadet uniform! She was nineteen when they married in 1942.

'Dot might never know where we were unless she rang up Old Quay Swing Bridge, and they could give her an idea. Sometimes, though, in winter if we were bringing a ship up from Eastham and the weather was bad or foggy, the pilot might decide to tie it up overnight at Old Quay; so we'd stop there and tie it up, and then we could get home for a few hours. The pilot would tell us when he wanted to start in the morning, say at six o'clock, and we could get back to be ready to start off then. That would be a lucky break, coming to Old Quay.

'We used to get our coal at Partington or Acton Grange, also just very rarely at Ellesmere Port, but that was really reserved for loading ships with, there. At Acton Grange they had those self-releasing boxes – they could swing them right over the bunker man-holes and open the bottom, and it would all go straight down the man-hole. There was tips all along at Partington where they could chute it straight out of railway wagons into ships' holds or bunkers. They'd just chute it to you, and then all the crew would be out – engineers, firemen, deckhands, all the lot – to share the work of getting the coal off the deck because it would go everywhere – all the towing gear would get covered in it. Then the firemen had to get down below and trim it in the bunkers. We had to brush it all off the deck and then get the hosepipe and wash all the dust off everything. We'd take about 15 to 20 tons, and then we'd be ready for action again.

When the ship canal tugs were coaled at Acton Grange the fuel was craned aboard in boxes with bottom doors, which meant that most of it went straight into the bunkers instead of falling all over the deck

'You'd need coal at least once a week. The control would try and get you to Partington with a ship if possible: they'd tell the skipper, "Take this to Partington and then get your coal, and when you've done that, come on the phone for orders." So he'd go in the office at Partington and phone for his orders, in the days before we had the ship-to-shore radio.

'We had to do all the maintenance, the chipping and painting and all. We had to make the fenders for the tugs, splice the towing ropes and all that kind of work – though we didn't do any of the fancy paintwork; that was reserved for the tradesmen painters. All the hull and that, we used to do all that. The paddle tugs had wooden decks, and they were all kept scrubbed white, teakwood decks they were. We used to do that every week, on a Friday if we got the opportunity. They used to mix this stuff, 'sooji-boogi' we used to call it, then spread it on with a mop and when it'd soaked in we'd get the hosepipe on it and start scrubbing off again. It was immaculate when it was done. We washed all the handrails at least once or twice a week, and in the summer months we used to paint it every few weeks. This was all done while we were on the move. We used to be in competition with the Mersey tugs, you see – and, of course, we always outshone them in my days!

'The skipper would get on the wheel and be controlling while you picked the ship up, and the deckhand and lad would be attending to the ropes. Once the ship got under way the mate would take the first trick at the wheel. He might have a length from, say, Eastham to Ince; then the deckhand would take over from Ince to Runcorn; and from there to Latchford the lad would have a trick with the skipper watching him. From Latchford the mate'd take over, and then it was the deckhand from Irlam to Mode Wheel. The skipper used to always come up at the locks to make sure it was all done right. When the lad was on, the mate and deckhand would be busy with all the chipping and red leading and all that. If we had any big jobs on, then the skipper would take over and let the lad come and get stuck in with us.'

Dot recalls that Tom could be away 'an awful long time sometimes. But I got to know when he was coming by, because I could recognise his blow on the tug's whistle. If I had the chance, when I could run down the street and wave, I would do! Then we had our son didn't we, Tom?'

'Yes, and do you know I spent *nine* Christmases away before I had a Christmas with him! That was through moving from one tug to another – maybe I had gone to a tug which had had the previous Christmas off, so when I was with them it wasn't *their* turn to be off. I went in the office in the end, to ask about it, and of course they hadn't realised what had happened so I had the following Christmas off. The way the job worked in those days I could be away from home a fortnight or three weeks, although I could be passing home two or three times in each week.'

Their son Peter was born in 1944. As soon as he became old enough Dot was able to go out to work again, eventually becoming the manageress of a dry-cleaning shop before moving on to a wool shop. This meant she couldn't dash down the street any more to wave at the tug when it blew the right greeting – but even if she couldn't wave, Tom's whistle was easily audible in the main street!

After school hours Peter occupied much of Dot's time, but she would always try to keep domestic chores under control so that she could join Tom on their pleasure boat. They have had about seven boats based on the Bridgewater Canal, each one an improvement on the one before – the present narrowboat is truly a home-from-home, with all 'mod cons'.

Tom would take a good supply of food and some spare clothes to work with him. Cooking was the responsibility of junior crew members on the tugs which would inevitably be on the move at meal times!

'Then I went back on a paddle tug. I went as mate on the *Irlam*, which was the last steam tug I was on. Then I went as mate on the *Nymph* and was on there another eight years. I was on twin screw tugs from then on, till I finished on the *Onset*; then I went to ICI for a few years, where I did scaffolding work and rigging lifting derricks and all that sort of thing.

'When the Ship Canal wrote I was back down to the tugs like a flash! They started the twenty-four-hour system in about the mid-sixties, and that made them short of men. You see, with that you were on board for twenty-four hours and then you had forty-eight hours off. That made them short of men, with there being three shifts for each tug. Then every three weeks we had what they called a long weekend off, say finishing Friday night till

(Left) 'That's the first pleasure boat I had on the Bridgewater Canal, the Betty. *I altered all that shed on the top and put a proper wheelhouse on. I was just showing the* Evening News *reporter how thick the ice was one winter.' Dot recalls that 'He was off sick at the time, he'd come off his scooter. See his hand is all plastered up. Off sick and the newspaper man takes his photo! It was in 1952 that we started pleasure boating.'* (Runcorn Weekly News)
(Right) 'That's one of the small diesel tugs, the Nymph, *that's the one I was mate on. It was still a ship tug. I'm in the wheelhouse.'* (Tom Kelly collection)

Tuesday, just according to which way the shifts worked round. So they sent a letter to all the old tug men they could find to see if they were interested in going back on. I was down like a shot, you know!'

Dot says, 'If they sent for him today he'd go straight back – not tomorrow morning, but *this afternoon*!'

'Of course I had to start as deckhand again because that was only fair to the others who'd been putting their service in. I came back onto the *Rover*. I worked my way up again and was mate on the *Udine* and the *Ulex* and the *Onset*, then *Rover*. They asked me then to take charge of the *Daniel Adamson*, and I was able to take that on and start the job on Preston Brook Marina.'

The Manchester Ship Canal Company's Bridgewater Department was entering the pleasure boating age. This smaller canal had been a busy commercial waterway in its own right since before it was acquired by the Manchester Ship Canal Company. Trade gradually disappeared until barges ceased to use even the Manchester end of the canal in 1973. Meanwhile the company built a new marina to cater for the new users, at Preston Brook close to the junction of the branch to the Trent & Mersey Canal. It was soon filled with pleasure boats whose owners enjoyed the security of a full-time warden living above the marina office. The first occupants of this new house were Tom and Dot Kelly. As Tom reflects:

'I wouldn't have been able to take the job on the marina if I'd been on the twenty-four-hour system on the traffic tugs – it wouldn't have been fair to have left Dot on her own because it was such a remote place at that time. We went into the house they built, with the marina office in it, from new. When we were up early in the morning there was every bird possible, pheasants, and partridge, and the fox used to come down our lane and into the field. Dot loved the spot there, in the country, but we got a bit tired of being on duty twenty-four hours a day, seven days a week. People didn't think you had any finishing time.'

Daniel Adamson was built in 1903 as *Ralph Brocklebank* for the Shropshire Union Canal

Tom steering the Daniel Adamson *to Manchester ready for one of the staff trips. He would put his uniform on at the last moment before the passengers boarded to be sure it was immaculate* (Tom Kelly collection)

Company, and was employed in towing their flats from their canal's entrance at Ellesmere Port across the river Mersey to Liverpool Docks. After her acquisition by the Manchester Ship Canal Company she served as a traffic tug before being adapted for passenger carrying as and when required. Gradually the removable passenger fittings became permanent and she was set aside solely for her more prestigious rôle.

'Part of my job when the *Daniel Adamson* wasn't doing trips was to take the various tugs out on trials. The tug superintendent would be on board, and they'd do trials testing the various temperatures and all that. We'd get onto a quiet length where there was plenty of room, like down Frodsham Score in the wide bit, and I used to have to give her full speed. We used to give her hells bells, you know, backing and filling and ahead and astern, bouncing her about all over the place! You could spin them tugs on a sixpence! Otherwise when the *Daniel Adamson* wasn't sailing I used to supervise the crew on all the cleaning, painting and maintenance and all that. They were all chaps who worked in Old Quay Yard, like apprentice deckhands, before they got a regular job on the tugs.

'Every few weeks we'd take a party of long-serving employees on the *Daniel Adamson*: not just tug men, but lock gate men, office staff, railway men, and everybody who'd served over twelve years. They'd be given a trip on the *Adamson* from Manchester Docks down to Bridgewater House at Runcorn. Coming down they'd give us priority over all the traffic. We'd leave No 6 Dock at ten o'clock and all the swing bridges would be off and the locks ready, so we could guarantee being at Bridgewater House for one. There were drinks all the way down, with catering staff aboard. The passengers would go ashore at Bridgewater House for quite a good feast, and then back aboard to go on down to Eastham. They'd travel home by coach from there. Meanwhile we'd run the tug back to Runcorn. Then we'd get all these big industrialists coming down, Russian timber merchants and everybody. We had MPs – Michael Heseltine at one time. You should have seen the guard he had! We picked him up at No 6 Dock. He landed by helicopter. When we left No 6 Dock and went down Mode Wheel Locks and passed Barton Aqueduct all the roadways were stopped off and there were cavalcades of motorbikes everywhere! There were police on the swing bridges. We only took him to Barton Lock, but I'd to pull in at exactly the right place and he was straight down the gangplank and into a car. All for security!

'When anybody came off one of the other tugs, the diesels, and onto the *Daniel Adamson*, they were always fascinated by the way there was no sound from the engine. You could just feel it surge along.'

Dot recalls, 'When Tom was skipper on that *Daniel Adamson* it was his pride and joy – he lived for that tug! I went aboard when it was Tom's long service award (he didn't have to steer for his own trip!) and the brass, the paintwork, the woodwork, everything absolutely gleamed. And the saloon down below, it was gorgeous, absolutely gorgeous. Tom was on

(Left) The Manchester Ship Canal Co acquired the tug Ralph Brocklebank *from the Shropshire Union Canal Co after the latter ceased to tow their flats across the Mersey to Liverpool from the junction of the two canals at Ellesmere Port. This photograph, early in her Ship Canal days, was taken at Runcorn* (Tom Kelly collection) *(Right) She was eventually renamed* Daniel Adamson *after the principal campaigner for the canal of the 1880s. Alterations to provide facilities for her passengers were carried out in stages from the late 1930s as can be seen by comparing the superstructure seen in this view taken in Manchester Docks with that in the picture to the left* (Percy Dunbavand collection)

it for its last trip from Old Quay to Ellesmere Port, to the Boat Museum. We went to see it there a while back, and they'd let it get run down. I've never seen a man so upset. They shouldn't have accepted it if they couldn't keep it up; it would have been better at Albert Dock [Liverpool Maritime Museum]. It was heartbreaking for *me* to see it like that, but for *Tom*, who'd worked on it…' Tom changed the subject:

'I was on the marina for eight or nine years and then was made redundant from the Ship Canal Company at sixty. I was redundant for about six months after that, but then I got that job on the trip boat *Kittiwake* at Wigan Pier – but I was only on that for about fourteen months before I had a mild heart attack. The doctor suggested that I should finish on health grounds and we moved back to Runcorn, where most of our friends are, and I retired. I found that trip boat hard work because all the crews were novices. I could never have a spell off because they needed supervising every moment. They were all on these job creating schemes and some of them had never seen a boat before.'

Despite the fact that Dot has severe eyesight problems they still undertake quite extensive cruises on their narrowboat: 'We're all right so long as there's nobody breathing down our neck! So write this down – if you're disabled, *don't* give up boating! Tom can't give it up because his love of water is too strong.'

"Dydle, to (Norfolk) to clean out": definition in *Bradshaw's Canals and Navigable Rivers of England and Wales – A Handbook of Inland Navigation for Merchants Traders and Others* by Henry Rudolph de Salis (1904)

CAUTION.
ENTERING FOULRIDGE TUNNEL WITHOUT A PERMIT.
NOTICE IS HEREBY GIVEN that at the Colne Police Court on Wednesday, 21st September 1921, the captain of a Motor Boat was **CONVICTED OF ENTERING OR PASSING THROUGH THE TUNNEL AT FOULRIDGE WITHOUT A PERMIT FIRST OBTAINED FROM AN AUTHORISED AGENT OF THE COMPANY AND WAS ORDERED TO PAY £2. 17s. FOR FINE AND COSTS.**
All similar offenders will be prosecuted.
BY ORDER, **FRANK H. HILL.**

Share Prices and Dividends:

Canal	Dividend	Price
Trent & Mersey	£75	£2,200
Loughborough	£197	£4,600
Coventry	£44	£1,300
Oxford	£32	£850
Grand Junction	£10	£290
Swansea	£11	£250
Staffs & Worcs	£40	£960
Birmingham	£12/10	£350
Leeds & Liverpool	£15	£600

The Gentleman's Magazine, *December 1824, quoted in* Canals and Inland Waterways *by George Cadbury and S.P. Dodds – 1929*

LANCASTER CANAL.
At Preston Police Court,
, John James Simpson, Charles Slater, John Beardsworth, and Francis Horn were FINED 2/6 and Costs, and Edward Walling and John James Whittle were fined 1/- and Costs,
For Bathing in the Canal,
And in default of payment were to go to PRISON FOR SEVEN DAYS.
E. & J. L. Milner, 'Guardian' Printing Works, Lancaster.

(BW Archives, Gloucester)

AIRE & CALDER NAVIGATION.
LIFE-SAVING APPLIANCES.
CAUTION.
THESE APPLIANCES ARE TO BE USED ONLY FOR PURPOSE OF LIFE-SAVING AND FREE ACCESS THERETO IS TO BE MAINTAINED.
PARTIES ACTING IN CONTRAVENTION OF THIS NOTICE ARE LIABLE TO PROSECUTION.

(Author's collection)

That every Boat or Barge shall give way to every Boat commonly called a Fly Boat and navigated by relays of Horses or Steam Power on this Canal, or the Cuts therefrom, on pain that the Master or Person having command of such Boat or Barge, and refusing or not allowing any Fly Boat to Pass, shall forfeit and pay the sum of Twenty Shillings.

Grand Junction Canal Byelaw – June 1863

COVENTRY CANAL NAVIGATION.
CAUTION.
On FRIDAY, the 17th day of MAY inst., HENRY WOODWARD, the Steerer of a Boat, was brought before the County Magistrates, at Coventry, charged with endeavouring to
EVADE THE TOLL
PAYABLE TO THE
COVENTRY CANAL COMPANY,
In respect of several Cases of Pipes which he had secreted in his Boat laden with Road Stone, on the 1st instant, and was CONVICTED of the offence, and fined in the mitigated
Penalty of 1s., and £1. 0s. 6d. expenses.
THIS IS TO GIVE NOTICE
That all Persons offending in a similar manner will be proceeded against under the Bye-Laws of the above Company, and the whole PENALTY OF FIVE POUNDS prescribed by the same sued for, and in addition
THE WHOLE OF THE CARGO IN THE BOAT,
Although partly consisting of Road Stone, will be
Charged with Tonnage.
BY ORDER,
CHARLES WOODCOCK,
CLERK TO THE COVENTRY CANAL COMPANY.
Coventry, May 25th, 1861.

(BW Archives, Gloucester)

(Euan Corrie)

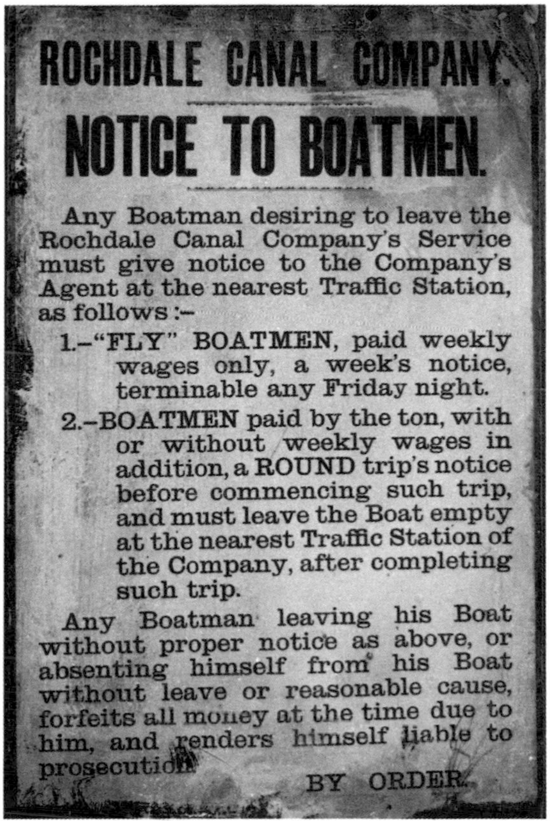

Tonnages conveyed on British Canals:

Year	Independent waterways	Railway controlled waterways	Total
1888	19,789,668	15,512,189	35,301,857
1898	20,070,769	15,940,472	36,011,241
1905	20,434,411	13,702,356	34,136,767

Canals and Inland Waterways by George Cadbury and S.P. Dodds – 1929

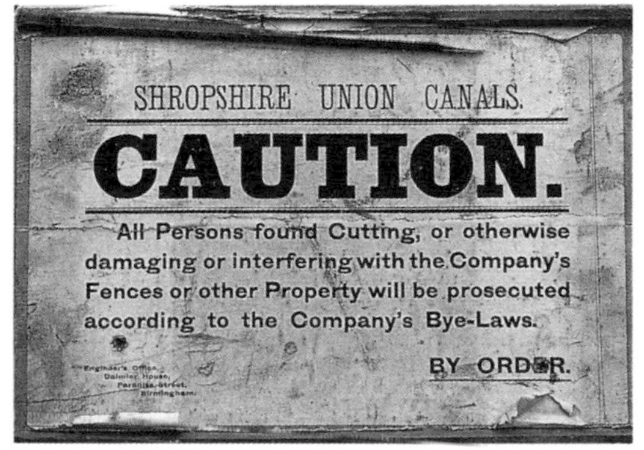

(Euan Corrie)

ROCHDALE CANAL COMPANY.

NOTICE TO BOATMEN.

Any Boatman desiring to leave the Rochdale Canal Company's Service must give notice to the Company's Agent at the nearest Traffic Station, as follows:–

1.–"FLY" BOATMEN, paid weekly wages only, a week's notice, terminable any Friday night.

2.–BOATMEN paid by the ton, with or without weekly wages in addition, a ROUND trip's notice before commencing such trip, and must leave the Boat empty at the nearest Traffic Station of the Company, after completing such trip.

Any Boatman leaving his Boat without proper notice as above, or absenting himself from his Boat without leave or reasonable cause, forfeits all money at the time due to him, and renders himself liable to prosecution.

BY ORDER.

A Priestman steam dredger supplied to the Grand Union Canal Company in the 1930s. It is built on a broad beam pontoon although others had narrow (7ft) beam hulls with additional detachable side pontoons to give the same stability whilst working with the additional flexibility of movement through locks and bridges on the canal's narrow branches. (BW Archives, Gloucester)

GEORGE & MARGARET WOOD

Canal Dredger Driver and Toll Clerk

The Staffordshire & Worcestershire Canal leaves the Trent & Mersey at Great Haywood, near Stafford, and runs generally south-westerly to join the river Severn at Stourport. It forms part of James Brindley's 'grand cross' scheme which he intended would link the Mersey, Severn, Thames and Humber estuaries. The Staffs & Worcs Canal was promoted by a group inspired by the Trent & Mersey Canal project, and obtained its act on the same day. It displays all the features associated with James Brindley's waterways: meandering along the contours, locks are randomly spaced as it climbs over the watershed between the Trent and Severn basins.

The canal was open in 1772, as was the Trent & Mersey from Stone, past Great Haywood, to the river Trent at Derwentmouth. The Birmingham Canal also joined the Staffs & Worcs in 1772, feeding in traffic from the rapidly multiplying mines and industries of the Black Country and Birmingham. The Dudley and Stourbridge canals were linked to it at Stourton in 1779 and there was rapid development of transhipment facilities at Stourport where dock basins could accommodate the Severn's sailing barges or 'trows' (pronounced as in 'crow'). The Staffs & Worcs remained independent, and paid shareholders a dividend until nationalised in 1948. The nationalised authorities, combining with those responsible for coal mining and the electric power station at Stourport, managed to remove the majority of the canal's traffic to roads and railways by the middle 1950s, although some continued to pass along the half mile between Autherley and Aldersley until the late 1960s.

George Wood's grandfather had started work as a bricklayer with the Staffordshire & Worcestershire Canal in 1885, and lived in the house at Greensforge Lock that George and Margaret were later to occupy. He was with the company for forty years, which was not an unusual length of service in those days. His son-in-law, Fred, George's father, came from farm work to general maintenance on the canal. The family moved into the canal company's house on the lockside at Rocky Lock.

Following George's retirement, he and Margaret stayed in their lock house for several years before moving away from the canal to Kingswinford. Anyone familiar with their previous home can immediately identify the house amongst its neighbours on the estate by its immaculate garden. George continues to enjoy his outdoor activities although clearly missing the conversations with boat crews as they worked 'his' lock.

His earliest memories of the passing boats date from his childhood at Rocky Lock, when the canal was busy with Severn & Canal Carrying Company narrowboats bringing grain and hay up from the river to the Cannock coalfield. Like many people then, they used to keep chickens in the yard, and the boats were always glad of a few eggs in exchange for some feed for the fowl.

'Stourport power station wasn't built then so there was no Element's boats [a Birmingham carrier] on; and the main traffic was Severn & Canal bringing wheat up. They'd fetched it from ships at Gloucester and used to take it into Wolverhampton, I think, most of 'em. They used to come with twenty-eight ton uphill in them days, and there'd be pretty well one every ten minutes. They all had mules pulling 'em, except a few with donkeys early on, you know. They had the donkeys side by side on the towing path; if they didn't, the one would stop to see where the other one was and they'd pull each other over!

'All the warehouses was full at Stourport then, and there'd be all sorts, lots of food,

A stoppage to rebuild the towpath side wall at the Hyde Lock early this century. George Wood's grandfather is on the ladder at the back of the group (George Wood collection)

salmon and cheese and everything, stacked full. It came up the river but went off by road from there. There was a lot of stuff went to Kiddyminster [Kidderminster], specially to Harvey's the seed merchants. They had a place in an arm below the lock where they could offload the boats right into their warehouse. They were corn merchants as well. Then there'd be coal into all the factories, too. The carpet works still had coal, and there was plenty to the local wharves then, though the lorries finished that in the end.'

When George was twelve his father became the toll clerk at Stewpony Wharf and they moved to the house there. This was a busy spot, immediately downstream of the junction with the Stourbridge Canal which leads up into the Black Country and Dudley. At the time that the Wood family moved in, many of the passing boats had to be gauged to check the weight of cargo loaded and assess the toll due. This was done by measuring the height of the dry part of the boat's side from the water level:

'The boatmen must have thought you were daft, because they'd stand on the gunwale of the boat chatting to you whilst you took the reading,' recalls George, 'and of course, when they stepped off, the boat'd bob up an inch or two!' The boatmen liked to keep the boat deep when they were paid on tonnage as opposed to by the trip.

When George left school at the beginning of the 1930s the depression was deepening and it was a bad time to be looking for work. He got a post round and was up early enough to deliver the letters and still be in the fields on his second job by mid-morning. (Even after more than ten years of retirement he still can't break the habit, and likes to be about and making the most of his day by 6am.) After a few years he was able to get work with the canal company, gaining job security and a steady income. He started on general maintenance.

For most purposes the Staffordshire & Worcestershire Canal was divided at Gailey Top Lock. One gang looked after the section from Stourport to Gailey, while another took over from there to Great Haywood, with close, but benevolent, supervision from the head office, in Wolverhampton. George would bicycle out to whatever jobs were in progress each morning; so a

(Above) Gauging a coal boat (BW Archives, Gloucester)
(Right) A busy scene at Stewpony Wharf with the Woods' house in the background and the small toll office, in which Margaret worked during the war, to the right

seven o'clock start could mean leaving home at five if the work was at the far end of the length. However, there was a chance to recover at weekends which, hopefully, began at lunch time on Saturday – that is, unless there was a major repair to be carried out on one of the locks, when you worked through. 'You got paid your time, though – no double-time or time-and-a-half or anything like that.' Weekends at home were not wasted either, since there was a large stable on the wharf at Stewpony. Once the power station was built at Stourport, numerous craft belonging to Birmingham carriers T & S Element came onto the 'Light Run'

to supply this new 'electric light works', as the boatmen called it, with coal. 'They had all single boats, some powered but mostly horse-drawn.'

It wasn't long before George was moved to work on the dredger. This vessel was known as a 'spoon dredger' and would have been recognisable to the canal's first maintenance man of 150 years earlier. It was a standard narrowboat hull fitted with a small cabin suitable for brewing up and, at a push, for kipping in overnight, though in no great comfort. A short mast supported a hand crane which lifted a long wooden shaft with a large iron spoon on its outer end. The first of the crew lowered the spoon to the bottom of the canal with the crane, and a second man at the inner end of its shaft directed the spoon into the silt. On many such craft this was aided by a second winch man pulling the spoon forwards into the sludge before the first man winched it up above gunwale height. Thereupon the shaft man overturned the spoon to drop its contents into the boat's bottom. The spoon might bring up a hundredweight of mud and water at a time. In order to get a worthwhile load aboard the water had to be pumped out at regular intervals.

'It was only a small boat. You'd only get twenty ton on, and you'd have about four inches of side showing then. We'd load that in a day. We often used to load it on a Sunday because there'd be no traffic, see.' In many places there wouldn't be room to work the dredger whilst boats passed, and there could be one each way every three or four minutes as they cleared the locks in quick succession at peak times.

'Then, if we was at Stourport, we'd take it to Wolverley on the Monday. It'd take you all day with the traffic, see, especially with the flushes coming at you all the while.' The movement of water from an emptying lock makes bowhauling difficult and tiring, and an uphill

A spoon dredger at work, showing the detail of the spoon and its gear, which is normally out of sight beneath the murky water of the canal

Bowhauling the spoon dredger to the next dredging job after unloading at the mud tip

boat keeps being stopped and pushed back as each 'flush' arrives. 'It'd take more or less the day to get it off again, and then we'd be back down for another load. It was a full-time job! We didn't do all the basins at Stourport, just a track round; there was birds walking on it in the middle in them days. The day boats going to the power station used to shaft their way round the edge, or pull from mooring rings on the warehouses – nobody tried to go across the middle until motors came in. In the finish they had the big dredger up off the river and cleaned the lot out. There were only one or two trows coming up then, to the middle basin. The Severn & Canal had them; they used to come to their warehouse at the top of the locks.'

All this required considerable muscle power, as did moving the boat by bowhauling along the canal to the tipping site. 'Ah, we used to bowhaul it from Stourport to the tip at Wolverley. We'd wheel it off then, along a twenty-foot plank! We'd no wellingtons in them days, so we'd take the slide [hatch] off the cabin and perhaps the other chap had a piece of wood and we'd stand on that to shovel. That kept you on dry land! But it'd go down with you shovelling all the while, so you had to stop and lift it out to move it from time to time.' The sludge was shovelled up into a large barrow standing on planks perched across the boat between the gunwales. When full, this was wheeled off along the lengthy gangplank George describes to the bank, and then onto the tip for dumping. The whole scene would have been familiar to those who had built the canal over 150 years before.

'We didn't dredge along the main channel then, the traffic kept it moving. We'd only to do the bad places, scours below the locks and the like.' The gentle swell from moving horse boats kept the silt in suspension and carried it into wide places. Some was deposited where the bywashes discharged water at the tail of the locks, and bars built up at these spots; it also accumulated at winding holes where boats were turned round, or wharves filled up with mud pushed aside from the channel. If the dredger kept these spots clear the passing traffic scoured the channel out.

Many of the narrowboats which kept all this silt moving were loaded at Lyttleton or other collieries in Cannock Chase, and would tie up overnight or at the weekend, at Stewpony; there is still a long row of mooring rings in the towing path opposite the wharf where the boats lay whilst their horses occupied the stables. George's grandfather looked after the stables by their house on the wharf until he got too old; then George and his father took over the stables and the eighteen horses they could accommodate at any one time. The crews were day boatmen and used the minimal accommodation on their boats as little as possible, travelling home, often to the Oldbury area, by tram on the Kinver Light Railway which passed over the canal below the lock at Stewpony Wharf.

And every Sunday the 'girl in blue' would be seen, passing over the road bridge beside the tramway: Margaret was a house maid at Stourton Castle and walked up the road to church in Stourton village each week. She had come from Ludlow to take up the position in 1936, and it didn't take George long to work out what time to wheel the barrow of muck out of the stable so that 'he would just happen to be emptying it' as she passed. 'He was a nice young man and always said "hello" and would smile at me' – and so she began to pause for a chat. They were soon married, and lived in the house at Stewpony until they got a house down near Rocky Lock. Their daughter, Audrey, was born there six weeks after the move, and they remained at Rocky Lock through the war, moving to the house at Greensforge Lock at the end of 1945.

Inside the toll office

The coming of war changed little for George and his colleagues since canal work was a 'reserved occupation' and they could not be called up for military service. In fact water transport took on a renewed importance as was demonstrated when Margaret, then twenty-two, was recalled from her war service at Prestwood doing domestic work for the army to help on the canals: in 1942 the canal company transferred George's father, Fred Wood, from the toll house at Stewpony out onto the length to assist with maintenance work to keep the heavy traffic moving, and then arranged for Margaret to take his place in the little office. She continued the work in much the same way, except that by that time she did not have to gauge the boats, simply dealing with the paperwork of their cargo tickets and recording the tonnages stated against the miles to be covered. Hours remained 'traditional', with Margaret opening her little office at six in the morning and working through until six at night. Boats that passed outside these hours would be checked through by the toll clerks at The Bratch locks or Kidderminster. She also had to walk up to the unoccupied Stourbridge Canal toll office at Stourton Junction every day and collect tonnage tickets posted through the door by boatmen trading from the Stourbridge direction up to Swindon Forge. Each day she would complete a large detailed ledger sheet and return it to head office in Wolverhampton, where credit accounts for the various carriers were made up and invoices raised for the dues.

'That's Mr Butler and all the committee come out to inspect the new dredger. You can tell that it wasn't working properly because they haven't put the shed on it. It came from Graftons with it but it mustn't 've been put on till they tried it out. The pontoons, at the side, could be taken off, to go through the bridge holes, or the locks, or anything. You'd take them off and their beams to get it down to 7ft wide. Then you put the grab in a boat. You'd turn all the driver's cab and the engine part right round and drop the jib on top of the cabin. You'd to wind it down by hand. It wasn't stable without the pontoons. Because the boiler's in the cabin with the water in it its weight is high up.' (George Wood collection)

'I had to fill in all the boats, the times they passed, the tonnage due and their loads and everything. Every day I'd to post that.'

George, too, was keeping the canal open for war transport. However, one of his duties was closing the canal each night with stop planks, to try to prevent it being seriously damaged in the event of bombing. Stop planks are stout wooden boards which can be fitted into grooves in the masonry at most locks and many bridges, thus forming a temporary dam which allows short sections of canal to be drained for maintenance work. These planks were inserted at vulnerable places every night so that any bomb breaching the bank would cause water to be lost from only a short length of canal, thus largely preventing the scouring which occurs at a major breach and the flooding of neighbouring property. It did, of course, stop all traffic during the hours of darkness, however.

'We always put the planks in at Mitton, above Stourport, because there's a good drop there from the canal to all them houses.' George spent many a night out patrolling with his little shaded hand-lamp checking for damage.

In the 1920s George's father had been the first to take charge of the company's new steam dredger. It was first used at Stourport, and a new tip was opened at the edge of the town, where a vertical boilered steam crane was used for emptying the mud boats. These were ordinary day

'This would be taken about the same time as the photo of the new dredger [page 75]. It's the emptying crane, at Stourport, I think.' (George Wood collection)

boats, ex-trading narrowboats, often with small cabins, down-graded to end their working life carrying the sludge away from the dredger. This now worked continuously, being slowly winched along as it cleared the silt. It was now possible to dredge the full length of the canal's channel as well as the wide places, and indeed this became ever more necessary as the increasing number of motor boats washed the banks in; about seven boatloads of mud a day were being shifted.

'I worked it right through from Stourport to Compton, doing below the locks where the mud built up. We used to dredge at weekends because you couldn't do it in the week with so much traffic going through. Then we'd move it in the week to get ready to do the next lock the following weekend. They kept the spoon dredger after the steam one came, but it wasn't hardly used after that. But it did come in useful when boatmen came complaining and saying "There's a scour up there" – meaning a sand bar – "and we can't get over it!" Then the foreman used to get the old hand dredger up to the place and tie it up, and next time that chap came down he'd say, "That's better, George!" But we'd not done anything except tie the boat up! We'd taken none out!'

The dredger crew was also responsible for the steam dredger's maintenance. Margaret recalls that 'They used to put "young" George in that one, didn't they – he was still "young George", right up till he was fiftyish!' When any leaks developed where the fire tubes, running through the boiler water space, were joined to the back plate of the boiler in the firebox, George was a convenient size to carry out the repairs. 'We used to throw the fire out first, but it was still a bit warm, I'll tell you! The fire-hole door was only about eighteen inches square, and I had to get in the firebox to expand the tubes. They had a big rod to expand the tubes from outside – it had to be done warm. I used to put the rod in the end of the tube and the foreman, he'd be outside, would connect it up and they could turn it from outside to expand the tube. It was tapered, so it could go into the end of the tube and would expand it tight in the hole and so stop the leak. We had to wash the boiler out every week as well, and get all the scale out of it.'

Expanding the tubes in the dredger firebox

George was on the dredger continuously once he'd joined the crew. 'Except for in the winter. You couldn't work it in the frost because you had to blow all the water out of the boiler and everything to stop it freezing. So then we went cutting trees, the overhanging ones, and the like – we did them off the ice when it got thick enough to stand on.'

George worked on the ice boat, too, a job that Margaret remembers well: 'George often used to be off at two o'clock in the morning up to Stourbridge for the Bantocks.' (Thomas Bantock

'Left his bowler hat floating.' George had knocked the general manager off the ice boat!

was agent for the Great Western Railway, and carried principally to, or from, railway interchange basins around the Birmingham Canal Navigations system.) George has clear memories of that time:

'Yes, they used to run three boats down to Stourton and up our canal to Swin – Swindon Ironworks, you know. Three load a day they used to do, and they were the last to work up from Stourbridge. They used to bring long bars up to the ironworks. There was a steam cutter on the side of the canal there, and it cut 'em up all into little lengths before they took 'em in the works. We used to get there for when they were ready to start and break the ice in front of them down to Stourton and up to Marsh Lock. We could turn our ice boat above there because it was only short, see, and then we could come back down again. Ours was a wooden boat, and some of them had a cabin on, too. It had a rocker bar in the middle and a platform you stood on, and we used to hang a fire bucket on the bar.

'One time we were above The Bratch locks and got something on the propeller, so I got off with the shaft, to pull it off again. When I'd cleared it the boat had got on the mud, so I pushed it with the shaft and of course it slipped, with the ice on everything, and I went in, shaft and all, through where we'd broke the ice! I cycled home for a change of clothes, and I was just one piece of ice when I got to Stewpony. Cycling was the only way to keep warm!' The episode had obviously impressed Margaret, too:

'He was iced all over, so he had a change of clothes and a cup of tea. I suppose you had some whisky in it, if I remember right! And then back you went again.' George laughed:

'One of the lads wanted me to borrow a motorbike, but I should have frozen to death on that.

'I knocked the boss in once, Mr Butler. Left his bowler hat floating on the top! He used to stand on the counter you see, right by the tiller, when we were ice breaking. It's ever so awkward trying to get your tiller over in ice, even without anybody in the way. We used to break it so far and it would stop the boat, you see, so we used to back up and have another run at it. Anyway, we backed up so far and caught a bit of ice in the rudder and the tiller whipped round. Nobody couldn't hold it. It knocked him off and in he went! He came up and he said "Now, you buggers ... have a good laugh!" He went home and got changed and then came back again, same as me. But you know, he stood in just the same place again when he got back! That was Butler the boss!

'Leslie Butler he was, the general manager, and his father was general manager before him. He was very particular, the old chap was.'

Margaret remembers the Butler family, too: 'But they were lovely days though, George. He knew each man and he knew what he were capable of. He was ever so fair. You weren't just a number, like you ended up, a number on a paper.' George nodded in agreement:

'They used to come down together, Mr Butler and Leslie, the son, he used to walk in front. Now, we used to have a smoke, and Leslie used to come and say "Put 'em out, he's coming round the corner!" One chap had his waistcoat pocket burnt out because he'd put his pipe in it and it wasn't out properly! Leslie used to smoke like a chimney, but the old man didn't and he wouldn't allow you to – I think he used to worry about losing time, because people would get a twist of baccy and be cutting it up and filling their pipes instead of working!

The Staffs & Worcs Canal Co inspection boat Lady Hatherton *was like a Victorian railway directors' saloon and had the company's monogram etched in the windows and fancy upholstery. It is still to be seen about the canals in use as a pleasure boat although its hull has been completely renewed* (George Wood collection)

'When the bosses came on a tour of inspection with the committee boat, the *Lady Hatherton*, there would be no dredging done for a week because we used to be sent out on the length getting everything tidied up. We'd have about three mile each, and would tidy it all up before they came. I used to have from Greensforge to Stewpony. We had to cut the towpath and the hedge, and get all the overhanging trees done. There wasn't too much grass then, with the traffic on, because the horses kept it back. Nowadays it's only a narrow path, but when the horses were walking it they kept it back nice and wide; they'd walk against the hedge very often in summer, when there were flies about, because that'd keep the flies off 'em, you know. If you were a lengthsman you had to go in front of the committee boat on your bike, and at each lock you'd to trickle a little bit of ash down behind the gates to seal up any leaks so that the bosses wouldn't see them! That way every lock they came to was perfect, with no leaks! They never knew there was a bloke just in front putting ashes to them!'

Margaret says, 'You were a crafty lot, weren't you!' George laughed again, and continued:

'Mr Butler, the general manager, put us on to that!

'*Lady Hatherton* had two horses on – well, two from Stourport to Stewpony, and another two from there to Gailey. Proper horses they had, no donkeys or anything like that. They used to go through in a day, though we only took them to Compton, and the top end gang would take them on from there. I've steered it for them. I used to bring it back empty too; two of us did that, but the gang was all on to take them up. There was just the one horse coming back. The boat was kept in a big red shed at Stourport, just by Stourport Lock on the right-hand side. We used to keep the pump boat in there too, the one we used to pump the locks out and everything.

'Those two horses are waiting at Stewpony for the committee boat, Lady Hatherton, *to come up. They're top end men and horses, come over from Gailey specially to take the boat back there.'* (George Wood collection)

'There was quite a bit of traffic going down below Gailey, to Lyttleton and those collieries. Of course some went off the other way, at Hatherton, and up into Cannock for the coal. I was about the last one to bring a loaded boat down there, I think, a load of slack for the dredger. There was no boatmen going up there by then. We used to clean the locks out, you see, and throw it on the bank; then we'd go with a boat and fetch it down for the dredger. We didn't go for boatloads from the colliery.' It seems that the Staffs & Worcs Canal Company never bought a boatload of good steam coal – almost everything the dredger burnt came out of the cut.

'Sometimes when a boat came down with good nuts on, Lyttleton nuts, he'd throw us some over. If the boss was about you'd have to cut the steam off a little or he'd want to know where you'd got the good stuff you were burning! Trouble was, if you hit something hard like that you'd struggle, because it wouldn't pick it up with the steam shut down – so you had to move on a short way and leave that bit behind. We used to get the slack out at Gailey because they used to throw it off to lighten the boats there. They were paid by the trip, not on tonnage, you see.

'They used to do the same down by Gothersley, where it was quiet. They'd start as soon as they'd got out of Ashwood Basin where the coal from the Earl of Dudley's collieries was loaded. Sometimes when we'd go down that way for a little walk we'd see all coal dust floating on the surface of the water. When we caught them up I'd say, "You've been busy, haven't you?" – and they'd say, "What are you on about, George?" because they couldn't see the floating dust with the boat moving. The canal company got a policeman to patrol on the towpath, and that stopped a lot of it.

'They were only trying to lighten the boat to get along a bit better. They were paid by the trip, you see – they'd not have done it if they'd been paid by the ton! If they made the boat lighter, and shallower, the horse'd get 'em along faster. Then when they got near Stourport a lot of them used to get water out of the cut and put that in and make the weight look right!'

Life changed gradually after the war. George continued to drive the dredger or the unloading crane. Then in 1948 the Staffordshire & Worcestershire Canal was nationalised, along with the majority of our inland navigations. The British Transport Commission was eventually broken up and the British Waterways Board formed, a new set-up that Margaret didn't like:

'You can't work for so many bosses; isn't that a terrible thing to say – don't write that down! When it was private they knew every man and what his capabilities were.' General manager Leslie Butler was transferred to the northern regional office at Liverpool. The trade had almost completely gone from the western part of the Staffs & Worcs. A diesel dredger was provided to replace the steamer, which George took to the Stratford Canal for further work.

George followed in his father's footsteps and was photographed driving the diesel emptying crane at the mud tip (George Wood collection)

George returned to the new diesel plant, which was made by JCB, and had a long reach arm on the grab. Eventually a man came from head office to 'pass George out on the dredger': somebody had realised that he'd had only forty years' experience!

By that time there was little trade since the power station at Stourport had ceased to take water-borne coal, and only the three daily Bantock's boats used the canal on their trip between Stourton and Swindon. Gradually pleasure boat traffic began to appear in the summer.

George would assist at stoppages when locks or other structures were closed to navigation for maintenance or repair. On these occasions the object was to get the waterway open to traffic and earning tolls as rapidly as possible, in contrast to the modern system of allowing work to drag on for months in winter when the pleasure boats are mostly laid up. A favourite time for stoppages was Whit week, or during colliery holidays, when traffic was lightest. Inevitably boats would be held up and their crews would work on the stoppage since there was no dole for a boatman who was laid off for a few days during the enforced delay.

'We used to start Saturday dinner and often worked right through – generally we'd be finished by Wednesday night.'

'You never used to come home, sometimes, did you?' remembers Margaret.

Stout stop planks were inserted into specially made grooves in the masonry at the head and tail of the locks, and the water was pumped out into the lower pound of the canal. There was a specially designed pump boat, kept at Stourport as George has described, which could be used to clear the water from the work in the bottom of a lock chamber:

Once stop planks are fitted into their groove beneath a bridge, any leaks can be sealed with a trickle of ash as the canal beyond is dewatered

'It was a paraffin engine on there. We used to have to start it by warming it with a blowlamp, and then you'd swing the flywheel over and if you caught it right it'd start and fire, and if not you'd have to swing it again until it did. There was one big flexible pipe you could put over the stop planks into the lock, and

Having drained off the water, a sheerlegs is used to lift new bottom gates into place

it'd run till it pumped the lock dry. You couldn't start it again if you let it run dry, you'd to fill it up again with a bucket of water before it'd pump again. It had a big valve wheel in the fore end you could regulate the water with, so if it was going down too much you could shut it off a bit and stop it running dry. There was a big cabin on that boat, and eleven of us used to stop in there if we were out on any stoppage or anything. There were no proper beds. You just had a lump of hay or straw and your jacket or something to sleep on.'

Often the culvert which carried water into or out of the chamber through the paddles would have become blocked with rubbish or driftwood. George was one of the smallest, so 'they used to send him up culverts. Tied a rope on to him in case he got stuck. He's got the legacy in his legs now!'

'Well, I'd crawl down from the top end because that's the way they'd get blocked. They're only a foot or two high. We'd drain off first but the bricks'd still be wet, you know, on your hands and knees. I'd tie the sticks or whatever it was to the rope so the others could pull them out. We'd only drain it off for a couple of hours for a job like that. There always used to be boatmen to help at stoppages, as they was held up.

'The gates were made at Stourport and fetched up in a boat to the lock. You'd keep 'em in the boat until you was ready to do the work, and then lift 'em with a sheerlegs, like a tripod. You'd to be careful to lift 'em straight or the tripod would be over and all the lot in the bottom of the lock. It's not like today, with the gantry they have now; you can run them up and down with that. It's on wheels and there's a chain block for lifting, you see. We used

The breach at Compton happened at 5.30am on Saturday 9 September 1972 and George was woken at 6am because the sound of the water running over the weir by the house at Greensforge changed. He set off on his bike to investigate (George Wood collection)

to put the boat into the lock and lift the gate over the foredeck; then pull the boat out and lower the gate down and lean it against the wall to one side. Same with the other gate, and then get the old gates out and into the boat. Then you could get your stop planks in and drain it all off.

'There was one time when they were working nights on a stoppage at Greensforge, and Grandpa came out playing the tin whistle to them whilst they were putting the top gate in. They had the electric rigged up there, and one of the boats had a dynamo on and Grandfather thought it was wonderful. It was all oil lamps in the cottage, then. The old gates usually went back to Stourport to get all the plates and ironwork off. They'd all be used again on new gates. Len, the foreman, wouldn't waste anything. We had days, sometimes, at Stourport, cutting those old gates up and getting the old pins out. We cut the heads off, and then knocked them through so we could get all the old ironwork off them.

'There was a carpenter and his mate there then. We used to fetch the trees for them – they were all stacked below the lock by the basin and marked with the date. We used to go down and push the one that he wanted into the water, float it up the lock and then it'd be winched out and lifted on the saw-bench. It would roll onto the bank with the winch. All the sawing was done by steam in my time. They had a circular saw and a bandsaw, and the engine drove shafting and belts in the shop; even the mortising was done by steam. It used to drive the lot, that one engine, even cracking the bricks up. We used them for concreting and making new anchor stones with. If we wanted a bit of a rest we just used to chuck a bit of iron in that and it'd fetch the belt straight off! There were no goggles or anything then, even with all this brick flying about, just a great jaw coming down and cracking them up. The blue ones used to fly a bit but the red ones didn't, being softer.' Margaret remembers a particular occasion:

'When there was that breach at Compton it was George's birthday and some friends were going to take us to Aberdovey. But George woke early and said, "There's something wrong somewhere".' George nods:

'You could tell by the water: it wasn't coming over the weir at the lock the same as it usually would.'

'George said, "I shall have to go and see what it is". So he got the bike out and went up the towpath – and by the time he was off, the phone was red hot!'

'It was below Compton Bridge, near Wightwick Mill. There was all steel pilings along there, I helped put them in, six-foot piles. There's a brook, the Smestow, comes down by Compton Bridge, and with there being heavy rain in the night it overflowed and got into the canal. The water couldn't get away down the weir at Wightwick Mill lock, so it burst through the bank; it got under the pilings and washed the bottom away, and they was all hanging there, like a string of washing!'

'So much for our outing to Aberdovey! But it was like that lots of times. The phone would go, and off *you'd* go and that was it! The work came first.'

'They put 800 tons of clay in there, in that hole. They brought it down the field and the crane put it in for us, then we drove 10ft piles right through the clay. You had to have the crane to fit the piles into one another because you couldn't reach the top of them, being 10ft.'

They remained at Rocky Lock through the war, moving to Greensforge lock house at the end of 1945. Margaret, sitting in her immaculate modern living room, recalls 'It hadn't the electric put in then. It was all oil lamps. There was that horrible brown-purple paint. Ooh, it was dingy! Admittedly there was a war on. It was then done out in that cream paper, wasn't it? I had a brainwave and stippled it all different colours, which made it a bit brighter, didn't it? It had mains water, George's grandfather had that put in. It had a pump in the yard, until Ashwood waterworks was put on, they had a bore hole and it took the water. The Staffs & Worcs company took him up to the court to fight the case with the water company. They took him up to London for that. We gradually improved it as we went along, but you couldn't get rid of the damp, could you? Cliff, who moved in after us, he's still plagued with damp. We were in there from 1945 till 1987, well after George had finished working. We had to become private tenants after George retired, but he was still very useful to the waterways. He used to clear the weir, to stop it blocking and everything. But we used to enjoy it, and we miss the company now. But you can't have it all ways. Now we've got gas central heating, the shops and even a bus at the end of the road. Everybody said we wouldn't like it, having neighbours, but they're lovely. They all stop and chat to George because he's always out in the garden.'

VIOLET MOULD

Long-distance Boating

Fellows Morton & Clayton Ltd was one of the largest general carriers to operate on the narrow canals. James Fellows established the forerunner of this business at West Bromwich in 1837. His principal trade was southwards from the Birmingham canals, along what later became the Grand Union system towards London. In 1876 his son Joshua, with partners including Frederick Morton, took over many of the boats and much trade from the Grand Junction Canal Company's carrying establishment. Their company expanded, absorbing the London & Midland Counties Carrying Company in 1887. In 1889 Fellows Morton & Clayton Ltd (FMC) was incorporated, bringing in craft owned by William Clayton of Saltley. The latter also operated special tank-craft for the carriage of liquids, which were transferred to a separate concern (Thomas Clayton Ltd, based at Oldbury, just north-west of Birmingham).

By the beginning of the twentieth century FMC was operating throughout the canal system from Ellesmere Port and Manchester to Birmingham, and along the Grand Junction Canal to the Thames. Their services also covered the Trent & Mersey Canal between the Bridgewater Canal and the river Trent extending as far as Nottingham, and the Leicester line of canals between there and the Grand Junction.

Many families worked for the company through several generations, with the younger menfolk finding profitable employment on the flyboats which worked non-stop to regular schedules. By the end of the 1880s many of these services were operated by steam-powered narrowboats, the last of which were not replaced by semi-diesel engines until the 1920s. Violet Mould was born against this background at the beginning of the twentieth century. Most of those who have kindly agreed to tell their stories in these pages have had to endure my intrusion into their homes, but Violet was keen for a change of scene and jumped at the chance to sit on my boat and look out at the occasional autumn pleasure boat passing whilst we talked.

Violet was a Griffiths before she married, her great-great-great-grandfather being a brother to John Griffiths, the carrier from Bedworth. But he didn't have anything to do with his family's boat dock at Charity as he wasn't the eldest: that went to the first son, another John.

'I weren't born on a boat, no. Me dad had got a steamer when we was young; going night and day, he was. Me mum and dad had a house at Braunston, on the Grand Union Canal, near Rugby, that is. I think the First War was starting and it caused quite a lot of people to come onto the boats. The young men was going off to the army, so we started to go night and day. My mum and dad kept the house at Braunston because sometimes when we were passing we used to tie up at the bottom of the garden and go up to the house. It was all right empty like that, but I expect they sold it after a bit, I don't know.

'Me dad had the *Sultan* new, and she was a steamer.'

Sultan had been built for Fellows Morton & Clayton, with an iron-sided, wooden-bottomed hull at their Saltley boat dock in Birmingham in June 1899. She was fitted with a Haines-type single-cylinder steam engine that may also have been built at the boatyard.

Violet Mould's father, William Griffiths, steers Fellows Morton & Clayton steamer Sultan *up from lock 11 to lock 10 at Long Buckby on the Grand Junction Canal, which was later amalgamated into the Grand Union's London to Birmingham main line. Note the length of boiler room and cabin which reduced the cargo capacity of these boats, and the crew of four to tend the steam plant and work the locks. They worked continuously in shifts whilst the boats were on the move and would be assisted by up to three further hands on the butty when towing* (BW Archives, Gloucester)

Steamer Sultan *and its butty* Kegworth *at Fellows Morton & Clayton's Nottingham Wharf after a trip from the City Road Basin in London* (Nottingham Historical Film Unit/Alan Faulkner collection)

When this was replaced with a Bolinder semi-diesel engine in May 1924, her cabins were rebuilt to increase the capacity of the cargo hold, using the space vacated by the bunkers and boiler of the steam plant.

'Me dad had the *Vanguard,* later; that was a steamer, too. Then the *Admiral.* Then he went into *Spain* and *Glascote,* which were horse boats. He used to wear white cords and a black velvet waistcoat on the steamers – every day he used to wear them; me mum had two pair, like, to keep washing one. He sometimes wore a drab-coloured cardigan. But the men used to look ever so nice on there.'

The steamers were the prestige expresses of the canals. Their crews not only drew the best pay, but were appropriately proud of their charges.

'There was four children besides me, and Mum and Dad: Lucy, Lizzie, Florrie and then me – I was a twin with William, but he died as a baby. Eli was the last one. We worked the locks and so on more or less straightaway, just as early as I can remember, really. But mostly we was at Braunston, going to school we was, while me dad had the steamer.'

Two of Violet's sisters married steamboat captains, so there was her father as well as two brothers-in-law on steamers.

'Dad had a motor after the First War, *Seal,* and we did the same runs with that. He said we should have to have another boat to get everybody in – we had a butty all the while then, the *Exe.* We had *Seal* and *Exe* from new: *Seal* was a wooden motor built at Uxbridge by Fellows Morton themselves; she was launched in June 1920. [*Exe* followed about twelve months later from the same builder.]

'We've been through up here [the river Soar] night and day, no stopping. We come through from City Road Basin in London, and we used to empty half at Leicester and the other half at Nottingham. Then if there was any goods at Nottingham to go back we'd load that and straight through to the City Road again. If there weren't no loading we'd go up to Shipley for coal and take that, but we didn't take coal every time; that mostly went back to Uxbridge. We've carried everything, everything you can think of. We've had spelter [an alloy used in casting and galvanising], in drums, and timber, and we used to bring tea up from the City Road. We used to get 50 ton on with the butty behind the steamer as well when it was a load like coal or spelter. That was in big drums which went to Fazeley Street, in Birmingham.

'They'd send you all ways from City Road; so you could go to Birmingham or Preston Brook as well. We sometimes emptied at Birmingham and then went off to Ellesmere Port – they didn't always send you back to London. It was the same after I was with my husband, Ralph. My mum and dad was dead by then.'

'That's me and me sisters on our motor, Seal, *at Brentford; the tallest is me mother and there's Eli, on the left. Jack Creswell and his Mrs [Alice] are on the butty* Amesbury *on the path behind. It's taken below Brentford Lock and round the corner a bit. We've got 25 ton of sugar on there. That's the school in the background. The boats are facing ready for going up the river Brent to get into the Grand Union Canal. There was a very high tide in the night and it lifted the boats on there and left 'em up there when the tide went out again. Dad hadn't got time to get her off. She floated off all right with the next high tide, she didn't leak. Dad wouldn't keep shoving at her because of hurting her bottom so he just left her until she floated. There was several boats got on that day because it was such a high tide in the early morning, before it was light.'* (BW Archives, Gloucester)

Routes from the south to Nottinghamshire and Derbyshire frequented by Violet Mould

Fellows Morton & Clayton were not known as coal carriers, or indeed bulk carriers of any material. I went over this point more than once with Violet, but she has clear memories of these cargoes. It is possible that the return loads of coal were consumed at the company's own boatyard and on their craft rather than being delivered to independent merchants. This trade, and much of the coal carried to canal-side factories along the lower part of the Grand Union Canal, was in the hands of a few factors and a large fleet of independent owner-boatmen until the later 1930s. These proud independents were gradually forced into the service of the big carriers, particularly by the Grand Union Canal Carrying Co, which, with its large fleet of new motor-driven craft, was able to undercut their rates. At the same time, this rapidly expanding company was desperate for the services of experienced boat crews and so was prepared to guarantee the former owner-boatmen employment should they sell their older craft. Thus the coal trade gradually passed to the GUCC Co rather than to FMC.

'We liked the lock keepers at Red Hill, where you come out of the Soar into the Trent. We used to take the tonnage ticket in the office here every time. We've been down here when the water was right up – I've steered down here when there's been water all over these fields because they was wanting the goods at Nottingham. You had to mind how you went on round here because you've got the weir on the Trent at this corner and it could fetch you astern over the weir. Me dad used to be on the motor and we'd all be on the butty. We'd just be on a short strap, say, 20ft, and he'd say, "Now have that lock ready". So me and Florrie, he used to make us get off at Ratcliffe and run down here to get Red Hill Lock ready. He wanted it ready when he arrived because it was running water, and it would pull you over into the weir at the top of the lock. The water could be on the towpath when you went into the Trent to get to Cranfleet Cut. There were gates at the top of that cut which might be closed if the water was too high, and you'd have to tie up. But we used to have to get down because they wanted the loads, you see.'

Ferrying horses across the Trent near the entrance to the Erewash Canal (Derbyshire Libraries)

There was a little ferry between the towpath from the river Soar and the Trent path near the junction with the Erewash Canal. 'It was like a punt, that boat, and we used to have to get the

This pair of horse-drawn craft were not so fortunate as Violet's family in making the crossing from the river Soar to the Erewash Canal. It appears that a horse towing line broke and the Trent current pushed them down to Thrumpton Weir. Except in time of high flood there is insufficient depth of water to float such boats over the weir cill. Nowadays the approach is in any case guarded by a substantial boom (Author's collection)

horse in it and get him across. Me dad used to work the boat, like. He just shoved the boat across with the pole – it didn't have any line onto the land or anything. Then one of us girls used to have to hold the horse's head while we went across. He could be a bit frightened. You see, we used to put the boat over first and then take the punt and fetch the horse. You had to go a bit upstream before crossing, and then push across. At least Ralph and I never had a horse to cross here because the *Seal* had a Bolinder in it!'

Ralph's father was in iron moulding, but he used to have trouble keeping in work because it tended to be seasonal; so then he would help out at Leicester Wharf with the loading and unloading, and in this way came to work a boat locally: Leicester, Nottingham and up the Erewash Canal to load coal for the electricity companies. Eventually this became his full-time employment, with Ralph as mate. When Ralph was old enough he took a boat of his own; he went to Fellows Morton & Clayton when he was seventeen. To start with he was given a single motor, but as he gained experience they found him a mate, and they were entrusted with a pair of boats.

Violet has described the necessity to boat down the river Soar and cross the Trent to the Erewash Canal, or to continue down the larger river to Fellows Morton & Clayton's depot at Nottingham whatever the weather and in almost any prevailing river conditions. Because stillwater canal boatmen were not used to the currents and changing channels of the rivers, FMC used to retain the services of an experienced local boatman; in the 1930s and 1940s the position of river pilot was filled by Bill Roberts. A postcard or telegram from the owners would advise him where and when to expect to meet craft requiring his assistance. Ralph's sister, Carrie, married Bill Roberts, and they went to live at Sawley.

'Ralph was on the motors with Fellows Morton – we was always on Fellows Morton's. We used to meet passing or at loading places. The steamers would be all finished before Ralph and me was married. I was married to Ralph in 1938. We was married in the church at Deritend, in Birmingham; my parents were married at Warwick.

Work under way to replace the twenty-one narrow locks at Hatton with chambers wide enough to take a pair of narrowboats together. When Violet first went boating the route from Braunston to Birmingham seemed to be all work, although it includes level pounds of eight and ten miles between locks, and she preferred the Nottingham run (BW Archives, Gloucester)

'Of my own children there was only Jill and Glenys was born on the boat, the second one and the last. Wendy was born at Brentford and Elaine at Braunston. Ralph and I never had a house, just the boats. We had various different ones.

'They would start on the cargo as soon as we arrived at City Road, or the other wharves. We've met some boats the other side of Leicester and they've said, "They're waiting for you at Leicester to unload". We used to like coming Leicester. It was better than going Birmingham – it was all work, was Birmingham! There was such a lot of little locks, they was little locks all the way from Braunston. In the end, they made 'em bigger, and then it was better because you'd get both boats in.'

Violet was referring to a government-sponsored, job creation scheme of the early 1930s when the fifty-two locks from Braunston to the outskirts of Birmingham were rebuilt into fifty-one large enough to take two narrowboats side by side. Many bridges were also reconstructed, and miles of bank protection carried out. But the scheme was never carried through to the extent that had been planned, which would have seen the introduction of bigger, wide-beam motor barges to replace the pairs of narrowboats.

'We used to load tubes at Coombeswood and take them to Brentford, and there they put them in a lighter and took them down the river. They used to come in bundles, and they'd

A pair of Fellows Morton boats loading overside from a ship in Regent's Canal Dock. Amongst those waiting astern is the motorised steamer Baron *whose steerer can just be seen trying to push the boat safely out from beneath the overhanging lighter. Violet was not keen on taking her home in amongst these heavy and roughly handled, outsized craft* (BW Archives, Gloucester)

tip your boat right over as each one landed. We could get 22 ton on the butty with them, and 20 ton on the motor. Then we'd go Camp Hill way back. We've took sacks of buttons from City Road to Birmingham, and bedsteads and timber, sawn deals. I helped to load them, off a barge. We used to take 50 ton of sugar from Brentford to Bournville; then they'd load chocolate, there, back to London. We'd load that crumb [part-processed chocolate] as well to Knighton, on the Shropshire Union, and that went to make the chocolate. We'd load back, I've forgot what it would be, I suppose it was dried milk. Some people used to like to get a bag of crumb from there, but we never bothered. The men that worked there used to bring a bit out to us from time to time. We did Guinness in barrels from Park Royal, as well. Ralph used to always keep one watercan empty when we arrived, and they'd fill it up for us!

'We went down to the ships in Regent's Dock sometimes, perhaps for copper sheet and that sort of thing. It was all right, but you had to mind what you did with those big barges about. I didn't like those cow-mouthed barges, as they call them – you see, they would come right over the top of your cabin. Ralph used to have to keep an eye on them, but the dockers used to put it in for you. They'd gauge you at Commercial Road, and after that each lock keeper would check your ticket up to Cowley where they'd gauge you again. Then Cowroast [above Berkhamsted, the summit of the climb out of the Thames basin] and the top lock of Bugby [Long Buckby, near Daventry]; then stop at the ticket office at Braunston, and then top of Wigrams [Calcutt Locks, near Southam] and to the top of Camp Hill, in Birmingham. Then down to Warwick Wharf.

'I've lots of relations at Braunston; it's a nice little place, Braunston. City Road was good for shopping, though. You wouldn't be more than two days in the basin there, but there was a nice little shopping centre on the top of the tunnel and you'd got time to go shopping whilst they was emptying you and reloading. The children would play in the warehouses there. They got playing in the top warehouse once and Elaine, she fell down a hole in the middle of all the bales of rags – they went to the paper mill with them. The men had to dig her out, but there was no harm done. Me uncle Ned was boating regular on the paper mill job, but we only did it very occasionally. They never had much sleep, they didn't, it was non-stop. [Fellows Morton & Clayton had craft on long-term charter to paper-makers John Dickinson whose Apsley, Nash and Croxley mills were alongside the Grand Union Canal. Some of the craft were painted in Dickinson's own livery and operated almost non-stop on short-haul work between the various mills and wharves.] We used to tie up of a night, but we might start very early.

'You could get some nice materials and that sort of thing at the shops near City Road; we used to make our own clothes, and Mum used to make the old-fashioned bonnets, printed material they was, then put lace over them, too. When she was doing them she'd say, "Don't touch that bonnet!" You hadn't got to touch anything. We'd got a little hand machine, a Singer it was. Glenys has got it now. I didn't wear a bonnet, but me aunt Ethel used to, and me uncle Jack Griffiths' wife. Folk used to get me mother to make them; they were usually white or cream with little flowers on, especially before they was married.

'If we had a nice day I'd do the wash because I had a little bath which I could put on the bank. When I was young, Granny was at Braunston and she used to do the washing for Mother. We used to leave all the dirty clothes on the way through, and pick up all the clean ones from her when we came back, all starched and ironed.

'Then when we was going I did all the cooking on the butty, and walked along to the fore end with it for Ralph. He could ease up the motor and the butty would catch up to the motor as the line went slack so I could pass his plate over. Otherwise you had to time it right so it was ready when you came in a lock with the boats together.

'Ralph kept a gun, and sometimes we'd get a rabbit or a hare and then we'd to hold the butty in and jump off and run to pick it up. The gun was kept on the motor, and there was a fishing net, too, because you could get

'He could ease the motor and the butty would catch up… so I could pass his plate over.'

eggs with that – swan's eggs were good. You could also get mushrooms and watercress, and raspberries or blackberries.

'We used to stand a jar of flowers against the watercan, some we'd picked along the way; when the brass bands were done on the chimney and that it used to look all right. We had three brass rims, not too much, and we'd a rod along over the range. The ticket drawer had a brass knob and some crochet work round the bottom. We used to call it "needle-bobbing that": I used to put the tiller under my arm or against my hip, and me dad used to shout back from the motor, "Keep the boat straight – you ain't needle-bobbing again, are you?" We didn't have as much as some of them do now; it's overdone, now, sometimes. I had a lot of them hanging-up plates. I used to have a nice brass lamp with a glass globe on it and a bow of red ribbon round. Then there was a row of plates down the back of the range. We didn't make any more dust from the range than we could help, so it didn't take you too long to keep it nice.

'When you went on a new boat at the dock, you see, there'd be iron knobs and everything, but you had to bring all your brass with you from the other boat. You had your own range. There was always a stove in, you see, but it was a straight up one, like a bottle stove, you know, and you couldn't cook on that. So you took that back to the dock and put your own cooking range in. We used to have a Larbert range – it was a nice range. It was as big as would fit in the space, like. You brought all your own things onto the change boat if your'n was going on the dock. It used to take less than half a day to change over. But we was always pleased to get our own boat back!

'At Uxbridge they used to do all the painting inside, and castles on the doors. They were nice painted at Uxbridge. You used to do one round trip whilst it was being docked, about a fortnight, and it would be ready when you got back. Some people used to like the change boat because it would be all cleaned out and nice, but really you never knew who had had them before, and sometimes you'd get one which had had a family in who hadn't kept it clean. Then you'd to clean it all out before you could take over. It would be about every two years that they docked the boats.

'Ralph always had everything in place on the boats: it was all neat, and you knowed where to get on and off, and where everything was when you was working. He used to scrub all the ropework and that, to keep 'em white, and the back fender on the motor; he used to get the boat brush and scrub them and give them a good doshing. But he didn't have any of those strings at the cabin side, he didn't like them. We just had the one to tie the watercan in case it got knocked.

'You'd get the inspector on sometimes, like at Birmingham where there was a lot of boats. He'd get on them all and check them all up. They didn't bother so much at Nottingham or Leicester. We never had any bother with them; they just stepped on the side and looked in, and said, "Oh, it's no good going in there, it's all right". They could see it was clean, you know. But some boats, they had big families on and the inspector didn't like that.

'Mac Anderson was the boss [the southern fleet superintendent for Fellows Morton & Clayton] and he used to like to come to us, he did. We used to generally give him a cup of tea. He was the head man. I don't think he had a cup of tea off anybody else. If he had somebody as wanted a trip on a boat, he used to send 'em with us. He used to talk to my dad ever so nice. We took a schoolteacher once.'

Ralph and Violet had a good reputation for looking after the company's visitors like that:

Once they had settled into their houseboat and the children were grown Ralph and Violet made extensive trips with their pleasure boat. Here Violet is steering Les and Freda Hales' boat whilst towing their own through some thick surface weed which was causing them engine problems (Leslie Hales)

'We kept that *Seal* and *Exe* till we came off the boats. We always got on all right on the rivers because we seen that everything was done right, all the lines in good order and everything.'

Ralph and Violet gave up working the carrying boats in about 1953; Ralph then worked for a number of years for British Waterways on maintenance on the Soar. At first, he and Violet lived in a converted narrowboat at Thurmaston: *Evelyn*, one of George Garside's former sand-carrying boats from Leighton Buzzard. Ralph and Violet bought it, the then British Waterways carpenter converted it for residential use, and they lived aboard with their four daughters for a number of years. Three went regularly to school, though the eldest was already too old. Then they bought a Victorian houseboat, which is still at Thurmaston, and lived in that until about three years ago.

'Me and Ralph put all new bottom in that houseboat when we got it – that might be forty years ago, now. Ralph didn't want to go in one of those lock houses. He did tug driving and moving the maintenance boats, and he also steered pleasure boats and trip boats from Thurmaston. They were a harbour-launch type of thing, mostly tripping in Abbey Park, at Leicester.

'We decided to have a pleasure boat later on. We bought the hull, and Ralph built all the cabin on it. We went different places with the pleasure boat, that we hadn't been with Fellows Morton's. We've been to Macclesfield and Llangollen.'

Following Ralph's death a few years ago, Violet found it impossible to continue to maintain the houseboat on a river Soar backwater, her home for forty years, and she was persuaded to move into a small flat in the village centre a few hundred yards from the river. This was the first time that she had lived 'on the land' since the beginning of World War I. It is significant, however, that whilst we sat on my boat and talked, she had smiled and sparkled as she harked back sixty and seventy years to the boats and her unceasing travels on the water; yet she visibly wilted whenever the flat was mentioned. 'I don't like it in here, it isn't like my houseboat,' she said in parting at her door. Friends around her were struggling to persuade her not to give up – but after a mere twenty years working on boats and waterways in between my writing, I can understand the bond with the water and just how she felt, even if I find it hard to explain in modern terms.

NOTE: *I am very sorry to have to record that Violet Mould died in December 1996 whilst I was preparing this chapter.*

JACK STRANGE

Blacksmith

Ellesmere in Shropshire was one of the principal maintenance centres of the Shropshire Union Canal system. What is now Ellesmere Yard was first established during the construction of the canal by Thomas Telford and his engineering team under the supervision of William Jessop. With expansion and amalgamation of the region's canal system this yard came to have responsibilities extending far beyond the original Ellesmere Canal. Not far up the road at Welsh Frankton, Jack Strange now joins with his brother Alf in demonstrating blacksmithing and guiding visitors around their fascinating collection of rural bygones. It was in this shady and low-roofed workshop that Jack and I sat and talked. All around were the tools and products of a blacksmith's trade. The only item out of place amongst the ironwork was the old church pew we used which usually accommodates a row of visitors who can watch in comfort just out of range of any sparks from hearth or anvil.

Jack, very dark haired and perhaps shorter and less solidly built than one expects to find a blacksmith, talked quietly with the gentle accent of the Welsh border country:

'I left school in 1935. I was going to be a blacksmith because my dad was a blacksmith; he had a shop just down the road here, at Welsh Frankton. The time came and I went to work for him but, well, you don't always get on, do you? So I was just turned fourteen when I went to work for another blacksmith who wanted an apprentice at a little place called Alberbury, by Shrewsbury. I worked for him for two-and-a-half years or so, and I got 5s a week. Hours didn't matter, though – I used to have to milk his cows in a morning – he'd only got three – and then I'd to be in the shop for eight. I finished in the shop for five and milked the cows, and then I'd finished for the day. But if there was shoeing to be done at night, then we were shoeing! There was no worry about overtime because I got none! Then, a half-day on Saturday was four o'clock!

'So, I'd been there about two-and-a-half years and there come a job on the canal for an apprentice blacksmith. I started about the beginning of 1939. It was the LMS railway then, that owned the canal. It was 16s a week! Quite a rise from 5s, wasn't it? After I'd been there six months they gave me another 6s because I was seventeen then! The inspector down there was a Mr Boyne, and the first morning he took me up in the shop to introduce me to the blacksmiths. Of course, he didn't come to work before nine so I'd to wait from half-past seven to nine. Then he took me in the shop and introduced me and told me that this was where I was going to spend me time; and he said, "Just remember tomorrow morning, lad, it's in the shop at half-past seven, not standing down by the clock!" So that's what I'd to do; though really, you'd to be in before that because you were supposed to have the fires going at half-past seven, ready to start work on the dot. So I went there as a "temporary improver blacksmith" and I worked there until I retired, near enough forty-nine years, and nobody ever told me any different! So I was a temporary improver blacksmith right through!

The blacksmith's shop

'We did all the ironwork for the boats, and the lock gates, and everything; and all the lift-up bridges, they had handrails going off them. There were handrails through the tunnels as well, to stop people falling in in the dark, and we'd to repair them, as well – they wore out in time with the ropes, you see, the towing ropes used to cut through them.

'I'd been at the yard probably about three days, and the head blacksmith sent me down to the paintshop; I don't remember what for, now. But as soon as I went through the paintshop door it was shut and locked. Well, I was only a lad and there was three big fellows in there as well as the painter, they just lifted up my shirt and painted SUC [Shropshire Union Canal] across my belly – in red lead paint. They said, "You'll never leave, now"! It wouldn't be possible now, it'd go to court, abuse, but then you daren't complain like. If you went down to the boss he'd just tell you to get back in the shop. But they were right, I never did leave, not till I retired!

'There was no such thing as a pleasure boat when I started. There were trade boats to Peates, who had the mill at Maesbury on the Montgomery Canal, as they call it now. They had a burst down Perry Moor, where they're building the new aqueduct at present; it burst there about 1936. Well, the LMS railway that owned the canal then did repair that because there were boats trapped up this canal [the Llangollen Canal] that were taking grain to Maesbury Mill. At that time Peates were gradually changing over to steam, they'd got quite a few steam waggons on the road. So I think the LMS must have had the idea that they wouldn't use the canal for long, and once Peates'd got their boats through they ran the water out again. You see, they filled it up to get all the boats past, and then let it all out again! It was never reopened again, until just now, in 1996.

'I know that because I lost my first job through that. I'd started work with Dad at fourteen but I had a paper round – I used to go up to the village shop early in the morning and do a paper round. I had to take a paper to the house by the hump-backed bridge, Lockgate

Bridge as they call it, and when I got down there, there was all this activity going on and no water in the canal – so I walked off down the towpath to see what had happened, and I didn't get back to the paper shop till two o'clock! So I was given my notice at the weekend.

'Then all this canal was legally closed about 1944, wasn't it, by Act of Parliament. It was a secure job when I came to Ellesmere because we worked for other sections, you see; so although the Montgomery was closed, we still made the lock gates and all that for the other sections, so they kept this canal open. But it closed in the war. I got called up, like, and I wasn't here, I went in February 1941, when I was nineteen, and I didn't come back until 1947. All they were really keeping it open for was to feed down to that reservoir at Hurleston.

'When I started at Ellesmere we could make pretty well everything in that yard. You see, when the canal was being built, Telford's idea was to plant trees on any banks and spare land, and by the time the lock gates wore out, the trees would be mature enough to renew the lock gates with them.

'The sawyers used to go out, you see, and they would fell the mature trees, ash, or whatever they wanted, and fetch them into the yard. We had a timber boat to fetch them: it was like an ordinary narrowboat, but it had quite a big hand-winch on it. They would cut the trunk into the lengths which they wanted for the heels of gates or whatever and fetch them into the yard. Well, there was a big gantry crane at the yard which went right out over the canal. It used to take five of you in the little box where the winch was for the grab, and you'd two fellows at each end on the chains; that was nine of you to work it. That's how we used to unload the trees, you see. Then the sawyer would number them and the yard foreman had a little book with all the details in. Then they were left to season for so many years. We made lock gates for the Trent & Mersey, Staffs & Worcs and so on, not just the Shropshire Union or even the Ellesmere and the Montgomery Canal. We made the gates for everywhere, all round the North West. We'd send them out, when they were made, on a boat, load them with that same gantry crane. If they were going to the Trent & Mersey, for instance, they'd send their own boatman for them. With a horse boat, of course.

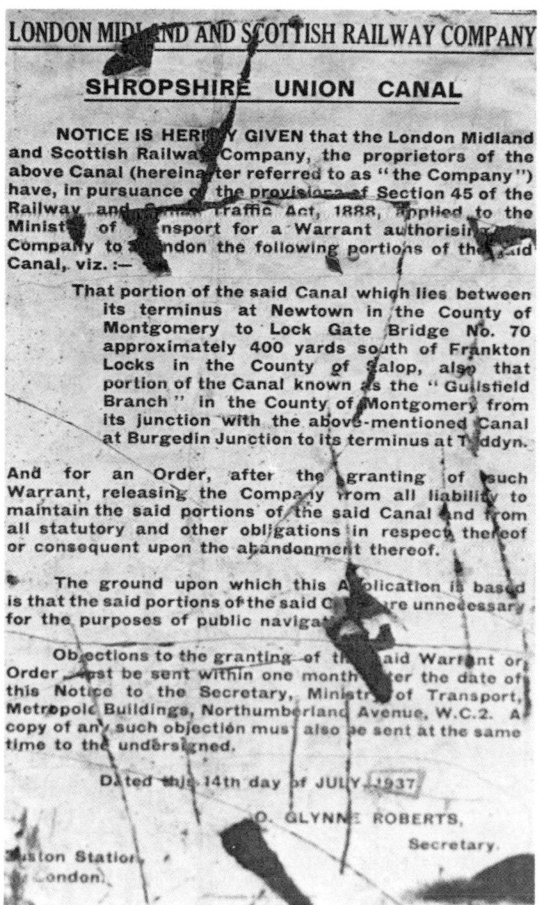

LONDON MID[illegible]ND AND SCOTTISH RAILWAY COMPANY

SHROPSHIRE UNION CANAL

NOTICE IS HER[illegible]Y GIVEN that the London Midland and Scottish Railwa[illegible] Company, the proprietors of the above Canal (hereinafter referred to as "the Company") have, in pursuance [illegible] the provisions of Section 45 of the Railway and [illegible] Traffic Act, 1888, applied to the Minist[illegible] of [illegible]nsport for a Warrant authorisi[illegible] Company to [illegible]ndon the following portions of the [illegible] Canal, viz. :—

That portion of the said Canal which lies between its terminus at Newtown in the County of Montgomery to Lock Gate Bridge No. 70 approximately 400 yards south of Frankton Locks in the County of Salop, also that portion of the Canal known as the "Guilsfield Branch" in the County of Montgomery from its junction with the above-mentioned Canal at Burgedin Junction to its terminus at T[illegible]ddyn.

And for an Order, after the granting of such Warrant, releasing the Company from all liability to maintain the said portions of the said Canal and from all statutory and other obligations in respect thereof or consequent upon the abandonment thereof.

The ground upon which this A[illegible]plication is based is that the said portions of the said C[illegible]re unnecessary for the purposes of public naviga[illegible]

Objections to the granting of t[illegible]aid Warr[illegible]nt or Order [illegible]st be sent within one month [illegible]er the date of this Notice to the Secretary, Ministr[illegible] of Transport, Metropole Buildings, Northumberland Avenue, W.C.2. A copy of any such objection mus[illegible] also [illegible]e sent at the same time to the undersigned.

D[illegible]ted [illegible] 14th day of JULY 1937.

O. GLYNN[illegible] ROBERTS,
Secretary.

[illegible]ston Station,
[illegible] London.

The LMS railway gives notice of its intention to apply for powers to close the canal below Frankton following the breach which amazed the young Jack Strange. The closure also threatened to put Bill Dean's father out of work unless the family moved to Norbury, as described in Bill Dean's chapter (Author's collection)

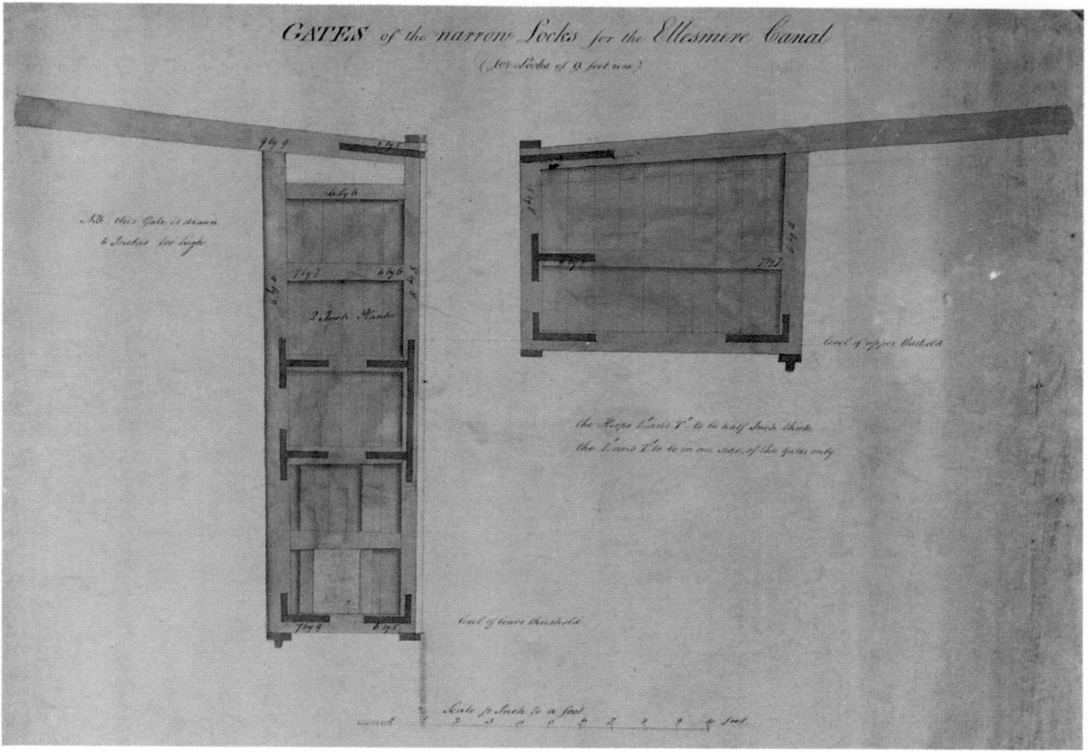

William Jessop's drawing of lock gates for the Ellesmere Canal – a design followed almost exactly for nearly two hundred years until the building of these items was transferred to Northwich in the 1960s (BW Archives, Gloucester)

'They'd all got carpenters on their own sections, but mostly it was Whitsun time that the gates were put in, and our lock-gate makers would go out there then. Often our blacksmiths would have to go too: we had a little portable forge. You used to have to renew the paddle-rod ends, where they were fitted onto the board that covered the hole to shut the water off, you know. You'd have made a selection of paddle-rod ends in our yard, and they'd be sent on the boat – but they were all different lengths. Whilst you were putting a pair of gates in you might stay there for a week or ten days. You could weld the rod ends when they were wanted to the right length, fire-weld them. We went out like that at every Whit and there were good sports on that weekend at Ellesmere but I never got to them because I was always out at a stoppage somewhere! You got a shilling a night for lodging. You might be out ten days, especially with those big gates down the Chester Canal where the locks are wide. The company would find you a lodging and you got a shilling a night, but you took your own food. Mostly the lady of the house where you were staying, she would cook it for you if you took bacon or eggs and things like that.'

A portable blacksmith's hearth for use at lock stoppages

Nowadays, of course, British Waterways carry staff to and from remote work sites day by day in minibuses. Much time which was worked in Jack's earlier days is now spent in travelling. Materials too come by road transport from centralised workshops at Northwich, as Jack was later to explain:

'In those days, you see, we had two sawyers; there was two

blacksmiths and two strikers in the shop; a fitter who worked the steam engine as well; a boilerman; also three boatbuilders, four painters, four in the lock-gate shop, two carpenters upstairs who made the patterns (they were the top notch), then of course six in the bricklaying gang (three bricklayers and three mates) and three in the dredging gang. They were all classed as tradesmen. Then of course you'd a man on every three-mile length of the canal. You'd got your water control man on at Llangollen. There was thirty-five to forty fellows on this section, that's from Llangollen to Nantwich.

'Our power was from an old railway engine because we were run by the LMS; they put it in, and set it up vertically so instead of it being on its wheels it was upright. There was a big boiler and the boilerman used to start an hour before everybody else, at half-past six in the morning to get steam up for when we got there. The fitter always started the engine up. Now, that drove one big belt which went to a set of bevel gears. The one of those cogs was made out of cast iron, and the other had wooden teeth, because if you had two cast-iron ones running together there would have been a hell of a noise. The teeth were made out of a wood which used to come from America, called hornbeam. It's very hard wearing, as hard as the cast iron. The actual wheel was made out of cast iron and the wooden teeth were fitted to it and wedged.

'The engine drove all the shaft which went through the length of the blacksmith's shop and the carpenters' shop – there were belts going off it in all directions. One went upstairs

The Ellesmere Canal lift-up bridge at Wrenbury, the ironwork for which, such as handrails, brackets and pivots, was produced by Jack Strange

Loading completed lock gates at Ellesmere Yard using the gantry crane described by Jack Strange

and drove the planing and thicknessing machine, a lathe and the bandsaw in the carpenters' shop. In our shop it drove two lathes, a planing machine, a screwing machine, the fan that provided the wind for the fires and the guillotine. Oh, what didn't it drive? There were the saws as well for the sawyers. But there was no electric light, we had gas, in the first instance. When the electricity come we thought we'd gone to Blackpool illuminations!

'Then of course they decided after so many years – it was well after the war – that the old engine had about had it, and so they put motors to every machine. That was all right in the end, but it took a bit of working out because somehow electricity doesn't work like steam. We had problems with getting it to keep going with a load on, or else it would be going too fast and smashing the castings. Eventually they got it worked out and it was all right then.

'Then, three years after, they took the lock-gate work away from Ellesmere to Northwich I got an electric welder to help with it! I had only had oxy-acetelene welding till then. That oxy-acetylene welding was slow, you see; the old blacksmith, he wasn't very keen on it at all. He'd do everything on the fire, and of course I was trying to persuade him that the electric welding would be just as good, but he wouldn't have it. The sale irons in a lock gate (which go down the heel of the gate) are the big ones, 4in by 5/8in, you'd got to weld those. We used to slot the one end into the bar, because where you wanted to join them you would get the iron hot in the fire. Then you'd make a chisel point on the end of the bar that was to go into the sale iron, and your mate would get that hot in the other fire; you couldn't get both pieces into the heat of the same fire. Once you'd both got a welding heat on you'd come out together, and bang the chisel end into the slot and give it a tap with the sledge hammer and under the steam hammer, and that would weld it all together flat. But you'd to be pretty quick. Now there's four legs in every sale iron, and the problem was that you might get three in and miss the last one. Well, that would finish that piece of iron because you couldn't get another weld in it, so you've got to start again from square one. Once you've had a welding heat and you've missed it, it won't weld again on the same spot. Well, nobody's perfect, you did miss it occasionally.

'I kept on to this old blacksmith about what he called "glorified soldering"! So I went to Crewe works, with the canal being LMS, on a welding course and started by welding the sale irons. The first one I did, I gave it to the head blacksmith, and he just flattened it and squared it up and then he decided that he would break it. Well, eventually he did break the weld, and said "I told you that it would break". But I said, "Well, we don't hammer our welds like that, those we've done on the fire. Once we've welded them you leave them go cold, and that's it, like. So why did you hammer that one?" So then he decided that it was all right; he just wanted to see how much it would stand.

'When you fire-welded those irons, as I said, you'd two fires going and two smiths with two strikers – all four of you working together to get the weld done before it cooled off. Well, one day I said to that smith, "Why did you suddenly take to letting me do all those welds?" "I suddenly thought," he said, "that there'd only be you losing any sweat!" But he was quite happy about it, and I used to weld everything after that. Oh, he was all right!

'The other thing we had to do was to shoe the boat horse. They were company horses that pulled the maintenance boats for carrying the lock gates and all the other materials. We had one boat at our yard, but you see, Chester section, for example, they hadn't got a blacksmith, Norbury Section hadn't either, or Welshpool. So they all used to work it so that their horse had to come to our yard to fetch something and it could get shod here. With the towpaths being metalled, as we called it, stoned over, we used to shoe them with the heels thickened up with a caulking and wedges across the toes to take the wear, and these used to last about ten weeks. Of course, as soon as you'd shod a horse with new shoes you made another set ready for when he'd come again. You always had a set for the Welshpool horse, the Ellesmere, the Chester and the Norbury.

'I shod the last company horse as come up here. She was a lovely horse, that Molly. She was only about ten or eleven year old, nice and quiet, she'd a lovely temper. Of course she was an LMS railway horse, and they used to send their vet every so often to examine her; about every three to six months he would come. Our old boatman at that time was Jack Roberts; he was turned sixty-five and there were motor boats about at that time, but he wouldn't have a motor boat – he wanted his old horse. Of course, with him turning sixty-five they wanted to get rid of him, didn't they, and have somebody that would drive a motor boat. Well, the vet came into the yard just as I finished shoeing this horse, Molly, and there was nothing wrong with her. He said, "Run her down the yard" – I could run in those days, too, so I trotted her down the yard and back up again. He got a doctor's stethoscope and he said, "Oh, she's likely to drop dead any time, she's got a weak heart." I said, "You can't

(Left) The toothed rack which engages with a pinion wheel to operate lock paddles is attached to a long iron rod extending down through the masonry of the lock structure to an elm board which closes the water culvert when required. All the ironwork was made by Jack Strange at Ellesmere before being fitted and adjusted by him on site during maintenance stoppages

Welding sale irons for lock gates

tell me that, I'm not daft!" He said, "She'll have to go" – but he couldn't even look at me. And I said "Why couldn't you have come an hour sooner?" He said, "Why?" and I said, "Because I've just put four new shoes on her." Well, she went the following day, back to Birmingham, and of course old Jack didn't have a motor boat, and he retired soon after. But there was nothing wrong with that horse. They grieve me, things like that.

'The boat builders in the yard only did repairs in my time. They built new punts for the lengthsmen and maintenance work and put cabins on, and they did a lot of repairs to boats off other sections as well. 'I mentioned before that they decided to transfer the lock-gate making to Northwich – they could weld much quicker than what I could in the fire. So of course I was to be made redundant then, after all that while. There was no room at Northwich to go to, see. But they didn't actually stop me immediately because we did a big repair job then. Ponty [Pontcysyllte] Aqueduct had got into a terrible state – a lot of the railings had gone, the towing path was non-existent – and I had the job of repairing all that and putting all the railings back, renewing all the ironwork of the towpath and everything. That was in 1964, and it took nearly nine months to do that.

'I had quite an argument with the personnel officer because I wanted more money to go up there. We hadn't got any scaffolding. Of course, these days you wouldn't think of doing it like that, with all the safety rules. I said, "What happens if I fall off?" "Oh no, you can't have any more money!" Anyway, I refused to go. After about a fortnight this personnel officer came and I took him up there and started to walk over. Well, I'd got about twenty yards across the aqueduct and he hadn't started to walk out onto it. So I shouted to him and said, "Aren't you going to come any further?" He said, "No, will you accept 6d an hour?" Well, 6d an hour was quite a bit then. So I went then, and I was in charge of that job. But as soon as we finished, which was on a Friday night, my 6d an hour stopped, on the Friday night. I didn't get it for that Saturday morning! It just stopped dead.

'Well, then I was for off, and where I was going I didn't know. But then the foreman's job came up at Ellesmere Yard and they gave me that job. Of course they killed two birds with one stone like that, because I was doing the blacksmithing and the foreman's job.

'I don't know why, but they'd let the aqueduct go very badly; they'd suddenly decided they weren't going to do any more repairs to it. Before that we'd had fellows up there in the winter doing nothing but ice-breaking because they didn't want the ice to get solid and bust it. But they suddenly stopped that. It was frightening for one or two winters because we thought it would burst.

'The aqueduct wasn't leaking when we started to do all those repairs. The horses had gone off the canal so they didn't need the towing path, and the tourists used to go down the bottom and cross the river by the road bridge. A lot of the workers from Monsanto's chemical works lived in The Vron, and they had been able to get a permit to go over the aqueduct because it was the shortest route to work. They paid the company, I think it was about 2s a year. Of course, once the holes started to come in the towing path over the aqueduct they couldn't walk or go on their bikes. I think that was one thing that started them thinking about repairing it.

'The castings were made at a foundry, in Widnes, I think. They were very good castings too; I believe the name of them was Platts. When we come to do the Ponty Aqueduct I found all the patterns in the pattern shop for all the standards and everything, the cross-members of the towing path, everything. The one cross-member was stamped something like 1894, which made me think that it had probably been renewed once before. The canal would be nearly a hundred years old then.

'Every 2ft there was a cross-member, like a T-iron from the outside of the trough to standards fixed upright from the trough bottom. Those had an angle bar running along their tops right through from one end of the aqueduct to the other, forming the front edge of the towing path. Then there had been an iron sheet shaped to fit over the top of those angle bars, but we used some old trench sheeting and cut it to size. We filled over the top of that with rubble and tarmaced the towing path surface. When we came to it, we found that each bay, between the flanges of the plates that formed the bottom of the trough, was filled up with ash; I think the reason was to stop mud collecting by giving it a level bottom – it kept the mud moving out with the movement of the boats. Well, we never refilled it with ash

A horse-drawn maintenance boat at work near Hurleston on the Ellesmere Canal on 4 September 1957
(Edward Paget-Tomlinson)

and I think that was a mistake. The most amazing part was that all those big bolts that are through the flanges, the vast majority, if you gave them a tap with the hammer, the nut would spin right off. The original ones couldn't have been made of ordinary iron. It didn't corrode, that's a certainty. We hardly made any new ones, perhaps two or three hundred of all the thousands that are in there. Ours were iron where we couldn't re-use the original ones. We didn't have to do any repairs to the trough: the only thing we did to the trough was to caulk some of the joints with a lead wool. Frank Rowland (he was our painter and plumber) did that with a caulking iron, like you would a boat.

'There was a lot of blisters on the cast plates and we knocked those off, like air bubbles they are. Then we had an epoxy resin which we could mix together and fill the holes in. The only thing was, once you'd put it in the hole you'd to stop with it, or it would just sort of slip out and hang there – so you kept pushing it back. Well, eventually you'd say, "Oh, leave it and we'll push it back in a minute." And then it would go off rock hard and you couldn't do anything with it! You'd got to knock that piece off then and do it again!

'There's two crosses cast in plates on that aqueduct, and nobody knows why. There's no engineering value to them. Whether there was two fellows killed building it, and somebody in the foundry made two plates with crosses, nobody knows. Otherwise all the plates are the same, and they are wedge-shaped so they wedge themselves in as well as being held with the bolts. Our carpenter, he put a wooden fender all along the edge of the towpath, made from greenheart.

Work on the dewatered trough and towpath (left) of Pontcysyllte Aqueduct in 1963–4

'It's funny, but I don't think anybody was really interested in what we were doing. We worked up there till half-past five, and by the time we got back to the yard the others had all gone. If I wanted anything I'd got to leave a note to Jim Howard, the inspector, and say how many bearers I wanted cast, and so on. We didn't really know how many we wanted until we'd uncovered them, like, and did each section. Then we'd know we wanted another dozen cross-members or whatever. We did a 30ft length at a time so that we never had more than a 10ft gap in the railings at a time. Also, you see, we had to fill the trough every other weekend to feed the water board reservoir at Hurleston. So we couldn't work that weekend. We only had it empty about five or six weeks altogether. During that time we renewed all the standards under the edge of the towing path and put the two angle-iron bars, under the front and back of the path, right the way through. We finished that by Easter. We used to close it at eight o'clock when we got there, and it would be closed till twelve o'clock, and although it had water in it we wouldn't let anybody through. You see, we'd got our own work boat on there, we couldn't keep pulling it off. But dinner time was twelve till one, so we'd pull the boat off and let the pleasure boats go across whilst we had dinner. Then they'd have to stop again for the afternoon, and then we'd open it again when we finished for the night.

'It was a marvellous piece of work, that aqueduct. They must have brought those plates by horse and cart from the foundry which was where Monsanto is now – but how did they get them across the top of those pillars? They're only 7 or 8ft by 10ft at the top, and over 100ft high – hardly room to stand. I can understand them getting them up on the top flat, but how do you hold the next one there whilst you get the bolts through the flanges? You're talking about 200 years ago, and there'd be no road crane to help you! It's an amazing piece of work. We were there hardly nine months: we started in the January and finished at the end of August or beginning of September, and we were there every day.'

The present re-asserted itself for a few minutes as Alf Strange showed a small party of visitors around the workshop, and talk turned to small items of ornamental ironwork. But soon our thoughts returned to one of the largest iron structures in Britain.

'As I've said, the aqueduct job gave me another nine months' work, and at the end of that time, just as we were finishing off, this foreman's job came up. Fred Thomas had been doing this job, and the engineer at the time was Mr Cotton, Bob Cotton. The first time I met him was after I'd been hanging out for that bit of extra money at the start of the aqueduct job; we got on very well, and after he'd finished work we'd have a couple of cans of beer if ever he was up here.

'Fred had been doing this foreman's job and everybody thought he would have it. Well, I thought there was no harm in asking, and I'd nothing to go to at the time. As I've said, Mr Cotton was a friend to me – and he gave me the job. Fred would be sixty odd by then. So I had twenty-two or twenty-three years to go, then. I didn't dislike the foreman's job, I knew what I'd got to do, like, but I've always liked working with my hands, you know. But you've got to rely on fellows. It's no good me trying to tell a carpenter what to do. If you're a tradesman you should respect other tradesmen and rely on them. Fred was a good canalman in general, you couldn't beat him on leaks or anything like that, but if he was in charge of a job, the carpenters and so on wouldn't take any notice of him: they'd no respect, because he wasn't a tradesman. If you were a tradesman you could say to them, so-and-so has to be done; and they would say, "How do you want it done?" and I'd say, "Well, you're the carpenter. If you want any blacksmithing doing, I'll do it for you." With Fred they would have played up more.

'On the other hand, if it was night-time or a weekend when you weren't working and you got a leak anywhere, Fred was the first one you called because there was nobody better than him to stop a leak. Brilliant. It was the same with puddling clay. It was only the year after I got the foreman's job that we had a major breach at Bettisfield, and it was up to me to be in charge of it. You have to rely on your canalmen to puddle the clay properly in a situation like that, so you have to have respect for them. They are the fellows that have been puddling clay all their lives. I don't really know why that one went; we didn't know there was any leak there, it just went out in the night. In those few years we had three or four major breaches in our canal, and every one went on either a Friday night or a Saturday night! It was

Puddling clay for leak stopping

The aftermath of the breach of the newly repaired concrete canal channel near Trevor, giving an impression of the scouring power of the escaping water which created this gash in the hillside. Contractors' plant is starting to break up the fallen sections of concrete trough, and surveyors are at work in the bed of the canal and on the towpath at the top left (Waterways World)

always when we'd all gone home and you'd to go round knocking people up and that, to turn them out.

'There was one at Bryn Howell, up on the feeder length towards Llangollen. That went about 1946 whilst I was still abroad, and it washed away the railway which was below the canal. All that along there is an embankment like a terrace along the hillside. The canal is in a clay channel, puddled, and it stands on sand. The sand is all compacted, it's very good for that; you can compact sand very hard. Well, that one went in 1946. There was another one up there in the 1950s, I suppose, and they fixed that the old-fashioned way with compacted sand. You make a wide base and then step it in a bit to make it narrower, and come up again with more sand, so you are making a base that is a lot wider than the water channel. You keep building it up and making steps in it like that, and then put your clay trough on the top. The sand will stay just moist, and well compacted, and it won't run like that. And it's not long before grass starts to grow on it like that.

'It went again, this breach did, in the early seventies. Well, not in just the same place, but about a quarter mile nearer Trevor. It was in the early morning, and so of course we shot up there and started to clear it all out and put the stop planks in and everything. Well, the engineer was Mr Haskins at the time, and he came up from Northwich, and he said "Do no more – it's going to be put out to contract." I said we'd made a start, but he replied: "I've got my orders – I'm not to get you to do it." Well, these contractors come in, and I used to go up there with Jim Howard and see what they were doing. They were building it up on sand, but I felt they were not doing it right! The base wasn't broad enough. But what can you say if you're not doing the job? They went and put a fellow in charge who was straight out of an office. I used to say to him (and he'd a better job than I'd got), "How on earth can you come out of an office and take charge of a job like this?" He said, "It's just professional jealousy with you!"

'Well, anyhow, they built it. Give Mr Haskins his due, he said, "What do you think of it?" I said, "I wouldn't like to say it'll last, and I wouldn't like to say when it's going to go, but I don't think it'll last long." He said, "What's wrong with it?" and I replied, "Well, they've built it too straight, there's no width to the base, they've come straight up vertically to the concrete channel walls, it isn't going to hold like that." Well, of course, this contractor's bloke out of the office, he said we didn't know what we were talking about. Well, all right, we don't; I was only a blacksmith.

'They had a big notice painted, a terrific thing: "This breach was repaired by such a firm at a total cost of three-quarters of a million pounds, and it was done in such a time" and all this, that and the other. Well, *we* never had a notice like that when *we* repaired anything!

'Anyway, the water engineers from Northwich put some *piezometers*, do you call them, in the bank at this breach, because when they put the water in first it leaked! Straightaway! These things will show them if there's water leaking, and well, they were registering leakage all the while, right from when it was first filled. So I was up there one morning, I forget just what for, and the lads from Northwich were there taking the measurements; and the one shouted to the others to come up on top of the bank and take a look. I went up on the bank too, and the water in the canal was going down like weirs. I said "What's causing that? There's no boats about!" And all of a sudden, whoosh! It was away, right where they had been standing! Concrete and all, down the hillside.

'The first job I had to do was get those notices down! After that they built it all up again, and decided to concrete it near enough all through to Llangollen. I was at Northwich a bit later for a meeting over it, with Jim Howard, and this office fellow from the contractors was there, and he said, "I don't want you to say anything, either!" And I said, "I shan't say anything, unless I'm asked."

'There's a lot to be said for listening to the old canal people like Fred Thomas who had puddled clay and fixed leaks all his life. When you went out to a leak with chaps like that, they'd find the leak while you were getting out of the van! It was almost like a dog with scent, they seemed to know where to go. You'd find water coming out, and naturally you'd think "It's leaking just over the bank, here". But they'd walk off up the canal and call to you "It's away up here!" They could find it yards away from where you expected it to be. But all that's gone, now.'

THOMAS TYSON

Carpenter and Lock Gate Builder

The Mull of Kintyre is a substantial peninsula which projects inconveniently over fifty miles across the shipping route from the Clyde estuary to the west coast of Scotland and its numerous islands. In the days of sail the passage round the Mull was often difficult and dangerous, since comparatively light winds set up a short sharp sea when blowing over the tide race at its south-western tip. As a result a canal across the peninsula seemed to have great potential.

Following the rebellion of 1745, the Forfeited Estates Commissioners were empowered to administer funds which might be used to provide employment and encourage stability in the north. In 1771 the commissioners appointed James Watt to survey a canal route across the Kintyre peninsula. Commercial interests, headed by the Duke of Argyll, prompted a further survey, undertaken by John Rennie, in 1792. The canal was to be financed as a public company and obtained its act in 1793.

There were immediate difficulties when it was found impossible to obtain labour at reasonable rates against the background of the canal mania in England. However, the canal was opened in 1801 with the aid of a £25,000 government loan. Its fifteen locks were able to pass craft up to 88ft by 20ft. Although it had opened with the water retained at a lower level than that originally intended, there was a breach and a reservoir dam collapsed, and by 1811 the company was seeking another government loan to resolve these and other problems. This concerned the Treasury, and Thomas Telford, engineer of the government-promoted Caledonian Canal, was instructed to make an inspection. He supervised improvements and the canal was reopened in good order in 1817, but under the control of the Caledonian Canal Commission. The opening of the Caledonian in 1822 completed a comparatively sheltered route from Glasgow, via the

The Iona *(left) joining David MacBrayne's* Columba *at Ardrishaig pier shortly before one o'clock on a summer afternoon.* Columba *was a large, and luxurious, answer to railway competition for passenger business between Glasgow and the West Highlands. The smaller steamer was returning from a circular route to the Kyles of Bute. In the extreme right background the pier head lighthouse can be seen. Tommy recalls the necessity to re-adjust the windows and lenses at the top of the tower after winter waves in the sea loch had broken over the 'lantern'* (Guthrie Hutton collection)

Crinan to Inverness, which stimulated trade on the older canal. However, at the same time steamers were becoming larger and more powerful, which allowed easier passages round the Kintyre peninsula, by-passing the Crinan Canal.

Passenger services were developed which utilised large paddle steamers between Glasgow and Ardrishaig. There the passengers walked up from the pier to a smaller steamer waiting on the canal, and this carried them through to Crinan and another change for the onward voyage. This service continued for ninety years, only ceasing in 1929. Cargoes meanwhile were carried successfully in small coasters and in the 'Clyde puffers' which became an essential part of life on Scotland's Western Isles as well as achieving wide fame through Neil Munro's *Para Handy Tales*.

The Crinan Canal passed into the control of the Ministry of Transport in 1919, and so to the British Transport Commission in 1948 and British Waterways in 1962. Nowadays few fishing or other commercial craft pass through the canal, which is busy with yachts heading for the islands in the summer season.

Tommy Tyson has lived all his life within a short distance of the Ardrishaig end of the Crinan Canal; in retirement he supervises the passage of yachts and the occasional fishing boat from his living-room window. Ardrishaig is a small community, its numbers

(Opposite) Regular users of the Crinan Canal are fishing boats avoiding adverse weather around the Mull of Kintyre, such as this one descending Dunardry Locks in June 1996. It was en route to drydocking at Leith via the Crinan and Caledonian canals (Euan Corrie)

10
SILVER CREST II

made greater in summer by the visitors to the grand scenery of Scotland's west coast. It looks to Lochgilphead as a regional centre, but is separated from the bright lights of the built-up area around the Clyde by the long inlets of Loch Fyne and the Kyle of Bute. Evening entertainment for many of Tommy's generation was more 'home-made' than it is now, and 'going out' was limited to trips to the local pubs and visiting friends. Even 'modern youth' finds it difficult to reach Glasgow in less than a full day's outing.

Tommy likes to fish locally, and he and some of his contemporaries occasionally go shooting on the nearby moors. As we talked I was distracted by canal traffic in the foreground, and sunlight on the wind-blown surface of Loch Fyne beyond the town's roofs.

'I was born here in Ardrishaig and went to school here. I was in the woodwork class one day when the canal foreman walked in. He walked round and looked at everybody's work, taking notes. Well, about three or four weeks after that I was asked if I'd come down for an interview, and I started work in August 1942. I was just turned sixteen then.

'When I started there was fifty-six staff on the canal, that's all along the length of it. There was twelve tradesmen, five apprentices; eighteen were operational, like the lock keepers and so on, the rest were on maintenance. The craftsmen were all at this end, at Ardrishaig, but there was a maintenance crowd at Crinan. They used to start from there cutting the grass and everything, and if nothing cropped up, they'd work their way right through to Ardrishaig. When they'd scythed all through they used to do all the hedges and everything at Canal House, you know, the manager's house down here – it's a hotel now. When they'd done there they used to go back to Crinan, and when the grass got too long they'd start over and do the same thing again. They had pushbikes and they got three bob a day for using them! When we went out we went in the lorry to wherever the work was.

'I worked with one of the carpenters. There were painters, blacksmiths, engineers and glaziers and everything else. Some days you were told "Go and give the glazier a hand", so you learned how you cut glass and how you put in glass. Then you might go to the blacksmith and you'd see him welding and mending sluices and all that. You got a bit of everything. At the start you were always in the workshop. Once you started to know something about it, you were allowed out, but always with a tradesman.

Hand boring lock-gate rails in the low-roofed workshop at Ardrishaig

'When you went in in the morning you went in through the joiner's shop – it was a small shop there, then you went through into the lock-gate shop. There were two tradesmen there and another apprentice other than myself, and we worked away in there, the four of us. I was lucky when I started because they were making a set of lock gates – that's, like, a pair for the top or bottom of a lock – each year, and they were renewing the lock gates all the way up the canal. On the likes of the sea locks the outside gates were usually greenheart. That's very heavy, and very hard to work; it's also poisonous – the dust is very bad for you. The

Pulling a gate out of the workshop and into the basin at Ardrishaig (page 114)

reason we used that was that the old carpenters that were on years ago they found that the salt water carried up into the timber. I think it was pitch pine they had years ago. It seemed to get into the pitch pine but the greenheart seemed to throw it, it was that hard. But those gates were very heavy, they were.

'The greenheart often came in a boat to the pier and was transported up into the yard. It wasn't squared when it came, just more or less off a tree, and you had to start with an adze and make a face and an edge. We had no power saw or anything like that; there was really no power in the yard. It was later on that they converted one of the buildings with a big power saw in it. They had a Petter engine, but that was for the electricity; I think they tried to drive a wee saw off it, but once you put the wood to it the belt would jump off. It wouldn't do for that greenheart because it was so hard. We cut the big lengths of that with a double-handed saw, but it wanted a lot of sharpening. Imagine you're putting the closing planks in a 27ft deep gate, you're talking about cladding at the sea locks which is 3in thick. You see, the top of the gate is broader than the bottom, so your closing plank is on a taper. You'd to cut that with a handsaw, 27ft along.

'All the boring was hand augers. They built a new place for making the lock gates, down there, and they put an overhead crane in it, but it had no ratchet on it. Their idea was that when you built your lock gate you could turn it over so you'd be able to do all your boring and suchlike on one side, and then turn it over to do the other side. But it didn't work. You could get it plumb, but not over, because there was no ratchet on the crane. It was only a hand-pull that, with an endless chain. Those sea-lock gates were eight to nine ton. So you had to do over thirty big holes in the heel and mitre post and the joints, all over a foot deep, into greenheart with a hand auger. The result was, because you couldn't turn the gate over, you'd then to knock it asunder and turn all the separate

By the time Tommy Tyson worked on the Crinan Canal the Conway *was only retained for ice breaking but he recalls the polished wooden seating in her cabins which had been provided for occasions, such as this, when she was used as a relief to the canal steamer* Linnet. *A relief was required because the* Columba *could bring far more passengers from Glasgow to Ardrishaig Pier than the* Linnet, *which fitted through the canal's locks, could take forward to Crinan. This photograph was taken a few minutes after leaving the top lock at Ardrishaig as* Conway *approached Oakfield Bridge near Lochgilphead* (Guthrie Hutton collection)

rails and then bore from the other side to meet your holes. Quite a bit of work, and you could only *hope* that you met your holes coming from the other side!

'When they were finished we'd push them out on rollers with big spikes to lever with. Then we rigged a ring right away across the canal and we could rig one of those endless chain pulls to that and pull the gate towards the ring. But the trouble with those greenheart ones was that when you got them in the water they were apt to sink! So you'd to bolt steel tanks onto them to make sure they floated. Then those gates were transported up the canal to wherever they were going; there was an ice breaker, the *Conway*, it towed the gates wherever you wanted them. Then there was the dredger which was wooden, with a steam boiler and crane: the old canal authority had built that themselves, and they used to hook the gate onto that and it would lift it up. That could carry it into the lock and they'd pull it into the hollow quoin where it fitted and slide it down the quoin until the pivot went into the pot in the bottom of the lock; then it could be fixed. They'd sometimes have a diver, just to make sure that it went in.

'The old foreman that we had, I'll never forget him. We put the gates in at No 2 lock, just outside the canal basin at Ardrishaig. I was only a third-year apprentice, I think, at the time. Everything was all right, we mitred the gates and set them up and then got a wee bit of water pressure on them. There was a wee boil showing below them. The old tradesman that was with me said, "If the water is coming up through between the cill and the gate you'd see it near the gate"; he said, "If it's coming up out between the mitres, the pressure will push it out and the boil will be away from the gate." Anyway, there was very, very little and he said "Oh well, that's good, we'll start putting all the gear away." But then the old foreman came along and just tapped me on the shoulder: "We'll lift it out," he says – 27ft long, and we'd to take 1/4in off the mitre post, with an adze, with the gate hanging on the crane! You adzed it and they lifted it with the crane and you adzed the next length. But that was his way – for 1/4in. Perfect! It was no use to him otherwise! And all the work I've ever seen him do I've never seen him put a pencil to a piece of wood: he'd a long thumb-nail and he'd just mark it with that. When he was finished he'd get a wet cloth and just rub it over the mark, and when he'd done there'd be no mark there at all.

'Then when the mitre was perfect we dropped the gate in again and put the balance beam to it and you'd a swing bar to go on the top of that. That was another thing he was very keen on, he wanted the gates perfectly balanced. They had what we used to call "the lock keeper's assistant". It was an iron bar fitted under the balance beam to keep it from moving. The keepers used to just take this off when a boat was coming: they'd keep the collars that well greased and the gates were that finely balanced that when a boat was coming up

The floating crane lifts a lock gate a little at a time as the carpenters adze the whole length of the mitre to obtain a perfect leak-free fit

pushing a little water in front of it, the gates would open. They don't bother to balance them now, they just hang them anyhow.

'We measured the gates each time before starting to make new ones. The mitre post and heel post were standard sizes on every gate except one where a mistake had been made and it was 1in narrow. Some you measured between the bars. That old foreman he wouldn't let you use a tape because he said sometimes that tape twisted. So you had two pieces of stick, and you put them inside the frame of the gate and you pushed them out till they touched the bars, and then you marked the sticks. You knew that your mitre post was 13in and your heel post was 14in so that gave you 27in which you added on. That give you the top size, and then you prayed that the divers gave you the right size for the bottom! Very occasionally, where it was a small basin between the locks, he would let you run the water out of the basin so that the tradesmen could get in. Otherwise, I mean, this reach is 4½ mile long so you couldn't drain that off. Each of the cross-bars was 12in square and there was about 18in between each of them.

'So the heel post was 14in and the round was on the back of that to fit the lock quoin. It was a 7in circle. You knew the bevel for the mitre was between 7$^{3}/_{8}$in and 7$^{1}/_{2}$in – if it was over 7$^{1}/_{2}$in there was something wrong. Just before I retired a set of gates came with the mitre posts and everything ready made and I measured the mitre – it was 13in. I said to the foreman, "There's something far wrong here!" He said, "Well, that's the measurements." When we put it in there was a mouth between them gates 8 or 9in wide.

'During the war, I don't know whether timber was getting tight or if it was the money that was tight, but one of the managers, Mr Walker, he decided he would try and take what he called the good bars out of some of the old gates and transfer them. Well, it was a waste of time and money – they'd done their life, and inside a couple of years they were falling apart.

'The top gate in No 2 was pitch pine. I installed the first metal gate in there. A metal frame came and we had to do all the woodwork on it, mitre post and all, and put that to it. The gate we took out of there was over forty year old and that was pitch pine. We did pitch pine gates for a year or two after I started, that's all. Then it was getting scarce and money was tight so we went on to a wood called jarrah: it's Australian mahogany, it's very hard. But I think we'd only done two gates with that and then we went into Oregon pine. But Oregon never lasted. With the pitch pine and that you'd be at least thirty year before you'd come back to the same set of gates again. I wouldn't see Oregon doing thirty year at all. It took about three months to make a set of lock gates.

'It's like a jig-saw puzzle now. The gates come with the body all made and you've to bolt on the mitre post and the heel post. We'd a terrible job with them at the start of that. Every lock gate has a taper in it, but the taper is in the heel post – the mitre post is square off your gate, but the heel post is tapered to fit the lock quoin. This is because when the pivot wore, the gate slid down a bit, but it would still fit. But, could we get them to understand that it had to be the heel post the taper was in, and not the mitre! With their gates, the bottom of the mitre touched first and when the water pressure came on, the gate started to lift up. I think they've got the message now and they've realised what they were doing wrong. But with all these things I don't think anybody knows the size of the gates now. They'll all have to be fully measured individually every time.

'The cills were all bedded into puddled clay, and when we used to replace them we used to have to dig it all out. They were 9in by 6in beams going right across the cavity and into

The puffers designed to fit the Crinan Canal's locks seem enormous in the confines of the waterway. Here is Glenrosa passing through the main road bridge into Ardrishaig sea lock (Guthrie Hutton collection)

each wall 6ft, and all that was puddled with clay to seal it and make it water-tight. That went round the beam and there was 3in cladding on top of the beam. Then the cill that the gates close to was bolted to that. At the bottom gates, which are deeper, the mitre cill goes about 3ft into the wall, but at the top gates it's only about a foot it goes in. We had to dig all that out, and by the time we'd finished a man could walk underneath all that. We used to pour concrete in where the clay had been. Then we'd put a complete new platform on the top and fit a new cill beam to that. The original bolts were "debtor metal", that's what the old chaps used to call it, you know, like brass. Anyway, we couldn't renew them because you couldn't get that any more, they don't make them; so we used to put in big iron bolts, right through.

'The canal used to close, when we were doing that, for the whole month of May, and I mind everybody was saying "Oh, you'll lose the trade, you'll lose boats, if you close all the month of May". But at the end of the month all the boats were coming through. They were waiting there to get through, they were still coming. May was supposed to be the driest month. Otherwise you had to contend with a lot of water, no' really from the canal, but it came in from the likes of the burns which run into it. If there was only a small amount of water it would go down the pipe under the cill and you would work in the dry. But if you're getting water building up, with the rain and that, the pipes wouldn't take it so we used to build a dam right across, with clay and timbers. We'd direct the water through one of the sluices in the gate. You couldn't build a dam very high because it wouldn't take the water pressure. Now they have a great big canvas and they put that in and the pressure of the water holds that against a frame.

'Then they'd have you repairing boats, putting planks in or caulking and all that. There's what we call the *Linnet* shed at Dunardry. The *Linnet* used to run trips through the canal, and there was a shed for it just by the first lock down from the summit there – you can see it from the road, though the walls are all crumbled now. We could make that a dry-dock – we could raise the basin there between the locks, and when the water was up we could take the boat in and then drop the basin back to normal level; the boat would settle onto blocks then. There'd be water round the blocks, but we'd put platforms round the boat to stand on when we were working. We could use the old sea lock at Ardrishaig as a drydock, too; it's right by the new lock that's used now. We could put iron beams across that. There was a navy base on Loch Fyne then, in the war, and they used to have smashed propellers and this and that wrong with their boats. So they used to sail them in there, close the gate and open a sluice and let the water out. You'd be right dry on that. But it's not been used for a long, long while now, that. They used it for fixing the asdic gear and that; it was an asdic training base up the loch here then. Once the diver had fixed the blocks in place we ran the water down for them, then the navy took over. They did the work on the boats.

Fitting new wooden decking to the swing bridge at Ardrishaig

'I was in the marines in the war – well, just at the start of 1945. I'd about two years of my time still to do when I went in. But the years in the army counted towards your tradesman's time. I never knew that until I came out and

Fishing boats crowd Ardrishaig Harbour

there was a big Union meeting and the delegate came up to me and says, "You're all right," he says, "your two years in the army will count – you'll go on to tradesmen's rates." I'd been in Hong Kong and China for a while. We were very lucky we got there when things had just started to calm down. I was married just after I came out of the army in 1948. I've a son and a daughter, both in Australia, one in Adelaide and one in Sydney.'

The coming of computer technology and the recent strides in telecommunications have helped to slow the depopulation of the Highlands, but so far this has been largely because of the arrival of those seeking refuge from the pressures of modern life further south. The region has never been able to recover its economy from the devastating effects of the Highland Clearances. The local youth must move to the cities if they are to obtain higher education, and many fail to return to their homes where employment is often seasonal and less well rewarded. In fact many follow in the footsteps of their clansmen of two hundred years ago by emigrating to America and Australia.

On Tommy's return from the forces little change was visible on the canal. The nationalisation of other island waterways under the Docks & Inland Waterways Executive of the British Transport Commission made no difference to a waterway which had been taken over by the government which had to subsidise its completion. However, after the break-up of the Transport Commission and the formation of the autonomous British Waterways Board in

Calm before the storm. The Crinan Canal office, left, presides over waiting chauffeurs and charabancs as the steamers (seen on page 110) discharge their passengers to change to the smaller Linnet, *or to road transport for the short journey to a further steamer at Crinan. This would cause twenty minutes frantic activity at Ardrishaig Pier and the demand for school boys such as Tommy Tyson to man the turnstiles. By the time Tommy was spending lunch hours thus employed, motor buses had replaced the vehicles in this picture and the canal steamer* Linnet *which would have been waiting above the locks behind the camera* (Guthrie Hutton collection)

1963, changes did begin to appear – for instance, work such as the making of lock gates began to be centralised at larger workshops at Stanley Ferry, Northwich and Bulbourne in England.

Tommy continues:

'When I'd done my time I became a tradesman and had an apprentice in my own right, more or less straightaway. We'd to look after all the bridges as well as the gates; even the main-road bridge here, at Ardrishaig, was a wood platform at one time. It was built by Sir William Arrol.

'There were two lock keepers on there, and I mind the old lock keeper, he lived just by the bridge, telling me one time he opened the curtains one morning and saw sixteen masts waiting to come in the canal – all boats in the harbour waiting to come in. And that was two men turning that big bridge by hand. In those days they were mostly puffers, a lot of folk call them lighters: the *Glencloy, River Cloy, Anzac, Raylight, Starlight.* The whisky boat, the *Pibroch,* had a white horse on top of the mast; he did nothing but the distillery, he took empty barrels in and took full ones away. Other boats brought the coal – it was only just up there above Ardrishaig, it was only knocked down a couple of year ago. A lot of that was transported down by horse lorry to the pier. The pier and that all belongs to the British Waterways, too.

'Loch Fyne was famous for the fishing too, you know: Loch Fyne herring. I've seen the harbour down there at six o'clock in the morning when you could walk across it on the boats, all waiting to discharge their herring. British Waterways had all dues for that. They had a harbour master and two fellows looking after the pier and that.

'The puffers used to come into the pier or up into the canal basin with coal. There was a weighing machine there, and you had to be sworn in by a Justice of the Peace before you could work that. One of the harbour master's assistants would generally work that and weigh the carts that came for the coal. There was another machine by Oakfield Bridge just before you come to Lochgilphead, there. The puffers with the coal for Lochgilphead used to go through and tie up at the wharf just there. The coal was all weighed there and taken away.

'The foreman used to come up to the school and pick five boys. He'd say, "Come down to the pier at dinner time and work the turnstiles". There were five turnstiles and the passenger boats used to come in. I mind, even now I can always remember, a game dog was 2d, an ordinary person was a penny. Folk used to come down in charabancs and walk to the end of the pier, and so one of your jobs was that you used to have to go and ask them for the pier dues. I asked a minister once, and got a penny off him, but I nearly got the boot for taking a penny off a minister! It was a penny to get on the pier and a penny to get off, whatever you did, whether you went on a ship or no. The *Linnet* had finished running through the canal by my time, but the *St Columba* still came. [The *Columba* had left the Ardrishaig run in 1936 as MacBraynes acquired the 1912-built turbine steamer *St Columba* which maintained the service into the 1950s.] It wouldn't look near the canal, it was a big steam ship, but it came to the pier, and two luggage boats came as well. The *Ardyne* was one, but I don't remember the other. They used to come in with luggage and it was all dumped on the pier; and then the shopkeepers would all come with their horses and carts and take it up the village wherever the passengers were going.

CRINAN CANAL

NOTICE.

CHILDREN and Others are hereby Prohibited from Running along the Canal Banks after the Passenger Steamer; and Passengers are requested not to encourage them by throwing Money on to the bank.

Children are further warned not to throw Flowers into the Boat.

SALE OF MILK.

THE SALE OF MILK on the Property of the Canal Commissioners is only permitted on the understanding that no annoyance is caused to Passengers.

Any person who, by urging to purchase, or otherwise, inconveniences or annoys any Passenger will be prohibited from selling, and, if necessary, dealt with according to law.

Passengers are requested to report any such case to the Purser, and also to point out the delinquent to the nearest Lock-keeper or Canal Official.

L. JOHN GROVES.
SUPERINTENDENT.

Crinan Canal Office,
Ardrishaig, 30th June, 1887.

Long before Tommy Tyson's time on the Crinan Canal the local children had found ways to profit from the tourist trade (BW Archives, Gloucester)

The traditional operating gear for Crinan Canal lock paddles which has now been largely replaced by modern hydraulic pump units

'We had to look after the lochs that supplied the canal with water as well; sometimes the sluices that controlled the supply would need attending to, and we'd to go all up there. It was no joke carrying the diving gear and everything, because there was no road up there at all. They used to get a horse with a "slape" – that's like a sledge with metal runners under it – and they used to put the heaviest of the diving gear on that and get the horse to take it. But the likes of the suit and the mask and all that, you'd be frightened that it

A view taken from the lighthouse of the canal dredger working in Ardrishaig Harbour, possibly during construction of a new, larger sea lock in the 1930s (Guthrie Hutton collection)

might get torn with dragging through the heather; so they used to carry that up. There were wooden sluices in the dams and channels up there. You'd call them "paddles" down in England, we call them "sluices" up here. Most of them were metal, running in guides, with a big screw at the top. The sluices on lock gates we found were best made from beech, though the runners for the sluices to move in were from greenheart; that greenheart is oily, and the beech and the greenheart seemed to suit each other – the beech would slide up and down nice and easy.

'The sluice gear we had then was like a bit of a death trap. You had a quill and a small cog which attached to the stem. You turned this up, and there was a pawl which kept going into the ratchet so that it wouldn'a slip back. But then to lower it you had to turn it to get out the pawl from the ratchet, and it came down like a guillotine. You see, you couldn't wind it down, you had to let it go. There were a lot of people got cracks with that, with the handle spinning, you know.

'We used to have to look after the dredger boat as well. It was a wooden boat you see, and we used to put that in the old *Linnet* shed; we'd to put quite a few planks in that. It was Russian larch 2½in thick by 12in, and we used to have to steam them to get them round the shoulder on it. We had the big iron ice-breaker too, the *Conway*.

'The *Conway* used to start at six in the morning and go through to Crinan and come back. They'd fill up with coal, and at six o'clock the next morning they were off again. I've only seen that big ice-breaker stop once, and that was in terrible weather. It was because of the snow: there was no' just the ice but snow, the snow had fallen on top of the ice. She was going up on the ice, to break it with her weight, but the snow was piling up in front. Eventually the crew had to walk ashore at No 13 lock – they couldn't make anything of it.

Nowadays they don't bother, and when the ice comes, that's it. That's except when one of MacBrayne's ferries comes through – they make good ice-breakers, being metal. They go down to Glasgow for drydocking. They were built small enough that they can come through the canal to get to the islands.

'The *Conway* was steam-powered, and she rose up on the top of the ice and her weight broke through it, and crushed it down. She was beautiful inside, all varnished, with lovely big scallop-shaped seats, the shape of your body. I don't know, but some of the old folk used to tell me that when the *Linnet* was too full they used to put some of the passengers on that ice-breaker and it would run through the canal behind the *Linnet*.

'There'd be a lock keeper at every lock in those days. Here there'd be two at the swing bridge, at the main road: one at No 2 who did that and No 3, and the one at No 4 was supposed to come down and help him with No 3. They lived in the cottages by the side. Quite a few of them had a cow or two just by, and they'd have their own milk and vegetables. When those puffers were running through, the lock keepers used to give them leeks, turnips and carrots and that for a plate of soup, and in return they'd get a pail of coal, you see. Everybody was quite happy with arrangements like that! But I never had a canal house: there weren't houses for the craftsmen, only for the lock keepers because in the summer nights they'd work till maybe eight o'clock. And the sea locks could be working later than that, because if anything was storm-bound or anything like that it was their duty to let them in. Also, the likes of Crinan, when the fishing fleet was in, they'd want to be out at six o'clock in the morning to get to the fishing ground. So the lock keeper had to be there then.

'The wee lighthouse was gas at first – they'd a gas plant at the side of the bridge and there was a pipe out along the pier from there. The lock keepers looked after that. But the Clyde Trust would come to do any adjustments: you know that it's got port and starboard glasses, red and green, which show the boats when they're on the right line coming up the loch, and the Trust men used to want them set just right. You'd to shift them back and forth, just 1/8in maybe. On a really stormy day the waves will go right over the top of that lighthouse, and vibrations seemed to shift those glasses out of place.

The lighthouse on Ardrishaig pier

'There's a lot of yachts now – although even that's dropping off – but not that the regular flow is drying out. Years ago you used to get the Clyde Yacht Racing Club which used to come in the second week in July, and you were talking about 200-plus boats. You don't get that number now – maybe it's too expensive. The big boats all go round the Mull now. But that's quite a trip, and it can be treacherous.

'When I started on the canal not many of

In 1964 the Duke of Edinburgh, Prince Charles (in the cockpit) and Princess Anne (on the foredeck) passed through the Crinan Canal on a cruise to the western isles in their yacht Bloodhound. *Behind the scenes there was much preparation, including raising water levels above their normal limits, to ensure a trouble-free passage* (BW Archives, Gloucester)

the boats had engines; they were mostly sailed. When the fishing was slack the men would all sit by the pier, in a crowd, yarning and that, down below the lock where it's out of the wind. If they saw a boat coming up they'd go to the end of the pier by the lighthouse and wait for the boat coming round. They'd shout across, "Do you want a man to work the locks and a horse to pull you through?" You see, they would make maybe a pound or something.

'We had that *Bloodhound* through once with Prince Philip and Princess Anne on board. They were drawing a wee bit more than the regulation depth so we had to put planks on the waste weirs to get the level up a bit and help them along. But oh, the photographers. They were everywhere. On the lock gates and everywhere, goodness gracious!

'I was a foreman for a while, about four year; then I was inspector for a while, but I didna really like it, I was no' really happy. I was inspector over the whole canal. I felt I knew the canal and the gates and everything better than the bosses in Glasgow, but I'd to do what they said. It was the time they were bringing in this self-service at all the locks, and I didn't really hold with that because it was becoming an international canal. There were Frenchmen, Dutchmen, and all sorts of yachts coming through, and they were wanting to hand them pamphlets in English to tell them how to work the locks and all. You see, when there was a lock keeper at every lock, if anything happened to his lock that made it harder to work, he would shout. Now, there might be nobody at that lock for two months, and if there's anything wrong there nobody's interested because it doesn't affect them in their work every day.

'I did forty-six years at the yard there. Now there's only one time-served tradesman, and all the rest are multi-skilled and do this or that as they need.'

JOE SAFE

From Day Boatman to Lock Keeper

A popular impression of canals is that they were only intended, or indeed used, to carry heavy bulk cargoes such as coal. In practice almost any commodity can be moved on water safely, economically and often surprisingly quickly. Joe Safe has carried the full range of cargoes in a lifetime afloat, and after moving ashore he helped to work as many through the tidal locks at Brentford where the Grand Union Canal reaches the Thames.

I visited Joe in his 'retirement' in Birmingham where he was busy, as ever, with boats. He has what many would consider to be a full-time occupation making rope fenders for the modern users of the waterways, pleasure boats: traditional hand-made rope fenders remain unbeatable for resistance to the abuse they receive on boats in inexperienced hands. But on the morning I was in Joe Safe's workshop, few hitches were added to the cover of the stem fender on the bench, as the memories of past cargoes and boats flowed.

'Me dad started me on the boats. I was six months old when I was took on the boats. I was born in a house not far from here, at Hockley. He was open boating before that, joey boating.' It is no longer clear why so many of the boats of the complex 160-mile Birmingham Canal Navigations system were called 'joey boats', but these were the craft used on short-haul work. Their journeys were usually completed in less than a working day and so if they were fitted with a cabin at all it was only sufficient for brewing up or for temporary shelter for the occasional night aboard. They were not registered as dwellings like the long-distance narrowboats.

'They started to have them tugs round the Wyrley [Wyrley & Essington Canal in the north of the Birmingham Canal Navigations system]. That *Enterprise* with the Gardner, he

Twenty tons, or more, of coal would be shovelled out of a BCN day boat by hand in less than a working day

could pull ten boats with that.' We talked about loading coal at collieries up the Cannock Extension Canal in the northern part of the BCN to carry down the Tame Valley Canal and so up into central Birmingham.

'Remember that jingle of the lock names? From the top of the Rushall Canal you come to "Mosses Two, The Ganzes Seven, The New Thirteen, and the Lousy 'leven, with a boat coming up, a boat coming down, and another one a-standing in the 'ospital pound". They called it the "Lousy 'leven" because all the dossers used to get in the boats there, to sleep. If I went with the old chap to collect a change boat there late at night he always used to chuck a bucket of water in first, in case there were any dossers sleeping in the cabin.

'It *was* busy round the Wyrley. They used to say that if you was going from somewhere like round here, or Oldbury, to get round there you'd got to be starting about twelve o'clock, midnight, to keep with the water. It was like a tide going up to Hednesford and Cannock; this end'd go down about 3 to 4in. Anybody what was at the top o' 'hampton

[Wolverhampton Top Lock] when the joshers used to go round to the mill at Pratt's Bridge, they never used to go round of an afternoon; they'd wait till next morning and "go round with the tide" they said. There was that many boats and tugs pushing water through the bridge 'oles. Then it would turn when they all started coming back. Then there was all them going up and down Walsall and Mosses and the Ganzes. They was going all hours of the day.

'When I was fourteen me and me dad used to reckon to go from Gravelly Hill up to Hednesford and back to Walsall Wood with a horse boat. We'd only to change over up at the colliery, not wait to load and bring the same boat back. We used to do four trips in a week, me and the old man, and empty three. We emptied our own. We slept on the boats a lot on that, though there was no proper cabin for living full time, just sleep on your jacket, like. We did the same down the Stour Cut [Staffordshire & Worcestershire Canal] when I was on that job; that was for Element's to Stourport Power Station. You had a bottle stove, you see, and you used to carry it across to the other boat, with the fire in and all. We used to let the fire go down, like, we had an old trilby to hold it with and stop you getting burnt lifting it in and out! Then you put it in the boat and fitted the middle pipe and of course a top pipe outside. Then you moved all the ellum and mast, boat shaft and gear. All the pubs had stables, and the horse stopped in them at night.

'Then dad ended up with no work and so he went long distance for Midland & Coast. He left them after a bit and went to Thomas Clayton's.' Thomas Clayton (Oldbury) Ltd was descended from one of the companies which had amalgamated to form Fellows Morton & Clayton Ltd. Their general carrying craft had been taken into the larger combine, together with much property in wharves and boatyards; but the liquid carrying business remained independent. The principal traffics were fuel oils, with tar and gas water more locally in the Midlands. Fuel oil was brought from Barton, on the Bridgewater Canal, close to its crossing over the Manchester Ship Canal on the outskirts of Manchester; or from Stanlow refinery, on the Ship Canal itself at Ellesmere Port to Langley Green. The Shell Mex depot there was near the head of the six Oldbury, or Titford Branch locks, at 511ft (156m) the highest level of the BCN system which remains navigable. These locks are often referred to by the boatmen as 'The Crow'.

'Well, there was about six on 'em from Clayton's, and they come to the bottom of The Crow; it was when the General Strike was on in 1926, and they couldn't get up the locks. But these six loads of oil had to be got up, and they had the police there. The lock keeper said he wasn't going to unchain the locks. The one copper said to my old man, "Can you unlock it?" He said, "Ooh, I can unlock it!" And he went and fetched a big hammer, and he hit the lock and it was off. They done everything to stop 'em getting up there, even throwed a lock gate out. That was soon back, however, and they got the six loads up. After that me dad and others was mentioned in Thomas Clayton's will as he could have a job as long as he wanted one; and if he ever left and wanted to come back they had to find him a job.'

Joe remembers that the Birmingham Canal system, where his family was working at the time, was generally very quiet during the General Strike itself. Naturally the long coal strike, which had sparked the wider stoppage, greatly reduced the short-haul traffic on the BCN. Traffic was most seriously affected during the General Strike by the lock keepers and the other canal company staff padlocking locks and stop places (where cargo tonnages on boats were checked) on the first night at the regular closing time and then failing to reopen them for some days. Joe does not recall bitterness between the boatmen, who were more

A Thomas Clayton horse-drawn oil boat ascends Oldbury Locks ('The Crow') on the Titford Canal

independent, and the land-based canal company staff, who do not seem, in general, to have been highly enthusiastic for the strike. After the strike, the boatmen from large carrying companies and those who owned their own craft continued to trade alongside one another in more or less friendly competition as before.

'We was on the Manchester run, going to Barton. Later, about 1934–5, they started going to Ellesmere Port for the fuel oil; but something upset me dad and he left, and went and had a pair of Grand Unions. Clayton's had no motors before *Soar,* which was bought from Fellows Mortons in 1937; she had been their *Lindola.* After that they started having them built at Uxbridge; *Stour* [now preserved at the Black Country Museum] was the first from there. Forrester Clayton was in charge by then because Thomas Clayton had died and he wanted me dad to have that boat. He must've thought well of me dad, you see.

'There was three on us – me, me brother and me sister, she was the oldest. Me sister stopped at home when she was old enough to go to work. She worked round Birmingham way, instead of on the boats.

'We went Grand Unioning around October 1934 – we had the *Hercules* and *Virgins* – well, that's what we called it. [The obscure names of many of the boats of the Grand Union Canal Carrying Co's Star class boats have always been a problem to boatmen, or indeed to many people with little interest in astronomy – *Virginis* is perhaps one of the less problematical!] Me eldest brother had been living on the land, with one of me mum's relations, I think. He got drownded New Year's morning 1936 at Maffas [Marsworth].

'When you was Grand Unioning you didn't take your range with you because the boats had them in. After we went down the north they started putting them in down there, too. Before, with Fellows Morton & Clayton's, you used to have to buy your own range, so you took it with you every time. Clayton's, they always found the ranges, but you always found all your drying rails and brasses and all that yourself. There was very little difference in the cabins themselves. The only one that I knowed that was any different was Clayton's *Forth*, which apparently was intended to go as a black boat – you know, just locally round Birmingham on the tar carrying. She had an extra beam half-way up the cabin before you got to the cross-bed hole. So we drilled a hole through the beam to get our top rod through and then the other rods hung below that. The cabin'd be clean enough that most time you could get straight into them. Sometimes you'd to clean up if it was a new docked boat because they'd made a mess in the cabin with working on it. But if you had a change boat, nine times out of ten you could put your stuff straight into them. You didn't have to work on your boat on the dock you see, you changed into one of their boats and went off for your loading orders. At Bull's Bridge, down there if you was waiting for orders in the lay-by they used to pay £1 a day. Well, if you was laid there you used to have to go to work on the dock, cleaning the boats up and things like that, or blacking the hulls.

'We didn't go many trips with that pair of boats before we had a brand-new pair, *Grus* and *Glaxy* – wooden boats they were. [The Star class butty *Glaxy* had obviously even confused the boatyard signwriter or a clerk in the owners' office who failed to spell 'galaxy' correctly – one of two craft in the fleet with mis-spelt names.]

Grus *and* Glaxy *in the warehouse at Sampson Road emptying cement*

'We went on the cement run, from Southam to Sampson Road in Birmingham. About 1936 that was. There was five pair on that, doing four trips a week each. If you loaded during the night and come out of the basin at, say, two o'clock, you would empty that day at Sampson Road [a trip of 31½ miles involving the operation of forty locks]; we used to average between twelve and thirteen hours for that run from Southam to the depot at the top of Camp Hill Locks. As soon as the men at the works had finished loading you'd to be away – sheet up the boats and gone. And when you was empty you had to keep the floors dry in the boats, so we had to turn them up to stop any rain getting on them. I've done some hours for them – and me and the wife have done some hours after we got married, too. We've been loaded at Bournville, that's Cadbury's at Birmingham, on the Monday morning and been emptied on the Thursday morning at Brentford – right through two-handed. 1941 we was married when I was nineteen.

'I met me wife, Mary, in this way: I'd been open boating around Birmingham with me dad. Well, I went down to Braunston on a weekend and came back by way of Birmingham and seen some mates there, and I stopped and had a week on the beer with them! When I got home me dad got on to me, so I just turned round and said, "Well, that's it, then, good day". And I never went back. I went as a mate on a pair of Fellows Morton & Clayton boats and I met Mary because I was working with her and her husband; but he died. She was a lot older than me, seventeen year older, but that never made no odds, we worked well together. I left Grand Unioning in 1945 and went on the shore because the wife had a baby, but unfortunately we lost her.'

All the boat people I have met preferred their children to be born in their own homes on the boats. This saved the worry of being confined to an unknown hospital away from the familiar ground of the canal bank, and where unknown doctors would be liable to suggest that life outdoors, doing heavy manual work well into the last month of a pregnancy, was not acceptable for mother or child. Nor did many medical practitioners think confined boat cabins suitable for giving birth or as a home for an infant. The boaters viewed this as simply contrary to several generations of successful experience!

Unfortunately, the midwife who, until the early 1940s, had assisted at the wharf at Tyseley in Birmingham, where Joe and Mary's first child would have been born, suffered a fall down the steps into one of the narrowboat cabins and afterwards refused to attend the boat people. As a result, and perhaps because she was older than average, Mary was taken into the local hospital, leaving Joe and his step-son living on the boats. The Grand Union Canal Carrying Co was unsympathetic, needing to keep every available boat and crew working in the last months of the war. Joe is still clearly distressed at the memory of being asked to work the boats back to the Warwickshire coalfield and London with a stranger as mate whilst Mary was abandoned in hospital.

Miscarriages and still-births were by no means rare amongst the boat people who often worked right up to the confinement. Mary was little different. After the loss of her baby she would have expected little rest in her cabin bed as cargo was loaded and the boats worked back to London through numerous locks. She would soon have been up and about, at least steering if not jumping off to open gates and paddles. Instead, Joe was fortunate to obtain work in Coventry and they lived in the cabin of S. E. Barlow's motor boat *Blake*, which was tied up nearby awaiting engine repairs.

'They wanted to send a boatman up from Bull's Bridge to work the boats with me whilst

Mary Safe polishing the brasswork in Carp's *cabin at Wolverhampton 1950*

Mary was recovering, but I'd got to pay him out of my money. So I went to work for Woodwards at Longford, Coventry, the boilermakers and engineers; I had about three years on the shore. Then Mr Veater, the Grand Union's traffic man, got me back. It was about the time they were nationalised and the British Waterways took over, 1948. So I had a pair of Erewash boats for them. I was on there about three year.'

The Grand Union's subsidiary, the Erewash Canal Carrying Company, had new boats similar to those built for the parent company except that they were about two feet shorter: this was so they would fit the chamber at Loughborough Bottom, or Bishop Meadow, Lock which was a little shorter than standard, without the need to remove fenders to swing the gates open.

Lifting the sternmost fender on the stern of a big Grand Union motor so as to get the bottom gates to swing past the boat at Bishop Meadow Lock, Loughborough

'We did all those runs round to Nottingham and Leicester from London. Then about 1950 they was took over by the Grand Union Depot at Bull's Bridge. Well, we still did the Erewash work but I didn't get on very well with them at London and so I swapped and went down the north. Then they was arguing that we shouldn't have the butty because of having no kiddies to make up the number of hands; so we changed with George Rooks because he had two single motors, a 15-horse and a 9-horse. I had the 9-horse, the *Carp*. That knocked our tonnage money down a bit, but we gained the other way because the working was easier and we could do each trip quicker. All the locks were narrow, you see, so with a butty you were always pulling it in and waiting for it; with the two motors you kept going because each one would drive straight in. Well, then they turned round and said we'd got to have a butty.'

Joe's two motor boats would earn him less cash for a given trip simply because he and Mary would deliver less cargo. The engine room of the vast majority of narrowboats was built in what would otherwise have been the 'back end' of the hold, immediately ahead of the living cabin. On a motor boat it occupies about five or six feet of the boat's length; the steamers built in the late 1800s lost more space to bunkers and boiler room. A marine diesel engine of the sort employed on the narrowboats in the 1920s and 1930s also weighs up to a ton and a half with its fuel tanks. Naturally the motor and butty boat hulls are virtually identical in overall size to fit the locks and so the lost space and weight in the motor boat means a reduction in total carrying capacity. If the depth of the canal allowed a horse or butty boat to load 30 tons and still move along efficiently, a motor could only be expected to carry a little over 25 tons on the same route. As a result Joe and Mary loading two motors instead of pulling a butty might carry up to 5 tons less than they had with the pair.

Like canal tolls, boatmen's wages were calculated broadly on the basis of ton/miles. The more one delivered to the destination, the more one got paid. However, as Joe says, the advantage of the two motor boats was that there was no waiting – they travelled as separate

FMC fish class single motor boats working together up Audlem Locks

units. Previously he had driven the motor boat into a lock and worked it through whilst the butty waited its turn. Once the motor boat passed out of the chamber the gates had to be shut so that it could be refilled for the butty to be laboriously pulled in and the lock emptied again before the motor could tow it to the next lock to begin the process all over again. There were fifty-eight locks to be passed in this way between Wolverhampton and Manchester (plus one which takes the two boats at once), so it will be appreciated that, unless the butty is manually bowhauled from lock to lock where they are grouped in flights, the waiting time with a pair could be considerable. A quicker trip with two motor boats carrying less tonnage might mean several extra trips a year with consequent extra earnings.

'It always used to annoy me that British Waterways traffic office people didn't make any attempt to stop our trade going onto road transport. They were always ready to say, "Oh, no we can't get it there that quick." They were all right, they got paid sat in the office with their tea cup whilst you were tied up outside waiting for a loading order and earning nothing. If we was asked we could easily get a load from the Black Country to Weston Point as quick as the railways, with all their shunting and everything, and often we were no slower than a lorry when you take into account the arrangements being made and everything.

'One time was typical: they'd got me sitting around with empty boats that could take 40 or 50 tons of steel tubes and they made no attempt to find a full load when they were offered 10 tons to go from Stewarts & Lloyds at Halesowen to Weston Point. You see, if there were a lot of small tubes you might get 50 ton on the pair. When you got them big ones you had more air space inside 'em so your weight was less.

'I was always one ready for a challenge. Dickie Tart, in the office at Wolverhampton, said to me one time, "There's ten ton of tubes at Coombeswood for the motor boat to go down to Weston Point." So I gets there and we had a night at Stewarts & Lloyds works.

'I asks the foreman, Joe, if there's anything I could put in the butty. He said "No", so we started to load the motor but then he comes dashing up and says, "Can you get her down to Wembley? I've got fifteen ton I can put in her" (they called that wharf at the end of the works "Wembley"). Anyhow, I gets the butty down there and the blokes was telling me as there was five ton of fittings to go, too. But the foreman says, "No, you can't have them, your bosses, they've told me it can't be done." This was a Wednesday and they'd got to be in Birkenhead by Friday afternoon. So anyhow I eventually kids him to put them in, but told him to say nothing to Wolverhampton till I was clear.

'So I gets to Wolverhampton and nips the notes in and Dick Tart plays hell into me about this five ton of fittings. He says, "It's tying up time isn't it, Joe?" "No," I said, "me butty's going down the locks!" I'd sent the wife on with the butty, you see, down first – Ronnie Saxon took the butty down. There was a horse to take it in them days. So I goes

DOCKS AND INLAND WATERWAYS EXECUTIVE
RATES PAYABLE TO CAPTAINS OF NARROW CRAFT

Per ton:		
Brentford to Wellingborough	3s 1d + 57% cost of living bonus	= 4s 10d
Brentford to Birmingham	3s 5d	= 5s 5d
Bournville to Brentford	3s 10d	= 6s 0d
plus bowhauling (total)	2s 6d	= 3s 11d
Baddesley Colliery to Dickinson's	2s 7d	= 4s 1d
Empty:		
Birmingham to Bull's Bridge (total)	33s 4d	= 52s 6d

The tonnage rates above were paid to the captain to cover the labour of his family and any mate on a pair of narrowboats which might load about 50 tons in total. The cost of living allowance had been introduced to cover the inflation of war time. Extra payments were made on some routes involving working the two boats individually through narrow locks as opposed to sharing the wide Grand Union chambers. To reach Bournville, boats from Brentford had either to use the nineteen narrow locks of the Stratford Canal at Lapworth, or travel further on the deeper Grand Union into Birmingham and then work six narrow locks downhill and nineteen up again to reach their destination. In all these flights the butty would have to be bowhauled with back-breaking effort by the crew in return for the 3s 11d extra payment. Should there be no southbound load from Birmingham, three to four days empty running back to London area was rewarded with the flat payment of 52s 6d.

Figures from a British Transport Commission Document; 31 March 1951

Loading British Waterways, ex-Fellows Morton & Clayton craft at Coombeswood tube works for Weston Point

down with the motor and I gets a mate with me to fill the locks like, telling him I was in a hurry. When I gets down to the bottom lock Ronnie Saxon's coming back with the horse and says, "It's round the Cut End, Joe." [A horse-drawn boat will move in and out of the confined lock chambers more easily than a motor-driven boat, and so it wasn't hard to gain the extra time needed for the butty to travel round the half mile to the beginning of the Shropshire Union Canal at Autherley Junction, 'Cut End', whilst the motor was still descending the Wolverhampton Twenty-One Locks.]

'So when I gets to Cut End the missus says, "Are we stopping?" I said, "No, we'll go below the lock" [at Wheaton Aston, 7¾ miles ahead]. When we got below that the missus said, "Are we stopping here?" I said, "No, we're going to Norbury!" [another 7¾ lock-free miles]. So we went to Norbury that night, about a quarter to ten, and I had a couple of pints! Then we were away about three next morning so we could be at the top of Drayton Locks [10 miles ahead] when it broke daylight. So we got down there [five locks, followed by five at Adderley and fifteen at Audlem and two at Hack Green], and then I gets on the phone at Minshull Wharf to the gaffer at Anderton, Mr Wilson. You see, I'd made arrangements at Wolverhampton with Dick Tart to tell them to get the lorry ready at Weston Point for ten o'clock on Friday morning. He had said, "That's all right, but I don't believe you'll be there."

Wilson, the transport manager, didn't either: "The lorry will be there, but I'll bet you won't!" he says. This was twelve o'clock Thursday. Anyhow, we keeps going and ties up that night at Anderton Lift, at the "lift hole", that little basin at the entrance. Me and the missus goes walking round to the pub for a pint. I puts the money on the counter but the landlord wouldn't take it. "That will be paid for in the morning!" I said, "Who's going to pay for it?" "Mr Wilson!" he said. Just like that!

'So we went back and had our supper and went to bed. Well, about ten to six in the morning I got up to get everything ready for the lift men because they started at eight o'clock. Then at that moment, bang, bang, bang, on the cabin, and "Come on," they said, "Get 'em in the lift!" Well, they weren't supposed to start 'till eight, but I know the river locks started at six so I said, "What about that lock at Saltersford?" "They are waiting for you," they says. So the missus gave me a cup of tea over in the lift tank while we were going down. She says, "Are we going down abreast today so you can have your breakfast?" "No," I say, "we're going in style, so keep it out of my water!" [Keeping the butty offset on its towline allows the motor's wash to pass by and so the two boats will travel a little faster.] And we did go in style.

'Being the first thing moving on the river right at lock keepers' starting time, we went flat out past all the ICI packet boats at Winnington and Wallerscote. Well, they was mad because they were all just getting ready to start off, thinking all the locks would be ready for them as they arrived, and we went down first so that they would have to wait for every lock to be refilled. I'll bet they would've been late for the tide if they was going over to Liverpool.

'When we gets to Saltersford I said to the keeper there, "What about Dutton?" "They're waiting for you," he said. Well, we went under the swing bridge at Frodsham and the bloke in the control box gave me a wave. There used to be a lower swing bridge at Rock Savage by the chemical works, in those days, which had to be swung off; there was a chap there to do it. As we came to the bend just above that I was about to give a good blow on the klaxon when I saw the bridge starting to move. Him from Frodsham had phoned and told him to get it off! So as we came into the dock I breasts the boats up together – and then I saw the crane was hanging over and the men were all standing on the quay side! I hadn't got a rope tied up before they were getting on and hooking those barrels of fittings out. I says, "You're in a hurry!" – and they said, "You've been in a hurry too, ain't ya?" And that was just eight o'clock, starting time for them, that's two hours for the thirteen mile down that river. I said I'd promised that bloke at Coombeswood that I'd have those fittings here for the ship. And I told them it was like a challenge, like: all the gaffers had said it couldn't be done, and I'd proved 'em all liars.

A motor narrowboat lies sandwiched between a barge and the quay wall at Weston Point docks, whilst tubes carried from Stewarts & Lloyds works at Coombswood are transhipped, to be carried across the Mersey for further transhipment into an ocean-going vessel at Liverpool for export. A number of empty narrowboats await loading in the background (BW Archives, Gloucester)

'Anyway, doing this trip so quick had more trouble in it for me than I knew!

'So I'm tied up and just before five

Mary Safe steers Prince Charles *whilst her son stands on the butty running planks and Joe regards the photographer from* Ipswich *as the empty pair approaches Marsh Lane bridge at the edge of Nantwich on the Shropshire Union Canal* (Edward Paget-Tomlinson)

o'clock that foreman comes and says, "Get them in the middle dock – we're landing them to the shore in the morning first off." So I was in the middle dock ready for starting time, and they emptied them, so I said to the foreman, "I'll go and tie up now." "Oh no you won't," he said, "you've got to stop here because there's a flat coming across at twelve o'clock and you've got to load." I said, "There's boats at Anderton that's on turn before me." "I ain't worried about them, you've got to load." So I loads and I said, "I'm going to be in a right row tonight when they all come down here – and I'm not going up this river to lay below the lift all weekend." [It was the system for narrowboats awaiting orders to load at Runcorn, Preston Brook, Weston Point or Manchester to collect at the traffic control office at the top of the Anderton Lift. This made it almost impossible for British Waterways to provide craft for loading the same day as requested in any of the docks. However, it was a serious offence against his mates for a boatman to jump the queue as Joe was being asked to do. Normal procedure would have been for an empty pair to be sent down from Anderton to load across the dock from where Joe's empty pair lay idle awaiting their turn, despite the delay thus caused.]

"No," he said, "you ain't, you'll be straight up that lift tonight. The lift men are going for their dinners and then they'll be back to get you up." That was Saturday, you see, so I was up the lift about four o'clock. He said, "You're going to be in Wolverhampton

ISWICH
IPSWIC

Monday morning." But I thought to myself that there'd be no one ready for me then.

'Anyhow, I come up to Wolverhampton for eight o'clock on the Monday and they emptied me. So I thought, "Thank goodness for that, now perhaps I can tie up." But the gaffer says, "Oh no, you ain't tying up, Joe, you've got to go straight into Coombeswood." By me doing that 5 ton of fittings, British Waterways had got a job for another 500 ton of tubes!

'This would be about 1957 or 1958. I had the *Prince Charles* and *Ipswich*, then.

'A bit after that Mr Houlder, who was at Bridge Street in charge of the south-western fleet, asked if I would go working under him. I was with him about three years carrying cocoa and all that sort of stuff. But they wouldn't load me back from Brentford very often, because I was having that cocoa regular. That was because it made a good return load for the southern-based boats which operated from Bull's Bridge. If they came up to Birmingham from Brentford or London with a load they could go round to Bournville, get loaded quickly with that cocoa waste and be back to Brentford in less than a week and a half. They'd get tonnage money both ways and no empty running getting paid next to nothing or having to go all round to the coal field and hang about there to get a back load.

Loading cocoa waste at Bournville

'Well, I phoned up one time from Brentford because I'd had enough of coming back empty. Well, when I gets to Bridge Street Mr Houlder says, "You've to go back to Cadbury's, Joe, and load cocoa." I says "No, I'm going to go to Hednesford for coal for Worcester. I've had enough of going down to Brampford [Brentford in Middlesex] with cocoa and coming back empty for £18. That's no good to me if I can't have a load from Brampford." He said, "Why can't you have a load?" I said, "Because the Grand Union men have kicked up about me have cocoa regular." So he said, "Well, you've got to go back, else it'll all go by road. And anyway you won't come back empty because there'll be two load of spelter for you."

'Well, we goes and I'm creating to meself all the way down. There was Mark Harrison ahead, my two brother-in-laws with us and George Radford, all with that cocoa waste. Well, George Radford had all his electric go wrong and he couldn't go throught the tunnels with having no lights, so he stops at Braunston to get fixed up. When we tied up the last evening, I rings up to see if they wanted us in the morning, and they did.

'Next morning, Mark unsheets going down the two bottom pounds, and when he gets to Brentford, they start unloading him straightaway. Well, they emptied Mark and they emptied Ted's, and then he comes along to me and tells me to unsheet. So I said, "Why, are you going to empty me?" "No, I only want sixteen bags out." "Well," I said, "I ain't unsheeting for sixteen bags." And he says, "You've got to wait three days for George Radford." So I phoned Mr Houlder, and he says, "Leave it with me."

When I came back the boats were on the other side, unsheeted. So we emptied, and I

(Opposite) Prince Charles *and* Ipswich *about to leave Anderton Lift for the river Weaver*

said, "All right, we'll tie up now." "You won't!" said the foreman. "There's five loads of spelter coming up, to be here just before five. You've got to load tonight." This was a Thursday. "You've to be in Birmingham by Sunday morning, they're going to leave the locks open for you." So of course Ted and Mark said, "We're before him!" "Ted," he said, "there's blokes at Bull's Bridge before you, but we can't load them because if we don't load *him*, there's nobody going to load." "What do you mean? He can't do that, stop us loading?" "No," he said, "he can't – but his gaffer can. We've had a right dressing down over not loading him with spelter all the while he's been coming down here. But that spelter's his gaffer's job, not ours, so we've got to load him and he's to be back in Birmingham Sunday morning. Then he's to load at Cadbury's Monday morning." They didn't like that.

'We did two years on that, and then I went back to Coventry living in the caravan. After that I came back on the coal job to Worcester that was from Hednesford; Cannock & Rugeley Collieries. I done that for eighteen months before it packed up. It was good money on that job in 1959 or 1960 – we made about £500 a year apiece, plus there was no rent, no coal and no electric light to find with living on the boats and not in a house. But you got to do the hours: it's like piecework, the sooner you done the trip, the sooner you got the money. The same as when we was open boating – if we used the barrow or the shovel we had more money. And if you did four trips in a week instead of three, you got more money again. I think it was three bob [3s: 15p] a ton for throwing it out at Worcester, that'd be for 48 ton. I used to do it in eight hours.

'I done two year and a bit at school, from when I was twelve till I was fourteen. I just got the basics, so I knew what they was writing in the settlements at Bull's Bridge and that. I didn't get on with him there because he tried to diddle me out of £5 once. I can think meself lucky in a way – but my lad, he never had no schooling, but you can't do *him* out of money!

'Well, then I went Willow Wrenning. I'd been on about three months with them when Mr Houlder tells me of a job going at Birmingham for Element's running from Holly Bank [Holly Bank Colliery] to the GEC, regular. Would I like it? I said I would, on one condition: that they took the side cloths off. Anyhow, when I gets to Braunston, Dennis Clarke, the gaffer there, wouldn't take them off. But I said "Those side cloths have got to come off or they'll be off in pieces with the grab. I've got to go round Birmingham, so I don't want no side cloths on.

'So we got up there and George Element set us on, three trips a week it was. The *Smew* was the butty. I don't remember the motor, it was an old Fellows Morton and they'd put a steel bottom in her. Billy Hindhead had it a good while. But it had a Seffle engine and it broke the bed bolts. He wouldn't get them fixed and I had propped the engine to hold it steady. So I asked British Waterways down the north for a job, and Joe Taylor said "Come down and put your things in the *Roach*." So I left the Willow Wrens at Element's Wharf at Gravelly Hill and we went. Well, Willow Wren's boss, Morton, wasn't going to send me me money and so I went to the Transport & General Workers office, at Broad Street. So they phoned up to Willow Wren, and Morton insisted he was going to withhold me money. Well, the TGWU chap says, "If his money's not in Element's office in the morning, Mr Morton will be up here in front of the magistrates. That's one thing you can't do, is to uphold the money off nobody!" The money was there with a registered letter the next morning. So we went down the north and that's where I finished up.'

Joe was unusual amongst boatmen in making use of his union representation. Few boatmen in general long-distance work bothered to join a union. As an isolated community,

Willow Wren Canal Carrying Co motor boat Sandpiper *and butty* Coot *lie loaded at Element's Wharf in Birmingham* (BW Archives, Gloucester)

always on the move and unable to read or write effectively, they relied on the paternal attitude of many of the carrying companies who owned the boats which were their homes as much as their places of work. The development of the larger and more bureaucratic carrying companies resulted in some changes to this.

Union influence did not always work to the boatmen's long-term benefit. For example, when the railway unions managed to obtain an eight-hour working day for their members in 1921, the railway-owned canal carrying companies, such as that on the Shropshire Union Canal, largely ceased carrying and their boats were sold off. Many of these Shropshire Union craft passed to the carrier's former customers who also took on the crews, and the long working hourse persisted.

In 1923 the large private carriers Fellows Morton & Clayton Ltd sought to reduce boatmen's wages as the post-World War I boom came to an end. The boatmen resisted, tying up craft and cargoes and blockading depots, such as that at Braunston. The strike lasted for

Brentford Depot in the early 1950s showing the amount of aluminium traffic handled then. Loaded ex-Grand Union Canal Carrying Co motor boat Badsey *at the wharf opposite carries the new British Waterways livery whilst her butty* Balham *retains that of their previous owners. The Fellows Morton & Clayton boats at the extreme left have yet to be docked and painted by the nationalised concern* (Author's collection)

seventeen weeks, after which a considerable time was required for boatmen to recoup their lost earnings, despite the fact that the company had not got its way entirely.

From the 1930s onwards one of the major problems faced by all long-distance carriers was that of obtaining good boatmen who were prepared to work the hours involved in preference to the attraction of carrying out mundane factory work in a regular eight-hour day for seemingly attractive wages. Those who left the cut were, however, to find that they had to pay rent and fuel bills, which whilst living in the company's boats and carrying house coal regularly as cargo, had not been a problem on the waterways.

Alan Faulkner (in his *FMC, A Short History of Fellows Morton & Clayton Ltd*, Robert Wilson 1975) compares a boatman's earnings on the London to Birmingham run (which had to pay the boatman's wife and family or any mate too) at £32 per month, with the national average earnings of £2 10s [£2.50] a week in other industries at the time. Whilst boatmen's earnings were entirely dependent on the effort they put in, they were not impoverished.

In case boatmen should feel that they were hard done by, from the 1930s onwards carrying companies began to keep an unwritten agreement not to poach one another's crews, as described by Harry Bentley. This in turn made it more difficult for any discontented family to move to a better employer.

'I finished at British Waterways because of a gearbox. I'd been reporting me gearbox slipping and they was supposed to be getting me another one. But all the while I kept managing with it they never bothered. Then they gave me an order for loading at Weston Point up to the Potteries, but I said, "I can't go to Western Point, my gearbox won't take me." He got the Union in and told him I'd refused orders. I told the Union bloke why, because I said, "He wants me to go down that river, at risk of losing all the power for my steering, and we'd be meeting coasters and the ICI packets coming up. If I lose power and gets across one of them we're going to be cut in two and drownded!" "Well," he says, "if you have an accident then we can do something about it!" That was the second time I'd been told that. Then they sacked me over it.

'So I went working on the shore on building sites and then onto the motorway. And when they was finished with the motorways I got the job at Thames Locks at Brentford. On there we didn't work on a five day week; only the Gauging Lock, next up the cut, did that. Thames Lock was tidal and worked the seven days, though Saturday was ordinary time and only Sunday was double time. But if we wanted time off on the Saturday and we had any days owing we used to have what they called a "lieu day". Thames Lock worked two tides a day so you were in your own time in between. If the tide was in the night you had two hours at double time, an hour before high water and an hour after. It was really for safety to get the boats in off the river. Later on they stopped that after ten o'clock. They made me retire off there at sixty-five.

'So I had a few fall-outs and left the jobs. But generally I was only ever on the dole if we was froze up; the most I was on it was after we left the boats before I got in with French's

Thames Locks, entrance to the Grand Union Canal from the tidal creek at Brentford, where Joe Safe was lock keeper after his time building motorways in the Midlands. This photograph was probably taken immediately after their opening if not at the actual ceremony on 24 October 1962. It shows the twinned locks in use by typical lighter traffic from London Docks leaving the tideway for Brentford Depot and the Grand Union Canal. Joe's house later occupied the vacant site beyond the left-hand chamber (Alan Faulkner collection)

RWBC

on the motorways. Then I had twelve to thirteen years with them, looking after the pumps keeping the trenches and that dry, day and night. We lived in a caravan all the while I was on that.'

Joe now lives firmly 'on the land' in a small house not far from the Birmingham canals where he had first gone day boating. He spends most of his time in a shed round the back where the floor is occupied by huge coils of new rope and bundles of heavy lines, more suitable for ships, and fenders hang from the roof trusses. There is usually an unfinished fender on the bench, often as part of an order for one of the many pleasure boat hire companies.

When not quietly at work in his shed, Joe will be driving around the boatyards delivering orders. For relaxation he is usually found where pleasure boats have gathered for a rally, chatting to the new users of the canals, sometimes gently showing newcomers how to keep their craft in good trim with all the equipment in the right places, or boasting with other old hands of the biggest load or fastest run from now-vanished trading days on the canals.

(Left) Joe supervises the arrival of pleasure boats in Thames Locks at Brentford on a round London cruise on 18 August 1986 from the coping of the lock wall outside his control cabin, to the right. Tree growth disguises the fact that blocks of flats have been built alongside Brentford Dock to the left, and Joe's house is now visible at the extreme edge of the picture (John Butcher)

DREDGINGS

FORTH AND CLYDE CANAL

NAVIGATION.

NOTICE.

That Part of the NAVIGATION between the MONKLAND CANAL BASIN and PORT-DUNDAS, commonly called the Cut of Junction, will be STOPPED, *on the Evening of Saturday the 3d of September,* for the purpose of Enlarging the said Cut and Completing the Works therewith connected, and will remain Shut for about Six Weeks.

☞ This Stoppage does not interfere with any part of the Navigation from Port-Dundas Eastward or Westward, and the Swift Passenger Boats will continue Running as usual.

CANAL HOUSE,
Glasgow, 12th August, 1842.

(Guthrie Hutton collection)

LIGHTS AND SIGNALS FOR DREDGERS, CRAFT ENGAGED ON WORKS AND DIVING OPERATIONS, AND FOR WORKS ON BANKS

Users of the Waterway are reminded that under the navigational Bye-laws the master of any vessel approaching or being near any place where dredging, piling, diving or any other works of repair, maintenance or construction of the canal are in progress shall navigate his vessel at such speed and in such manner as shall not imperil the safety of any person or cause any damage or injury to any of the plant or equipment employed in such work or to any of such works or to the canal.

In order to assist users BRITISH WATERWAYS have decided to introduce the code of signals set out below, which must be observed by all vessels navigating the waterways.

(a) Dredging

Dredging craft working or moored ready for working in the navigable channel will carry:

(i) By day

A metal square 18 inches by 18 inches of cruciform construction and painted red will be displayed from the yard arm on that side of the dredger on which craft may not pass.

(ii) By night and during periods of low visibility

A red light will be displayed from the yard arm on that side of the dredger on which craft may not pass. A white light will be displayed from the yard arm on that side of the dredger on which craft may pass.

By far the easiest way to ensure complete dredging of a waterway to remove the water and so get a clear view of the task ahead. This clear out of the Grand Junction Canal's Buckingham Branch near Deanshanger was undertaken in about 1902 and the method of shovelling the mud up the banks by putting it on to ever higher bends would certainly have been known to the canal's builders. (BW Archives, Gloucester)

"The owner or person in charge of any Boat Barge, or other Vessel, navigated, with the Rudder foremost, upon the said Canal or any collateral Cut therefrom, shall forfeit and pay, for the first offence, the sum of Twenty Shillings, and for every subsequent offence the sum of Forty Shillings."

Grand Junction Canal Byelaws – December 1824

"In regard to the use of the company's ferry boats: ... in rowing ferry boats passengers shall sit down and keep quiet."

Manchester Ship Canal Company General Bye Laws – 1963

A Grafton dredger working at Gayton Junction with the Grand Juntion Canal's Northampton Branch entrance in the background. (BW Archives, Gloucester)

LANCASTER

CANAL NAVIGATION.

REGULATIONS

TO BE

OBSERVED BY BOATMEN,

Passing the Locks at Tewitfield.

All Boats to be provided with strong Check Lines, and to be well checked on entering a Lock, and not to strike either the Gates or the Forebay.

The Gates to be put quite back into the Recesses before a Boat enters a Lock. The Rudder to be fastened over to one side, and the gates to be put quite back into the Recesses before the Boat is allowed to pass out of the Lock. The upper Gates to be shut before a Clow is opened.

CLARK, PRINTER, GAZETTE OFFICE, LANCASTER.

"Any person employed in navigating any Boat, Barge, or other Vessel, on the said Canal or any collateral Cut therefrom, who shall permit any dog belonging to him to go loose on the towpath thereof, or on the adjoining land, shall forfeit and pay, for the first offence, the sum of Five Shillings."

Grand Junction Canal Byelaws – December 1824

SHROPSHIRE UNION RAILWAY AND CANAL COMPANY

NOTICE

THIS BRIDGE IS INSUFFICIENT TO CARRY WEIGHTS BEYOND THE ORDINARY TRAFFIC OF THE DISTRICT BY ORDER

(Euan Corrie)

TEN POUNDS

REWARD.

WHEREAS,

Three Men did, on Sunday, 2nd November, instant, violently

Beat and otherwise Maltreat

(so as to endanger his Life,)

One of the LOCK-KEEPERS, belonging to the REGENT'S CANAL, at JOHNSON's LOCK,

STEPNEY.

This is to give Notice that THE ABOVE REWARD will be paid to any Person who may give such Information as may lead to the Apprehension and Conviction of either of the Offenders, by Application to Mr. HANLEY, Constable, 112, White Cross Street, St. Luke's.

Nov. 12th 1823. BRISCOE, Printer, 207, White Cross Street.

(BW Archives, Gloucester)

FLOWER & EVERETT

(Successors to Farnham Flower and Wm. Flower, Bow, London),

Contractors to H. M. Admiralty, War Office, and London Corporations for

DREDGING

ALL KINDS OF MATERIAL FROM

DOCKS, HARBOURS, AND CANALS

WITH

STEAM BUCKET DREDGERS,

BAG and SPOON BARGES and GRAB DREDGERS,

making from 6 feet to 40 feet depth of water.

69, King William Street, London, E.C.

(992 AVENUE),

SHOOTS–

Charlton, Kent (33 Woolwich). Rainham, Essex (8 Rainham).

Purfleet, Essex (Tilbury), and other places.

LONDON WHARVES AND SHOOTS–

Rennies Wharf, 60, Holland Street, Blackfriars (1646 Hop).

Westminster Jetty, 7, Grosvenor Road, S.W. (5272 West).

Fisher's Wharf, Millwall, E (394 East).

BARGES BUILT AND REPAIRED AT MILLWALL.

An advertisement from Bradshaw's Guide.

SAM & GLADYS HORNE

Boating 'til the Last

During World War II the Grand Union Canal Carrying Company was desperately short of crews for its long distance carrying narrowboats. Various outsiders were recruited, including a number of young middle-class women who formed all-female crews, initially under the guidance of instructors. Several of these women, including trainer Kitty Gayford, were profoundly affected by the life of the waterways and have subsequently written accounts of their experiences which have been published elsewhere. To those born and bred on the boats they remained something of a curiosity and are still referred to as the 'trainees'.

When I first met Sam and Gladys Horne at their canalside home in Berkhamsted, Gladys quickly made me aware of Sam's inexperience on the cut after a mere half century: ''Course, he's only a trainee, you know. He didn't come on the boats till he was seventeen. He wasn't born to it.' Thus Sam is condemned never to *really* know how to steer a boat! Sitting in their kitchen with the sound of boat engines and the rattle of lock paddles coming through the window, I set out to discover if Gladys was qualified to appear in these pages since Sam would apparently not be able to tell much of canal life!

'I was born on the boats, in Birnigum [Birmingham], on 13 December 1931. My mum and dad was on the boats and all the families before them, right back, they'd always been boat people. They was working for Fellows Morton & Clayton when I was born. I was born on the butty *Fazeley*, that's still about on the canal. When I was small we had a motor which was a boat built new, at Uxbridge, for my dad, the *Elder*, a wooden boat.

'People working for Fellows Mortons had quite a lot born in Birnigum where they loaded and unloaded. I was born at the first of their wharfs you come to; coming from London, it's called Warwick Wharf, close to the HP sauce factory. We used to carry a lot of HP sauce and the stuff that went to make it.

'I remember as I got a bit older that my mum had a baby at Cosgrove, on the Grand Union Canal. As you come round to New Bradwell from Wolverton, there's a long straight across the valley to Cosgrove Lock. I remember my dad got off at that first bridge and biked ahead and got the midwife on the lockside for when we got there! My mum had the baby while the lock was filling! That was one of me brothers. Then I had a brother and a sister born in Northampton. Another at Kingswood, at the junction where the Stratford Canal goes off just before you go into Birnigum. Me second oldest sister was borned at Wolverhampton and my oldest sister at Leicester. We were born all over the place. The older kids used to have to help.

'We stopped at Cosgrove just that one night for the midwife to come back. I remember that midwife telling my mum, "You can move off tomorrow, you'll be all right because you've got the kids to help you!" She was telling my mother that she went to a gypsy camp and borned a baby. She said to the woman there, you must stop in bed today and I'll come back tonight. Well, she went back that night and this woman was chasing her old man round the van with a frying pan!

'My own dad was Ted Price, but he died and my mum married again, when I was eight,

Sam Horne and his 'steerer' Gladys, during the period when they unofficially operated a pair of Samuel Barlow Coal Co boats together. This now battered photograph was taken at Sutton Stop, officially known as Hawkesbury Junction, at the northern end of the Oxford Canal (BW Archives, Gloucester)

Following the ice-boat: Cairo, Malta *and other Samuel Barlow boats lead a train to assist one another through the thick ice of the Coventry Canal at Griff Lane in the winter of 1947. Several of these craft were on the short-haul power station coal traffic on which the Skinners and Sam Horne, with his 'steerer' Gladys, were working. At least fifteen boats are visible on the original print* (BW Archives, Gloucester)

to Philip Ward. There was no way a woman could work a pair of boats, not with a Bolinder engine. You need a man to start it, you see! Not like when we used to have the Nationals and Petters. There was no press button or winding handle to start. You had to pull that pin out of the flywheel, put you foot on it and then kick it over to start.

'I never did that. I started a Petter once, and I nearly went mad! It was after I'd left home. We was at Braunston and we'd to take an extra boat round to Sutton's Stop [Hawkesbury Junction, near Coventry]. You used to have warm the top of the engine up with a blow lamp before they'd start – well, Jack [Skinner] said to me, "Go and get the lamp on. I'll have a cup of tea and then we'll start it and get going."

'Well, those Petters aren't like a Bolinder; you don't have to lift the floor plate up to get to the pin in the flywheel, you can just swing them over with your hand. So whilst it was warming up I was just stood there playing with the flywheel, swinging it back and forward and singing to myself and she started! Oh, I was going mad, shouting, "She's going, she's going!" I did go mad, hopping about all over. I'd be about sixteen then. Then we had to take that boat round to Sutton's for a bloke working round the Moiry Cut because something had happened to his. [The Ashby Canal is often known as the Moiry or Miry Cut because it was never completed beyond Moira to Ashby de la Zouch.] That was the *Wasp*. I'll never forget it.

'As far as I can tell my mum's maiden name was Payton, Elizabeth Payton. I stuck with them about five years after she was remarried but my stepfather got worse and worse. When he wanted you to wake up to get the locks ready and that he would never say, "Come on" – no, he'd go in the cabin and hit you with a belt or smack you round the face and say "Get up". He got so violent with us, and I can't understand why me mum never done nothing about it. I said I'd had enough, but my oldest sister had went first, then my second oldest sister went. It came on to me worse when they'd gone. He was a sod, he was.

'When he died, ten years or more ago now, my sisters and brothers, they said, "He's died, are you going up to his funeral?" My oldest sister was alive then, living down at the next lock below here, and she said, "If we go it'll only be to kick him down the hole!"

'So I left home a bit after my mum married again and went to work with Jack and Rose Skinner. There was just them and me grown up, but they had two children. Sam had worked with them before. He was bred and borned on a farm. He had a job for a little while, and then he decided to go onto the canal and he went with them. They learned you how to boat, didn't they?' Gladys glanced over at Sam.

'Yes, that was in that big frost – what was it?....1947. My family lived on a farm at Kidlington, near Thrupp, a little farm just across the field from the cut, and of course we used to see the boats coming down there. I got talking to one or two of them and to one of the girls, you know. That's how I got interested in the boats. I used to go with the gas boats [which collected the tar or waste gas water to take up to Birmingham] to Banbury and then come back home. Then Jack come along one day and asked me if I'd like to go with him. He had the Barlows then. [The Samuel Barlow Coal Co of Birmingham ran a fleet of boats and a boatyard at Braunston which delivered fuel as far as Oxford and London.] So when I left school I went with Jack until I was just over army age. If I'd have stopped with him I'd have never went in the army, but I didn't, and as soon as I got back home of course they got me for the National Service.

'When I came back home I couldn't settle and I went Barlowing again. I had a pair of my own with a young chap from Leicester. He didn't know nothing, a trainee. We worked up and down the Moiry Cut then for a long while together. He left in the finish. Then I went and worked with Jack Skinner, the two pairs of boats together, and Gladys steered the butty for me for a while.'

'If it had been now I'd have went and lived with Sam. But you couldn't do that then! That wasn't allowed on boats. No, you'd got to be married and that was it. It was an instant dismissal otherwise! I was just steering the butty for him. That's how it was put into the bosses, "steering". We was just on short journeys, down the Moiry Cut to the Longford Light Works [Hawkesbury Power Station, on the outskirts of Coventry].'

Gladys recalls that the Skinners had left Barlow's by the time she went to work with them. 'Jack and Rose had British Waterways boats when I went to them. Rose was born and bred on the boats, they used to have two-horse boats on the Oxford Cut. But for some reason after she had the kids she hated the boats and she kept harping him and harping him to go and live at Banbury in a house which he didn't like. Well, I thought I'd go with them and I think I was there about six months, which is when I met Sam. As soon as he got to know they was at Banbury he came up to see 'em and that's where we met.

Gladys uses the mast line to slow the progress of her Willow Wren butty Wagtail *as it enters Baddesley Lock on the Atherstone flight of the Coventry Canal. Motor boat* Warbler *waits behind; it was usually quicker to send the butty down a flight of locks where it has to be bowhauled first with the motor steerer refilling the locks for the second boat. Sam and Gladys were on their way to load coal either at Baddesley Colliery basin just below this lock or Pooley Hall a few miles and five locks further on* (Sam Horne)

'Jack, he tried his hardest to settle down there, he went to work in a brewery. But he just couldn't settle away from the water. So we decided to go back on the boats and he went and had another pair of Barlows again. Sam had his own pair of Barlows, too, and during the time that happened the Willer Wren's [Willow Wren Canal Carrying Co] started up and we were the first captains for them.'

Sam: 'One day, whilst Gladys was working with me as "steerer", the Whitlocks was tied up at Heyford Bridge. They must have just stopped a moment for something because the boats were only tied up by the mast line, which is only thin, you know. Well, his string broke and he said we was going too hard. Well, we couldn't have been going that hard because I was right up behind Jack and so I had to pull out of gear so as not to catch his butty. I happened to run into Bill Whitlock in Barlow's Yard just after and he was carrying on about this so I threatened him. Because it was on the premises, like, I was sacked for that.'

Gladys: 'A bit before that Barlow's had given Sam a roll of lino for the motor's cabin, a thick green lino. So when they told him he'd got to get out of the boats, he rolled the lino up, it was thick stuff, and opened the office door and threw it in.'

Sam: 'I said, "You'd better have that back then." And it sprung open and everything flew everywhere, papers all over the floor, everything off the desk! Then the Willow Wren job came up and we had the *Warbler* and *Wagtail*.'

Gladys: 'There was a painter at Braunston that was very thick with Jack Skinner and knew Morton, who was Willow Wren's boss. Well, we was round the Blisworth Pound in a frost, Linford it was, and he knew that Sam had had the sack for hitting old Bill, and he come over and seen him and told us that there was this new firm starting up, and give Sam the address. He wrote off and we got the job straightaway.'

Sam: 'We got married to go to that, at Oxford, and Leslie Morton came over and picked us up.'

Gladys still remembers the optimism of the start of her new life on new boats with a new carrying company: 'Ooh, yes. We'd got a boat at Rickmansworth, because the dock there was going then, Walker's. And the motor, *Warbler*, was at the dock at Leighton Buzzard. Just before we got to Leighton, they'd varnished all the cabin out in the motor. We stuck everywhere! Well, we were lucky that there was another pair of Barlows laid there because her husband wasn't very well. We knew them quite well and she said, "Come and sleep on our motor tonight. You can't lay on there!"

Sam recalls that not all was right with the world: 'Next morning, when we come to start the engine, we found the big ends had gone. Nobody had told Morton – they'd brought it down and just tied it up. Leslie Morton had to come over again. He came from Paddington, they had a caravan in the basin there as an office when they first started. He had to come over and fetch us, and some of our things, and take us to the butty boat at Walker's. But, you know, we had a lovely welcome there. They'd even got a fire in it for us, the dock people.

Warbler *and* Wagtail *awaiting orders to load from the coalfield traffic office at Sutton Stop near Coventry. Sutton Stop, where the Coventry and Oxford canals join, is so-called after a family who kept the office where the boats stopped to pay their tolls there for several generations* (Sam and Gladys Horne)

Gladys poses on the running planks over Wagtail's *coal-filled hold as she is towed along the Oxford Canal in 1954 by* Warbler *which is visible in the background* (Sam and Gladys Horne collection)

'Then me and John Hemylrick, who had that *Peacock*, we had to come back to Leighton and tow *Warbler* back down to Uxbridge. They took the National out and put a Bolinder in it, and we laid there whilst they done it. Len Hough, the fitter at Uxbridge, he was a good bloke for them engines; he took it out of one of the old Fellows Mortons and put it in *Warbler*.

'Then we went down to Limehouse for our first load. That butty had been empty so long it had all dried out, and the seams between the planks open up when they're like that, you know. So when we loaded, the water poured in everywhere! It was a good job there was a lot of boat people there. They helped us pumping and chucking ashes round it.'

The caulking between the planks of a wooden boat dries and the planks themselves shrink with exposure to wind and sun if they are not regularly soaked by immersion in the canal when the boat is deep laden. A well placed shovelful of ashes or sawdust will often be drawn into the worst of the cracks by the water movement and this helps to form a seal until the timbers swell again. But, as Sam described, this was an anxious time in the deep water of the Regent's Canal's ship dock.

'You see, when you had a load off a ship like that, the last boats loaded had to stop and get the customs clearance papers for all the lot. Sometimes you could be stopped there three or four weeks or more. You could never tell how long it would be. Well, we should have stopped, but old Sam Beechy, he said, "You get out of this dock. If you go down here you'll be out of sight! I'll stop in your place." Well, that was good of him because he didn't know how long he'd have to wait and not be earning any money.

'Well, once we'd got out into the canal, it hardly leaked a drop. You see once the planks got soaking up the water they swelled up and the gaps closed and then it was in canal water which is full of mud instead of clean so that went in any cracks and helped to seal it up.'

Gladys remembered being an onlooker on a similar occasion: 'There was one chap, Charlie Atkins – that's old chocolate Charlie's son – he used to like those old wooden boats. Well, when he was on British Waterways he went mad for one that was lying empty. But it hadn't had a load in it for ages and we was at Longford, by Coventry, loading coal, and they all betted him that he'd have to call the men out to it from the dock at Hillmorton. He said, "I bet you I don't", and they all said, "We bet you you do!" Well, we knew what Charlie was like. He sat in the deck locker at the fore end because he knew that's where she'd leak first, they always do. You could see through between those planks! He had three packs of his missus' sanitary towels with him, and as soon as the water started to come through he was furiously hammering them into the cracks!

'Those wooden boats, you know they'll tighten up with keeping the planks wet. I remember we was going down to Talbot's Lock one time when we had that *Kingfisher*. That was an

Sam steers Warbler *out of Black Jack's Lock, near Harefield on the Grand Union Canal, while Gladys shares the butty with her brother Jake who had been riding ahead on the bicycle preparing locks until meeting a pair coming uphill which had left the next few ready for the Hornes' boats. They were loaded with cocoa waste which went from Cadbury's, at Bourneville, to the Thames for export* (Sam and Gladys Horne collection)

old Fellows Morton, but Willow Wren used to name all their boats after birds. We had Jack Skinner's dad along with us. He used to look after his boats like they were glass. Sam went in the lock so fast, and I jumped off to stop the butty with the checking strap and it broke! Oh it did hit the gate, bang! and I thought, now I'm for it for knocking boats about. But he didn't moan, he just said, "That does a wooden butty good, it tightens up the planks!" They do say that would tighten up the joints between the planks. I didn't much care about that, it broke a lot of my pots, that did!'

Gladys recalled that whilst working for Willow Wren, the first of their family put in an appearance.

'I had my first son, Barry, born on the boat at Tusses Bridge, just as you get to Sutton Stop, near Coventry. 1955 that was. The midwife still came out to you in them days. The second one, Roy, I had in the hospital at Bull's Bridge [the former Grand Union Canal Carrying Co fleet depot near Southall which had been operated by British Waterways since nationalisation at the beginning of 1948] because British Waterways used to have five beds to be kept for boat women to have their babies. You used to have to register when you was pregnant so that they could have the bed ready for you at the right time. They used to let you tie up for the last three months by those days. See, with Fellows Morton's, like my mother, they used to get pregnant and they used to carry on and carry on until it was time to have it. In them days you could guarantee there would be a midwife to come out more or less

Gladys and Barry Horne pose with their British Waterways' butty Ayr *at Sutton Stop before carrying another coal cargo southwards* (Sam Horne)

wherever you were. Then they used to have the baby and off the next day. Now look at it these days. Tablets and injections and I don't know what! The kids were better in them days than what they are now. Stronger.

'When I was expecting my oldest one I used to carry on as normal, jumping down off the lockside onto the cabin top of the boats. We were tied up for about six weeks with him. Leslie Morton, our boss then, used to be called "Whip and Windlass" because he wouldn't let you stop too long! I was lucky to have a little bit longer off because it was in the winter and we got froze up so we couldn't move. I had my third one, Robert, here, after we moved into the house.

'Sam later asked Mr Wood, at Bull's Bridge, if we could have a pair of Waterways [British Waterways' boats]. I always wanted to get back down there because that's where my friends was. I didn't like the Barlows because they didn't get down to Bull's Bridge a lot; they only used to go to the jam factory and empty and go straight back up. You never got a night at Bull's Bridge.'

Despite Gladys' enthusiasm: 'That didn't start too well because the first run we had was with a little Woolwich motor, *Virgo*, up to Rose's at Boxmoor with lime juice, and when we got there that run a big end out. That was a National and I used to like them better than Bolinders. But there was no worries with Waterways because all you'd to do was get on the phone and their van could come anywhere.'

Sam found life changed in the bigger carrying fleet, with a greater variety of trips. 'At Bull's Bridge you wouldn't get any choice in the orders except, perhaps, the first skipper that arrived. You had a ticket given you for what you'd to load and where. If there was a steel ship, then they was all the same and there was such a scratch. They'd all come running along the lay-by from the office to try and get going the first. Lime juice wouldn't necessarily be a very good order because it was low pay. And then sometimes you had to go on up to the coalfields for coal so you wouldn't get back for another quick order. Nobody would want that. Also there used to be maize to Fenny [Stratford] to the brewery which was very low pay.' Gladys remembered that 'There used to be a buffer depot up here at the Cowroast, and maize to there was low pay. My dad would never have a short journey if he could help it. Birmingham was always the best paid. People used to break their necks to get that. Wheat at Whitworth's mill at Wellingborough wasn't too bad.'

A young Barry Horne on the wharf at Brentford; with little space for toys on the boats a wheat grab might come in handy (Gladys Horne)

Sam recalled that there was also extra work required: 'Only a lot of work cleaning up your boat afterwards. You had to turn all your floors up after emptying to try to sweep it all out. You had cloths like sacking under the wheat to keep it off the floors and sides of the boats, but it still got between and under the floors. When you got to the mill and they started to empty it, it used to stink – like stale wine – as you got down into the load. Then you used to have to try and sweep it all out. But even so after a couple of days it would start sprouting everywhere. If you got just a little bit of moisture in the boat it would sprout green shoots two or three inches long in a couple of days. We used to hate that.'

Gladys: 'We would never come back to Bull's Bridge from that far away, we used to go for coal then, except when the coalfields had their regular ten days' holiday at the pits. At one time of day you could stop up there for ten days to wait for a load, but later on they made you come back down to Bull's Bridge. They wouldn't pay you to stop up there. Then just before the Waterways finished they come up with the idea that the quicker you done your trip the more you got.'

Sam: 'We done a quick load back from Birmingham one time. It was just 19 ton of dog spikes for the railway – they were going on a ship abroad somewhere. Anyway, most times when you got a back load like that at Birmingham it was urgent to catch the ship, you see. So we worked day and night to get it back, but then when we got it there they put it in the warehouse, didn't they! They said "Well, nobody told you to go mad, rushing down with it!" I'd had me own back anyway, because at Tyseley they said, "There's only 19 ton, so you can leave the butty here and work single motor." Well, we lived mostly on the butty, you see, so I said, "I ain't leaving that here – it won't make that much more work." He said, "Oh well, please yourself." The loaders at the works put a bit in each boat. So then we got paid for 40 ton. That was the minimum for carrying in two boats; it was meant to compensate if you got a very lightweight cargo that took up all the space. If we'd have had it all on the one boat we'd only have got paid for the 19 ton!'

Gladys: 'I remember going for that because Sam had never been along there, Black

Awaiting orders at Sutton Stop, time was easily filled with domestic chores – Gladys busy aboard Ayr *in the late 1950s* (The Boat Museum)

Country way, so he said, "You've been there with your dad, haven't you? Tell me when we get to it." Well, I'd been, but only when I was young, about ten, and then it was all a new galvanised building and lovely. Well, I looked and I thought, "It's got to be here somewhere"; but I never said anything to him, I just let him keep going. There was this rusty old shed all hanging down in the canal, and I thought "This looks a bit like it". So I said to Sam, "I think that's it, back there." "Nah," he says and kept going; but it was! By that time he was well gone by it! There's an awful lot of turns and arms in Birmingham there, and I had only been about those parts when I was small.'

Sam: 'One time I tried to go through a bridge that had no water in it. That was at Cannock Chase, wasn't it? Just before you got to the loading basin at Anglesey. There was a turn to the left and a side bridge on the right of the canal, and a lock through it. Well, this lock and the canal beyond had been shut up years ago. It was dark and you couldn't see where you was going, so I thought I had to go straight in there and of course there was no water. Well, we stopped a bit quick!'

Gladys: 'We'd been sitting in the cabin when he went on in there, and we wondered what the heck he'd done. We had a struggle to get the motor out of the mud.

There could be waits for loading orders at the southern end of the Grand Union too. Here Gladys stands on Aynho's counter deck whilst tied stern on to the wall with numerous other boats in the lay-by at Bull's Bridge depot. Here orders for loading in the London Docks and at Brentford were issued (Sam Horne)

'When we got into the basin there for loading they poked the boats about just like they did the joey boats there. They'd get the point of a shaft and poke it in your cabin side to move the boats about when they wanted them for loading.

'Dickinson's used to pay for a full load of coal but I don't think they ever got one. You should have seen our load in 1963 when we was frozen in all that time – there was a blooming great hole in the starn end. Thirteen weeks we was frozen up. It was weighed in and they gave us a ticket but it was never weighed out at the other end. Sam stopped me burning coal from the butty cargo in the end. British Waterways took all the boatmen out hedge cutting and he started to bring bags of wood back. Otherwise there'd have been nothing left!

'At Bull's Bridge you'd all be laying there in the lay-by, in a row. There might be thirty boats there. The mums all used to be standing in the door holes chatting while they did the washing and cleaning. There was a loudspeaker there and I remember the chap in the office saying, "Calling all steerers, boat numbers so and so"!'

Sam would be looking after the engine or the boats' equipment. Gladys recalls: 'Every night at about four o'clock they used to call you up for your orders. You listened for your number. If it came up, the first thing my mum used to do – and I must admit I used to do it too, later – was to get all the water cans and get them all filled up. Because Sam'd come back and he'd start straightaway, tonight, and not wait for morning. A lot of them would come out of the lay-by and go down to the next bridge, to the pub, the Grand Junction, instead of stopping in the lay-by. What they used to come out for, you see, was so that they didn't wake anybody on the other boats by setting off early in the morning.'

Sam is more concerned with the boating: 'You could be so tight in the lay-by in that line that you'd got a job to get out sometimes. We nearly always used to go down to Brentford and leave the beer. You could go steady down the locks without having all the others on top of you breathing down your neck, see. That was better with being two-handed.'

Gladys recalls: 'Those locks wasn't too bad because there used to be a lock keeper to help you at every lock. But two-handed at the Northampton Arm with a pair of loaded boats, and two or three pair behind you with three crew on each, it was hell down there, trying to keep ahead of them. I used to have to bowhaul our butty boat by myself, like a horse! I had nobody to steer it while I was doing that, so sometimes it would get stemmed up on the bank. I had nobody old enough to steer. Then you'd got them behind you, flushing all their water down, and that could fill up your cabin if you weren't careful.

'I could stop that if I was crafty. You see, they could get their boat into the lock behind, above mine, before I'd got my butty into the next lock because there was more of them and so they'd got a steerer. They they'd draw the paddles up, and the water would come over the top gate at my lock and might get in my cabin. So what I used to do was wait and not empty the lock. Then when their lock was empty and all the water had gone, I'd wind my paddles up and get down, and they'd just have to wait.

'I did that one particular time on one of my step-uncles, and when we got to Wellingborough his missus was going to do this to me and that to me for keeping them waiting. Well, we weren't unloaded when they got down to Wellingborough Mill with the grain. Down there there used to be a little raft because the mill was built straight down into the water. So you tied up against this little raft and the bloke from the mill got down onto it to look after the elevator in your boats. Well, she came running on there to give me a good hiding, but I went and jumped onto the raft – and she couldn't run back up that ladder fast enough! She didn't think I'd get off the boats to her!'

I wondered why Sam and Gladys hadn't thought of taking on a mate to ease the

Barry in the butty cabin doorway and Roy out in the hatches learning to write numbers by looking at the large numerals that were clearly painted on the locks of the river Nene. Gladys, here looking after the motor boat in the background, recalls that 'when they were young the children used to be tied. You know round that coaming in the hatches in the butty they made me a rail at Bull's Bridge and they threaded a steel ring onto it and fastened the rail to the woodwork. Well, then you used to be able to buy a harness for the kids and you just clipped that to the ring and they could walk about but they couldn't climb to get over the side' (Sam Horne)

workload and speed up their trips, but naturally they had. Gladys well remembered the days when life was easier for the womenfolk.

'The like of us, there was fifteen of us kids, they wasn't all old enough to work; but I was ten when I was getting the locks ready and that. Fellows & Morton's used to have plenty of mates so we always used to have a mate along. We would never have gone two-handed with a pair of boats like Sam and I did. One of my sisters was nineteen and the other was eighteen so they used to help a good bit, but you never used to see a Fellows & Morton's with just two people on. If they hadn't got nobody of their own they used to pay a bloke to come with them, a mate. We did when we was Willer Wrenning, we used to have one of my brothers with us, especially when we had the first child. But you used to have to pay 'em so that made you short of money, then.

'If we had a mate on and did a load both ways in the late fifties – say we brought coal down and then went to Brentford and loaded to Birmingham – he'd get £3; but if we took a load of coal down to Croxley and had to go back empty with nothing, they'd get thirty shilling. When I worked with the Skinners they used to give me £3 whatever we did. So I was all right with them and I used to save a lot of money. You used to get treats off them, as well – like they took you to the pictures, and if you went in the pub they'd buy you drinks. Every young girl that was a mate on the boats, they was envious of me because I always had money when they hadn't because I'd such a good skipper.'

Gladys continues: 'I think that before the war Fellows Morton's was on their last legs. But during the war it was all nationalised, well, under the government, and there was so much stuff to move, it made them. There wasn't one boat stopped in the war, they was always on the go. We took it all over the place. After the war a lot of places kept their work on the canals, like Tate & Lyle's and all them, they proved it could be done on the canal so things was better for a while after the war. That was until the M1 was built – as soon as that was built, places like Croxley [John Dickinson's paper mills] they didn't want the boats, they wanted the lorries. I think that's what did it. You see, there could be a string of boats waiting there at Croxley, with a pair emptying, and if a lorry came in they'd just leave you and go off and empty the lorry. The motorways did it.'

Sam, too, was frustrated by the way boats were kept waiting: 'All they saw the boats as were store warehouses. Those lorries could do about two trips a day. We used to be two-and-a-half days from Suttons to Croxley. See, I had this argument once with one of those lorry drivers. I said, "I've been waiting here to be emptied fourteen days. Now *you* get in that queue then we'll see who's the quickest in terms of delivering the bulk!" He shut his mouth and never said no more. You see we brought 52 or 53 tons each trip.

'I went down there a bit before I retired, taking a boat to Bull's Bridge – well, when I went round the turn to Croxley there was nothing there, just a grass hill! I said, "Where's the factory?" There's just nothing left.'

'It's the roads that's done it,' affirmed Gladys.

'Then at the finish, about 1963, Gladys and I got called up to go carrying the piles from Marsworth. Me and Sam Brooks, that was. They more or less sold all the other boats up and put everybody off. I didn't want to take the job on. I said to the boss, "There's older captains here than me, it's not fair." He said, "That doesn't matter, we can trust you when we wouldn't trust some of them. We know that you'll go and do your job, and not be tying up here, there and everywhere for half a day or a day."

The prolonged freeze at the beginning of 1963 confirmed the British Waterways Board's decision to withdraw the nationalised narrowboat carrying fleet. Here Sam Brooks stands on the Oxford Canal towpath at Sutton Stop chatting to Gladys, aboard Aynho. *Sam's boats lie across the canal where they froze in with several other pairs beyond* (Sam Horne)

Gladys was pleased to get the pile-carrying job: 'They wanted us and Sam Brooks for piles and Ernie Humphries, Tom Humphries and Fred Powell because they kept the contract on for lime juice to Rose's at Boxmoor. I didn't want to do the lime juice. You could always tell when you'd got that on in the summer because you'd got a cloud of wasps following you everywhere!'

Sam: 'We was mostly carrying them piles out from Marsworth, but sometimes, if they had none to go out, we had to go out and work on the length, on maintenance.'

Gladys: 'That was OK, because if they had none to go out for a while Sam went working on the length and the headmaster would let our kids go in the village school there. My first two boys went there, and then when we'd got a load and we was ready for going away, we'd go in and tell him and he would give the kids enough to do to keep them going till we got back. So the two boys could read and write before I could.

'We didn't go round on the Lee at all before we started on the piles. Sam was ever so scared!'

'No, I didn't want to go round on that big wide river. I was scared stiff!'

From 1963–66 the Hornes were based at Marsworth maintenance yard from which concrete piles were despatched to bank repair sites on several of the southern waterways. Barry (left) and Roy spent much time with Sam Brooks' children (whose parents also boated piles away from the yard) playing along the towpath at the head of the branch canal to Aylesbury (Gladys Horne)

'It was Charlie, the store keeper at Bull's Bridge depot, as persuaded Sam to go on the Lee. He'd been before. He said, "You come down to the depot and we'll fix you up with a horn and whatever else you want. You'll be all right round there." This was the first place he got frightened, because there's a huge turn there, at Lee Bridge, it's a bad bridge. That's as soon as you got on the river, just after you turn out of the Ducketts Cut, by Old Ford Lock. There's a very low railway bridge there, and if the water's high you go round that turn and by the time you realise you can't get under that bridge it's too late! You used to meet those big lighters coming with a tug, as well; they never used to steer them when they were empty. The last one used to trail all along the bank.'

Sam: 'Then, the agreement was that if a house came empty I could have it. Well, this one came empty and I applied for it and they let me have it. Then there began to get less work for carrying the pilings, so towards the end there was really only just enough for one pair of boats. We come in this house in 1966 after three years on the pilings. That was with the same boats all through, *Aynho* and *Ayr*.'

In an attempt to reduce the amount of unproductive waiting time they paid boatmen for, BW employed a number (including the two Sams) cutting overhanging trees along the Oxford Canal, which was easily carried out from the ice. Sam Horne photographed George Wain, Sam Brooks, Bert Wallington, Ronnie Hough and Les Lapworth standing on the canal near Hillmorton (Sam Horne)

Sam was thereafter employed on general maintenance work, involving little actual boating. The in-house manufacture of concrete pilings was phased out by British Waterways in favour of the use of galvanised steel trench sheeting for bank protection. Sam spent over 25 years looking after the banks and towpaths, in between assisting at stoppages for lock gate replacement and other work in the area supervised from the Marsworth maintenance yard. He made the headlines in British Waterways' house journals, with three successes in the lock and bridge competition for keeping his house frontage and lockside immaculate.

'I had three cups for the lock and bridge competition. I wasn't really no gardener, the only experience I'd had was with the farm when I was young.'

In 1970 the last long regular distance trading narrowboats passed through his lock *en route* to Croxley Mills and the Kearly & Tonge jam factory at Southall. Then for over twenty more years Sam presided over the passage of pleasure craft.

Gladys: 'Our son, Roy, died in the February, and then British Waterways put Sam off work in the April; two years early, that was.

'That was when I was having my left hip done, before I'd even had any trouble with the right one at all. It really annoyed me, that, because there was no way anybody knew whether I'd work again. I hadn't had any trouble with my right hip then. It broke my heart that did really, because there was still plenty of jobs I could have done full time, even if I wasn't really allowed to lift. After $35^{1}/_{2}$ years that was, you know.'

Gladys remains unsure of the advantages of life in a town-centre house with all its conveniences: 'We haven't really got any good friends in Berkhamsted except on the boatyard just up here. We still miss that after the boats, because when you were on them it didn't

(Above) A small mobile crane and stacks of new concrete piles form the background to this photo of Gladys and Roy encouraging their dog to pose for the camera (Sam Horne)
(Below) A favourite game at Marsworth was always Cowboys with occasional ambushes from the deck of motorboat Aynho (Gladys Horne)

matter where you were, you knew you'd always got friends nearby. You never used to go a day without speaking to somebody. Round here, people just don't seem to want to be friendly.

'I'm proud of being a boat person, I am. But it was difficult when we first come on the land, with not having been to school and all. But since then I've been to night school. When you was all on the boats you were nearly all of you the same so you never used to take no notice. The lock keepers used to write letters or anything for you. You see when I first met Sam he used to write letters to me and send them to the toll offices and when I got one I used to open it and the toll keeper would read it to me. Then if there was any answers they would write a letter back. They always used to do that, the lock keepers or toll keepers did.'

Sam received many such letters written for Gladys. She recalls: 'The one at Cut End [Autherley Junction, where the Shropshire Union joined the Staffordshire & Worcestershire Canal] was the best one at that, Sam Lomas. And him that was at the top of the Marsworth Locks never used to be too bad. But the letters Sam used to send to me used to be like a writing pad. So I used to say to the lock keeper, "Just tell me the interesting bits and skip the rest!" But, you see, when I did come into the house here I found it difficult not being able to read and write because of mixing with other people. When Robert was five I took him down the infant school and the headmaster said, "You'll have to fill this form in," I said, "Oh, I can't do that, I can't read and write." He said "Would you like to?" I said, "Yes, I would!" So he got me in with his colleague.

'I wasn't sure about it at all, because I didn't want to be the only one who couldn't read and write. But when I saw her, she had quite a lot to teach, all adults. She said, "It's better with you, because we can start from scratch; a lot of these have been to school but have learned nothing of it." She said, "Let me take you into the Dacorum College at Hemel Hempsted. We'll get a coachload up and go, and you'll see how many people can't read or write." I was amazed at all those people who couldn't read and write. I got in with a bloke who used to live just up here and he was with the post office putting telephone poles in the ground. He and I used to sit together and help each other. If he didn't know how to spell something he'd ask

me, and if I didn't he'd help me out! I got through pretty good but he didn't, he didn't make it.'

Sam: 'Now she does all the writing, I do detest doing it now, I don't write any letters any more.'

'No, now Sam's retired and got all the time in the world, he doesn't do it!'

Looking back over the years Gladys is in no doubt as to which way of life she prefers: 'You never used to get a lot of money on the boats, but I reckon it was better. You could save, because you'd no rent to pay, and no electricity to pay and you could burn as much coal as you liked! What money you got was yours – you didn't have to pay it out to nobody else like you do now for gas, electric and rates; it was yours, no matter how little it was, you could do what you liked with it. That frightened me, when we come in this house and we had the first bill come. I thought, "Oh, my God, I'm not used to these things. I'll have to start saving for them" – and that's what I've been doing ever since!

'I liked the canal I did, I loved it. I don't regret being on it at all. If I could spend my time back, to like it was, I'd do it all again! But not like it is now, you couldn't get your living on it now, with all the pleasure boats.

'I used to love the boats. When we was teenagers we used to have so much fun on them. When you got to the ends of your trips nearly all your mates was there, and you could go to the pictures or off to a fairground. I used to love all that.'

(Above) On seeing this shot of the Dinkum dredger being used to ease the work of delivering the Hornes' cargo to the latest bank re-enforcement job Sam recalls that, 'You wasn't supposed to unload them with the Dinkum'. Health & Safety regulations only reached canal maintenance work in fairly recent years (Sam Horne)

(Left) A boatman's view of his wife, at the far end of seventy feet of boat towed behind him, attached to up to a further seventy feet of line. Gladys knew what had attracted Sam to take the picture, however: 'I'm sitting on the side because it's a straight pound washing all me legs. We must've been going out somewhere so I was getting ready.' (Sam Horne)

(Overleaf) After leaving the boats and becoming lock keeper at Berkhamsted, Sam still had regular contact with former Willow Wren colleagues. Here he is (in white shirt) assisting the skipper of Ascot *who was towing the broken down motor boat* Stirling *on 27 August 1967* (Alan Faulkner)

BERKHAMSTED LOCKS
WILLOW WREN

BILL DEAN

Canal Inspector

The Shropshire Union Canal is nowadays generally taken to be a through route from the Wolverhampton area to the Mersey at Ellesmere Port, with a branch to Middlewich. However, its history is much more complicated than this suggests, and at the height of its commercial power the Shropshire Union Railways & Canal Company operated a far-reaching network of waterways.

The earliest part of the system was the Chester Canal, from Chester to Nantwich, built under an act of 1772; it was a waterway broad enough to take the local estuarial sailing barges, or flats. The Ellesmere Canal obtained its first act in 1793 and was intended to connect the Mersey, opposite Liverpool at a village which later developed into the town of Ellesmere Port, with the Severn near Shrewsbury. Finance became a major problem, however, and several changes of plan were made. The first section to be completed linked the Chester Canal to the Mersey at Ellesmere Port. The Ellesmere's main line was completed in 1805, from Trevor near Ruabon, to Weston Lullingfields where the money ran out; a branch from Frankton was opened to Newtown in 1821. Meanwhile the Ellesmere Canal eventually extended from Frankton to the Chester Canal just north of Nantwich, in 1806.

The last major link was the Birmingham & Liverpool Junction Canal which opened throughout from Autherley Junction on the Staffordshire & Worcestershire Canal near Wolverhampton, to Nantwich in 1835. This new canal was built much in the style of a railway, running directly across the country with deep cuttings alternating with high embankments. It incorporated one major branch, from Norbury to Newport, which connected with the Shrewsbury Canal and so gave the Shropshire system an outlet to the rest of the inland waterways.

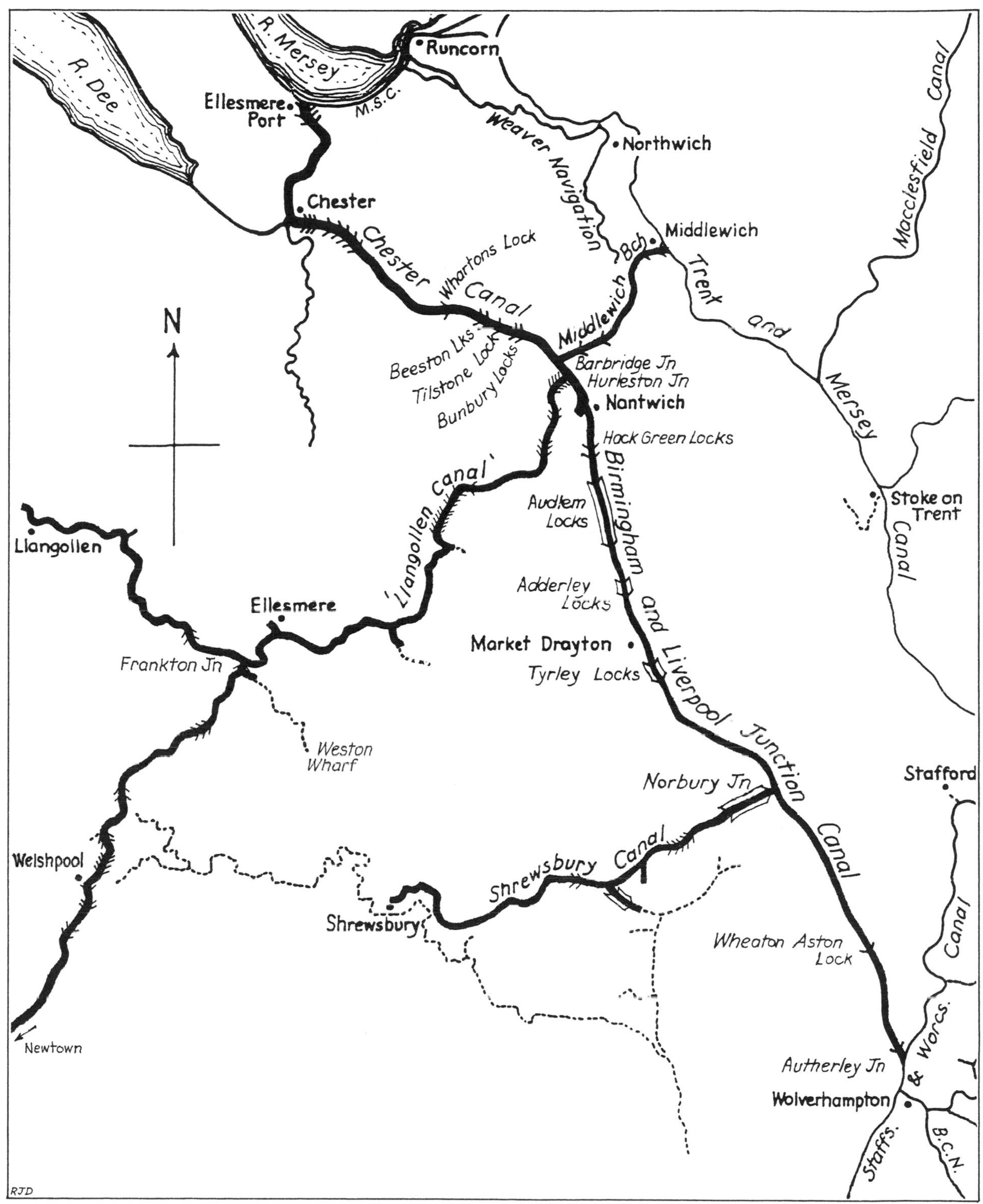

The Shropshire Union system

Unloading the Deans' furniture from an LMS maintenance boat at the Vernons' cottage at the head of the Newport branch of the Shropshire Union Canal at Norbury

In 1846 these canals became part of the Shropshire Union Railways & Canal Company, with the Montgomeryshire canals being acquired by 1850 and the Shropshire canals in the Shrewsbury area being leased to complete a 200-mile system. The newly formed London & North Western Railway in turn leased the Shropshire Union company from 1846. It did, however, work the canals enthusiastically because they penetrated rival railways' territory.

As Jack Strange tells in his chapter, a breach in 1936 below Frankton locks severed the Llanymynech branch, isolating Newtown, and was never repaired. In 1944 the London, Midland & Scottish Railway, successor to the LNWR, was able to obtain parliamentary powers to abandon many of their canals; amongst those closed were the Ellesmere Canal above Hurleston, all the Montgomeryshire section and the Newport branch with the associated Shropshire system. Only the main line from Autherley to Ellesmere Port and its Middlewich branch remained. However, the Hurleston to Llangollen part of the Ellesmere Canal survived since boats were used to maintain it as a water feeder to the main line and a reservoir at Hurleston – and so it, too, entered the pleasure boat era.

Bill and Frances Dean live quietly in retirement in Newport, although numerous memories of their time at Norbury Junction are perpetuated by a painting of the workshops which hangs on their living-room wall. However, our conversation started with recollections of earlier homes.

Bill Dean comes from a family of 'company' men, as those who worked for a canal's owners were generally known. His grandfather was a lengthman on the Weston arm of the

Ellesmere Canal. There was a pit where clay could be dug to seal leaks in the canal bed, a short distance along the arm from Weston Lullingfields, and Bill's grandfather worked there, as and when required. Grandmother's family were coal merchants and had coal brought down to Westonwharf. Bill was born in a canal company house at Weston Lullingfields, at the terminus of the Weston branch of the Ellesmere Canal. Bill's father was later lock keeper at Frankton Locks.

'It was about 1930 or 1931 that he was transferred to Norbury Section. When we first came from Weston we had to lodge with Mr and Mrs Vernon, the blacksmith at Norbury, until our furniture came; it had to come by boat. It was carted up to the top of Frankton locks and loaded up, then it was boated all the way round to Norbury. It would come in one of the company's boats; they had three at that time, all horse boats.

'It was a change there from being at Weston; you'd hear the motor boats chugging by in the night when we were at Norbury. We were to live in the lock house down on the branch to Shrewsbury – we had the middle house, at No 9 Lock, and it was being all painted and done out. There were seventeen locks there, in that first mile and a half. My dad looked after the seventeen as lock keeper, and he also had half a mile on the main line, at the top, as lengthman, from Norbury Junction towards the High Bridge, going into the cutting. There weren't a lot of boats, but there were the Howards who used to go down with coal, and three women, called Beck I think, who used to go down to Long Lane, or somewhere down there, taking coal to the wharves. They had a big black mule pulling the boat.

'The company boats used to go down to Shrewsbury, when they could still get that far, to the wharf at Shrewsbury Station. There were also the Thomas Clayton boats which would go down and fetch tar from Newport Wharf; it came from the old gas works that were down there. They had a cart with a big iron tank on it, and a horse pulled it to the boat, and the boat was filled from it. Then the boat used to come back up our locks again.

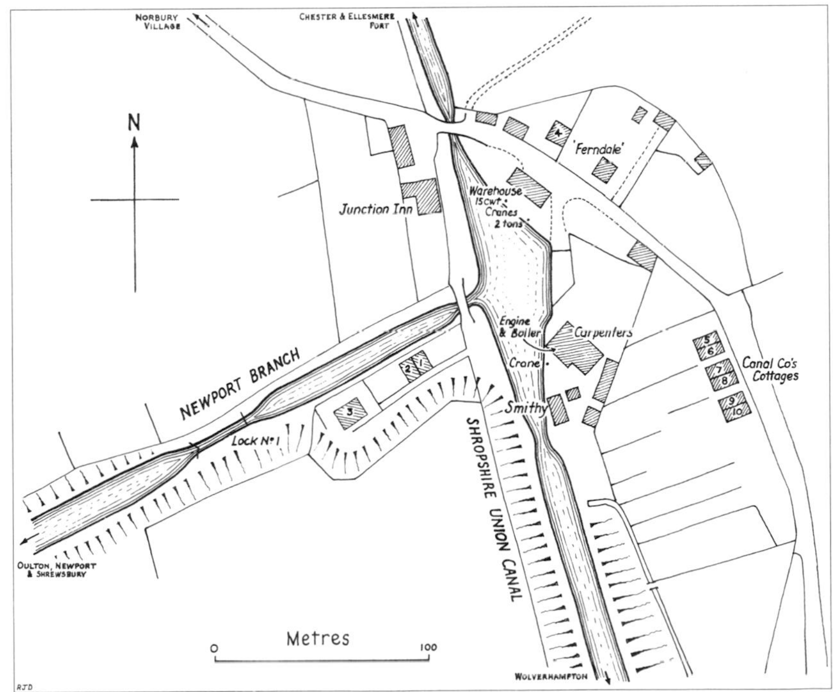

A plan of Norbury Junction and the canal maintenance yard showing where the Deans first lived at the top of the Newport branch, the family's later cottage down the lane from the yard entrance, and Bill and Frances Dean's last canal company house Ferndale; *a complete, self-contained canal community*

Cadbury's milk boats making their daily delivery from local farms to the Knighton factory a few years before Bill Dean first saw them passing through Norbury. Road transport had superseded them by the time he started work (Author's collection)

'Me father was there until some time during the war. I was in the army when they moved up to No 9, in that row of cottages below the yard across from the junction. You see, they are all company houses at Norbury Junction, all except the pub; there's only the one down by the aqueduct which was an estate house.

'When I was little we had a shop in the village, Mrs Morley's sweet shop and a post office. That was in a private house – there was nothing at the junction, only the pub. Eventually the post office was stopped, and the shop went too, so then there was nothing. When we lived down the locks on the Newport branch we would walk into Newport for the May Fair, down the towpath and back. We used to go to Norbury school in the village; it's a private house now. When you were eleven you had to go to Forton so I had to go the other way, down towards Newport and across the fields.

'We had a very big snow in 1933, on a Friday, market day; I'd be eight or nine. I was at school in Norbury, and it started to snow about eleven o'clock in the morning – by dinner time, when the bus was supposed to be coming back from Newport, everywhere was snowed up. There were huge flakes coming down, and all the roads were full up. I came down from school with a girl who lived across the field from me. We came down at Oulton Bridge to go down to the next bridge, and it's a deep cutting down there; my dad's length hut used to be in the cutting, between the sixth and seventh locks. We started down there, but you couldn't get down that cutting: it was all snow. So we had to clamber up the bank and get into the field and go along it to slither down and so make our way home. But when I got home there was nobody there, so I went across the field to where this girl lived. Of course my folks were stranded in Newport, as were a lot more.

'Some had walked up the canal to Norbury Junction. My mother was stranded in the market hall, and she'd got my brother; he was about eighteen months old. Anyway, my dad went down to meet them, and picked 'em up and started up the canal. Then he saw the canalman who lived there: "Come in and have a warm drink." So they went in and my father had a tumbler of elderberry wine. Now, he was a chap as could take some drink, but apparently when they got loaded up with the groceries and the little 'un he'd had it! He couldn't go – he was all over the place! Mother had to struggle along with the shopping and the baby and all, and him straggling along behind!

'When I left school I went onto a farm for sixteen or eighteen months, something like that. I worked for a chappie who used to work Cadbury's milk boats collecting milk. The various farmers used to take it to these wharves, and then it was collected by the milk boat and taken to Cadbury's works at Knighton. But by the time I worked on the farm it was being collected by lorry.

'Then I went to Norbury as an apprentice carpenter; the 15 August 1938, that was. You see, in those days you could only get on the company when a job came up. There was no vacancies when I left school – but when that apprentice job came up they put me in for it.

'When I first started at Norbury, I walked down from Oulton to Newport for my tools and me mother come with me to Burgess's in Newport. They'd given me a list, at Norbury, of what I wanted to start off with. I'd to have all me own tools. So we went there and I had me bag, and saws, tenon saw, wooden mallet, chisels, hammer and lump hammer, wooden plane, jack plane and hand plane. I don't know what else but I do know they were blooming heavy! I put 'em on me back and carried 'em all the way from Newport back up to the lock house. Then I took 'em to work, and the first job then was to make a toolbox to put your tools in. Then when you went out to work, even if you went to Autherley Junction, you'd to take your tools with you on your pushbike: tools on your handlebars and dinner bag on your back.

'There was a steam engine at the yard then; it was behind the big carpenters' workshop and it had a huge great flywheel on it. There was a bloke to look after the boiler house and he kept it all polished. The boiler house was separate from the engine.

'The yard man used to mix the black mortar. They used to mix the ashes and lime, and mix that so there was always a pile of black mortar. You can still see the pointing done in it on some of the locks and bridges.

'There was a drydock in the workshop, you could take a boat right inside. They used to send a company boat round Penkridge way to fetch a boatload of coal at a time, and that was stacked outside the boiler house. The boiler was fired up with that, and the engine drove the big saw, a big circular saw. There was also a small circular saw, and a drill, and a big grindstone. We used to do the holes in fence posts and we had a machine to cut them out. It was all big pulleys and shafting under the floor; there was a pit for the sawdust underneath the floor as well.

'We used to cut those big balance beams at Norbury for the lock gates; they were 21ft, oak, and they were done on the big circular-saw table. It had rails to it and a little trolley. They used to be cut straight until you come to the heel of the gate, and then it was at an angle to throw the beam off, away from the lock side, so that boats didn't catch it as they went into the lock. It was difficult to cut them as they were 21ft long and 12in by 12in oak. I shall always remember when once we dropped some round timber along the valley by the first aqueduct, in G.W. Lloyd's time – he was our boss, the Section Inspector. [His father, G.T. Lloyd, was

A Marshall tractor and thrashing box delayed by a newly felled oak tree across the lane below Norbury embankment

Inspector before him.] There was a big oak tree there, and Mr Lloyd said to the carpenter, "We'll have that oak tree down, Walter, and have a beam out of it." We weren't timberfellers or anything, we'd only got cross-cut saws. We'd got ropes and tackle, but you'd got nowhere to anchor them unless you went right across the canal. Well, we cut the tree, as we thought to drop it up the bank. But it didn't go to plan – it spun on the butt, and went down the bank and into the road! All the full top of an oak tree! And who should come steaming down the road but Geoff Bucklers with a big Marshall tractor and thrashing box, and this tree was filling the road. So we all had to set to with saws and axes and saw it up. Then we had to get it round and get it up planks onto the back of a little Dennis lorry we had at the time to carry it up to the yard. We had a scratch to get rid of that!

'We'd let 'em lie in the yard to season, and then we'd have to adze them along to get a flat side on them and get them up onto the bench. We had a chain block to lift them up onto the trolley, and you had to push the round timber through the saw on that. Anyway, one time we had a terrible accident when a timber fell off and smashed the cast-iron table. Oh, George Lloyd went blue and when he came back! "Negligence!" he shouted, "negligence!" So we had to have a big new table. But eventually it got where you didn't dare do that sort of thing because it was made illegal to cut timber like that, on that sort of a saw, with all the new safety rules. They were tremendous things to cut.

'We had a steambox as well, outside by the edge of the canal, so that we could bend timbers. We used to put the timbers for doing the bridges in that. There used to be convex guard irons fixed round the edge of the towing path as you came into the bridgeholes, and there was a timber fixed to the stonework behind them. There were holes right through the iron, the timber and the copings, and you put a big bolt through and screwed it up at the back of the stonework. You dug out the towpath to get to the back. Well, we used to steam the timbers in that box to make them pliable so we could pull them round to fit the stonework.

The towpath through bridges on the Birmingham & Liverpool Junction section of the Shropshire Union canal system is protected by a wooden fender with an iron guard

'We used to make all the wheelbarrows and that, when the mud boats were working: navvy barrows for the bricklayers and the mud barrows. That was my job when I started, making wheelbarrows. The mud barrows were big, deep ones with wide handles, the navvy barrows had only little sides for a bit of sand or some bricks, like an ordinary barrow. Then we had timber trucks and trolleys: we did all the wheels for them and the iron hoops round them. George Hanson did them, and a bit of welding in the blacksmith's shop. I had to strike for him with the sledge hammer. It *was* hot in there, and he used to call me all sorts of names! We could do most of the jobs there until they started to take the work to Northwich. When young Mr Lloyd came he had more modern equipment for a lot of it, and he set a lot more men on. He had no end of men on, fifty or sixty at one time. He hired and fired.'

The control of manning levels and decisions about what work was necessary to keep the canal in good order were more localised before nationalisation than they are now. And whilst motor transport was available centrally to the major workshops, this was slow to reach local section depots. Before such luxuries arrived, the men's concept of a reasonable journey to work was totally different to the door-to-door service they expect now.

'We had a company lorry at Norbury, after the war. Frances and I were living at Aqualate, near Newport, then. I used to bike from there about half past five in the morning and be at Norbury for six. We used to go to Audlem then, six o'clock in the morning, and Cecil Debney would drop us off; then he'd come back in the afternoon and pick us up.' Frances recalls that, 'They didn't have the lorry, you know, until the Germans were prisoners, during the war. The waterways men complained, saying that if the prisoners could have a lorry to take them about the place, so could the men! That was while you were away in the war.'

'That's right, we didn't have a company lorry at first, they hired the coal merchant's, Jack Parr's. He kept the pub at the junction and ran a coal boat for his business. His brother Tom Parr used to fetch the coal from up Penkridge way, Lyttleton Colliery probably; they'd one of those deep-sided coal boats and a horse. He used to bring it like that and unload it onto the wharf. That was used until the pleasure boats took over the whole of that side. Cecil Debney used to work for Jack Parr before he came on the company and it was his dad, Bill, that was the bricklayer.

'When I started I was apprentice with the carpenters; there was two carpenters in those days, and we went further on Norbury section than they do now: we went down to Nantwich, and right back up to Autherley Junction the other way, and we also had the Shrewsbury Canal, right down to Shrewsbury. So we could be anywhere. But we used to go to Tyrley, mainly because there was a carpenter, Bob Williams, at Audlem and he used to do Audlem Locks and Adderley. So if we were out to Tyrley or anywhere we used to be on the old push-bike, you know – and in those days we used to start at half-past seven and work till five. Then there was Saturday morning; we used to start at half-past seven and worked till twelve.

'Sometimes we used to go the other way, to Autherley Junction. Old Sam Lomas was toll keeper, with his office and that, there. You had to be at Autherley Junction on time because Mr Lloyd (that's the older one, G.T. Lloyd) used to ring up at just gone half-past seven – he would have the excuse that he wanted to speak to the carpenter who I was working with.

'Of course, Mr Lloyd used to get around a lot himself. He used to travel by train and his old bike, and many a time I had to take his bike, when I was at Norbury, to Gnosall station. He might walk down and catch the train say to Shrewsbury, and then I'd have to take his bike and meet him coming back. It was some while before he had a little car, but he did have one eventually, towards the end of Mr G.T. Lloyd's time. Then the company had one, perhaps getting into the late forties, that.

'When I started, the company didn't have any vehicles at all, and as a result you had a job getting materials. If you wanted to repair anything, a window, or a gate or anything, you had to measure everything very carefully, and then the order had to go to Crewe. The materials came back in bits and drabs for each job, you know. It'd come to Gnosall, or Newport station. Then it was delivered by the railway people, because they used to have lorries. A lot of the bulk stuff used to go to Calverley, and the company boats used to go down there for it. All the sand and gravel and that sort of thing was fetched from there. The chaps on those boats used to live on them originally so it made no difference where they were. But eventually they had houses as well. Hugh Williams went in the lock house at Wheaton Aston, and Jack Watkin had a house at the junction; but they really lived on the boats and just came home when they were back from trips and the like.

'When the war was on I joined up, in November 1940, so I didn't finish my apprenticeship. After the war I came back, in 1945, and they took me on as a carpenter although I hadn't really finished doing my time. I was on the lowest rate, of course – which was *nothing* in those days! We used to have to scratch. Frances and I had got married when I was in the army and the housing was terrible then. The first home we had was a round army Nissen hut which Stafford Council had set up, at Aqualate, just on the Stafford Road out of Newport. That was our first home – but eventually we had No 8 at Norbury Junction which was next door to my people. Just a few doors away was my wife's family. I was back at Norbury as a carpenter until 1955.

'There were lengthmen about every two-and-a-half or three mile when I first came to Norbury. There were men that worked in the clay hole at Grub Street; they had a little rail track made out to the canal so they could wheel the clay to the boats and then tip it in. There

Norbury Yard in the 1960s with Parrot *and* Uranus *tied at the maintenance yard on their way from Weston Point to Birmingham with aluminium. Behind the boats a pile of coal awaits consumption in the boiler house. Pleasure craft have taken over the warehouse and wharf in the left background. The Section Inspector's house*, Ferndale, *is just visible behind the fuel tank* (Mike Webb)

were three bricklayers and then labourers, a boilerman to look after the steam engine at the workshops, and a sawyer. Blacksmiths were just finished when I went there, although the smith's shop and all that was still there; then they'd strikers to work with him. Oh, I would think there'd be more than a couple of dozen.

'If they were working locally, everybody would be in on a Monday morning, in the shop at Norbury – where the Shropshire Union hire boat people are now. There'd be bricklayers, bricklayers' labourers, us carpenters, painters, the clay-hole men, yardmen and some of the local lengthsmen. They'd all be lined up in the shop there and the old man would come out, old Mr Lloyd, with his list of work, and he would call on everybody and detail everybody.

A view down Audlem Locks at stoppage time; with the nearer lock dewatered for the bricklayers, the carpenters can replace gates further down the flight

He'd tell the two or three from the clay hole how many boats they'd got coming for clay (the boat men would be there as well) and he'd detail them off and they'd go off to walk down to the hole. Then he'd come perhaps to the bricklayers, and give them their work for the week, they'd perhaps have to go out, so off they'd go on their bikes, perhaps to Wheaton Aston, or the other way to Tyrley Cutting. They used to have to do a lot of work down there. Then he'd come to the carpenters, and so the yard men, and the boy.

'The gates were all made at Ellesmere by that time, and they used to have to fetch them in a company boat, then. It changed over to Northwich when British Waterways was set up; they used to bring them out by road from there. Ellesmere did have lorries, and if they came on one of them they had to come to Norbury. We only had craneage at Norbury; you didn't have road cranes then. Sometimes when they came round in the company boat they could stop on the boat, and then they'd be unloaded straight off at the lock they were to fit and they could take the old gates out and put them straight into the boat. The old ones used to come back to Norbury for breaking up. All the ironwork was kept and it went back to be re-used. We fitted all the gates. If we needed more help sometimes they'd come out from Ellesmere, if we had a lot of gates to fit. They would do certain locks and we'd do some.

'In those days the stoppages were always Whitsuntide holiday time. Other areas would have other times so that if the Shropshire Union was shut the traffic could go by the Trent & Mersey, for example. It was always Whitsun for Norbury. There might be two or three jobs on at that time. For example the bricklayers might be working at Tyrley, or doing a lockside somewhere. Otherwise the carpenters could be in Audlem, with the bricklayers being further down that flight at the same time. You spaced them out a bit so that the water could bypass the jobs and you wouldn't get flooded out. You wouldn't work in every lock. In modern times they tried to do locks adjacent to one another and somebody'd be flooded out. The men used to lodge Whit week until the work was done; they'd lodge with the local canalmen and they'd work long hours. They'd start at six o'clock and work on when the nights were light.

'I wasn't allowed to do that when I was an apprentice. At that time, before I went in the army, we did those stop gates by Boulton & Paul's aircraft factory at Pendeford – the carpenters went out early in the morning but they wouldn't let me start till half-past seven. They stuck to the rules in those days.

'Otherwise, when I was an apprentice and everybody was away, lodging like that, I was usually found work in the shop. When the boss was there he used to keep his eye on me and come round and have a look at what I'd done and tell me if I'd made any mistakes. Everything had to be done right in those days or else you had to knock it apart!

'The dredging was all done by hand spoon, with three men on the boat. I used to make those, that was one of my first jobs, making the handles. It was an iron spoon, and they had different sizes of them. Then it had a long ash shaft and then a Tee handle on the end, two-and-a-half feet long probably. I used to have to make them and get them smooth and round, comfortable to use, sandpaper them and just leave a little nodule on the end to stop the hand slipping off. I used to have that job. And then to put the hooks on them and bolt through to fit them to the spoon. I also used to make the big stake, the big wooden shaft with a spike on the end as they used to have on the front of the boat. They used to stick it down into the mud to hold the boat out and then have a line into the bank to keep the boat steady. I used to repair the decks and planks for them to walk about the boat on. They used to dredge Norbury basin a lot then with that; they did Shebdon Wharf and Park Heath. They did that for

Engineering Spot

Etruria

Etruria stands on the Trent & Mersey Canal in the busy city of Stoke-on-Trent in North Staffordshire. At this point is the junction with the Caldon Branch and the base of the Potteries Section.

Section Inspector Jim Bailey, who is in charge of the forty miles of the Potteries Section and 14 miles of feeders, has 46 on his staff, among them carpenters, bricklayers, painters, excavator drivers and labourers.

Equipment on the section, including that at the Red Bull District Office, comprises: Hamster hydraulic dredger, drop-hammer piling rig, excavator, bantam motor-tug and four motor-boats.

Most of the work of the Etruria Section is outside; and with 53 double and single locks, the $1\frac{3}{4}$-mile long Harecastle tunnel, and a big piling and lock renewal programme, plus the reservoirs at Rudyard, Stanley and Knypersley, it's a busy job. Last year they put in over a mile of concrete piling on the section, and dredged about 30,000 tons.

Traffic on this Section of the Trent & Mersey is mainly coal, and pottery materials such as china clay, flints, felspar and china stone. Though not heavy, traffic is up by about ten per cent on last year – an encouraging sign. And pleasure-boating is on the up and up.

In the picture strip: Section Inspector Jim Bailey; Length Foreman Albert Arrowsmith, Red Bull length; Length Foreman Bill Dean, Trentham-Caldon length; Dredger Captain George Smallwood; and Water Controlman Ted Parrish.

The men of Etruria Yard made the back page feature in British Waterways' house magazine Waterways *January 1961 issue* (Author's collection)

Cadbury's because they used to come with a motor boat and often four butties behind. They used to bring the coal to the works at Knighton, and you should've seen the barrows they had! We thought ours were big, but theirs had tremendous high sides, you know.

'You didn't get a lot of money in those days, but I think everybody was a lot more satisfied than people are today on the whole. It has always been a good job but not very well paid. I think they're very well paid, today!

'After the war I was carpenter and had to do everything, lock cills, gates and all the lot. In particular Tyrley cutting had a lot of fences and gates round about because the company own the land outside the cutting there. We used to have to put the posts in and then hang the gates and put all the furniture on them. We took one of the bridges down below Nantwich, the other carpenter and meself. The old Blue Bridge it was, which was a wooden-topped bridge. There's only the abutments there now. You used to get quite a variation of jobs then.

'We did repairs at the cottage beyond there as well: we did the roof there, and we used to do all the laths and the end rafters and that sort of thing then. We used to get a lot of odd jobs in between wood-working ones. One job we used to hate coming was when George Lloyd started concrete walling. When the concrete gang was working away from Norbury the cement and that used to all come to the yard. Where the Shropshire Union Cruisers shop is now we used to put the cement in the warehouse there. It used to come by lorryloads, and it would be red hot when it came. Of course the only people in the shop when it came were carpenters, so all of you had to turn out and go across there and unload this cement – all by hand on your shoulders. And of course if one burst it'd stick all over you, mad hot! Those were jobs we didn't used to like, but you were the only ones there, so you had to do it. When loads of timber and that come, well, that was our job so we had to unload that as well. That came by lorryloads when British Transport and then British Waterways took it over, in the fifties and sixties.

'In 1955 I went from Norbury and up to Etruria, in the Potteries, on the Trent & Mersey; we went to live on the Caldon Canal at Planet Lock. It was a very damp place. We were in it for fifteen years, from 1955 to 1970. It was handy for the school and college and so on, for the children, but it was noisy, with the buses over the bridge there shaking the house. The pot banks made it very dirty.

'I went up there as chargehand carpenter and worked from Harecastle Tunnel, this south side, down to Trentham and up the Caldon, down to Leek and Froghall. But when there were stoppages I used to have to go down to Middlewich, as far as King's Lock or Rump's Lock. We had that depot at Etruria and there were four other carpenters, but two of them worked mostly at Red Bull. They used to do the general repairs down from Red Bull, but if there were stoppages and that down there, then we would all be down there, you see. I had to decide most of what needed doing and put it up, through the Section Inspector. I'd put it to him and then he would okay it, whether we would go ahead with any particular gates and what we would repair or renew. I would have to order the timber, and then again that would have to go through him. I would measure for repairs and so on, but not for new gates. When Northwich took over making them they would come and measure for the new gates and that was their responsibility. Orders from the Section Inspector used to have to go to Northwich to the area office in those days, everything was ordered through there.

'We did a lot of work on the reservoirs, especially Stanley Pool. That was a very complicated one. We had to empty that to attend to the valves. There was an old man there who was the top end ganger, Alf Shaw, and he was the man as knew all the workings at Stanley Pool. You can't beat the old ones for finding out things like that! It was quite complicated because there's a lower pool, which feeds the mill, as well as the main one. We wouldn't have known, us carpenters, what all the workings was, only for Alf Shaw telling us. You had to drain the lower pool and then there's a big stone tunnel which goes under the dam, to the main valve. They used to call it "Big Ben", that was the main one, on the dam – a big round well-hole. You used to go up some steps and through this arched way, and then you came to a big pipe, and on the end of that was a big wooden valve, almost like a lock paddle which hinged up – you could open that up and it would take you into the well-hole where you could get at the valves. All that'd be under water when the bottom pool was full. At the time I went up there the top, main reservoir was empty because they were doing a survey on it, so you could get at all these valve chambers. I think it's the only time a lot of people have seen that right empty.

'I can remember doing the other valve on that dam. Mr Freeman was the engineer. He became Area Engineer at Wigan, he was doing this survey. At the time there was an old bricklayer on Trent & Mersey, Albert Arrowsmith, and he was working there, and Mr Jim Bailey, he was my Section Inspector, and Albert's, too. Anyway, Freeman was doing this survey and he'd done the big well and he wanted to go down this small one, but it was getting late in the afternoon. They put some small sheerlegs up and Mr Bailey put a rope round Mr Freeman, fixed it round him, and he'd to be lowered down this small well. He kept messing about with his papers and doing his calculations and one thing and another. And Albert kept on to him, saying "If you don't go down there you're going to be left down that well-hole, because," he said, "you see the time. We've got to go and catch our bus." The bus went from the bottom of the lane at a certain time – you see, they came from Kidsgrove. Anyway, they lowered him down this well-hole and he was down there tinkering about. Albert kept looking at his watch and the other chaps as were from Red Bull, and he kept shouting down to Freeman, "Are you coming up? If you don't come up you're going to be left down there!" Anyway Albert, he says to Mr Bailey, "We're going!" They got their bags and away they went. That left only Mr Bailey and meself and Ernie Johnson the reservoir keeper, and Freeman was still down the well-hole; we had to get him up. Albert said to Freeman next day, "I told you I should leave you!" Albert Arrowsmith, he was a character. Mr Marsh was the manager of all our region and Albert used to talk to him just the same as he talked to us, and his language and that ... ooh! Every other word was a swear, and Mr Marsh only used to laugh at him.

'I worked quite a lot at Red Bull, but I didn't like working there very much. It was an old warehouse with a very low roof in the workshop because it had three floors in it. There was an office on the first floor. But we had one of those portable diesel saws, and it used to be terrible working in there with the sawdust and the fumes. It'd get so you couldn't see people in there. There was all electric at Etruria and the ceilings were high because they used to make lock gates there at one time.

'Then in the mid-sixties I was made foreman on the same area. I used to be in charge of all the people out on the section and have to do their work plans for the whole year, and then see that they had all the material they needed, and tools and so on. Then there were the blokes' time-sheets to check and make up and take in the office for the Thursday pay-day. Friday I used to do most of my paperwork.

'I got the job as section inspector at Norbury in February 1969. I had to travel until the

May, from the Potteries; I had a little van on the company. I was there until I finished in 1987 – that was a change from being there as carpenter! I should have gone to Chester – there was a vacancy at Chester: I applied for Jack Venables' job when he finished and I got that. But then I was at Northwich one day and someone told me the inspector at Norbury had passed away, and so there was a vacancy there. I had to apply for Norbury and be interviewed again, and I managed to get it, like. There were a lot of old hands that I'd worked with before, and I had some problems, but we overcame them; besides, I had a good insight into what I was letting myself in for because I used to stand in if ever Mr Bailey was off when I was at the Potteries.

'We lived at *Ferndale* when we went back to Norbury from the Potteries in 1970; we were there ten years, and then we moved to Newport. By then, all the budgets and that sort of thing was beginning to come in, and you had to do all the work programme for the year. But you didn't have to handle any money, only the petty cash. Of course we didn't have any office clerks in those days, so you had to do all that with your foreman. Frances was my telephone operator. When you went out you could switch the telephone from the office across to the house, and if there were any calls she used to take them – unpaid, like. But sometimes there'd be nobody in the yard. Perhaps just the carpenter, Stanley, he would answer the phone if he was in. Frances used to get quite a lot of abuse, didn't you, dear?'

'I certainly did, off one lady in particular. She was a farmer along by the canal, and she was an old battle-axe!' Bill remembers her too:

'The fishermen used to get behind her hedge and do things they shouldn't do! Anything like that she used to ring us up and complain; and then she got a leak. Our water was in her field. She was a regular. She used to say to me, "I'll ring Liverpool!" – and I'd say, "You go ahead and ring Liverpool then!" Because of course by then the area office was at Northwich!

'She did have one or two leaks, but whilst I was at Norbury we did a tremendous lot of steel piling and that cut out a lot of those leaks. Hers was one we stopped, along the valley there; we piled along there, and back-filled with clay. She still used to complain, but a lot of the trouble after that was her drains, you know, they were blocked. I sent a chap down to have a look, and he found her drains were blocked; so he rodded them all and cleared them all out. She rang me up just after and was complaining as usual, and I said, "Well, Mrs, I'm afraid I shall have to send you a bill because my man's had to rod all your drains and that out," I said, "even down the fields to get rid of that water." Well, she told me then what she thought about me!

Before Bill Dean's piling programme the towpath of the Shropshire Union Canal had been eroded away by motor boat wash in many places

'But that was only one. You know, we had a lot of places where the motor boats had washed the towpath in – there were places where the water was right back to the banks in the cuttings. But by the time I retired from Norbury we'd done them all, right from the top end at

Autherley; we did all down through Betton Wood at Market Drayton and at Adderley – down there they were washed away completely. We piled all the way through there and then back-filled 'em. By the time I finished in 1987 I'd say you could walk right through from Audlem to Autherley Junction on a good footpath.

'You see, we were allowed so much money each year, and I spent more or less all the allocation as I had on steel piles. I got told off a time or two because I was piling places I shouldn't be. We had an engineer, he came to Norbury and he said I'd piled in places where there was no need to pile. They were places where there were no towpath at all, that I'd piled; then we'd back-filled with dredgings to make the path – instead of boating the dredgings to the tip, the dredger had put a lot straight behind the pilings to back-fill. But I reckon we did a good job! I've got a note somewhere … here, see, from 1969 to the end of 1984 we drove 67,203 steel piles and dredged 341,534 tons.

'It was up to the different Section Inspectors what they spent their allocation on. Different ones spent it on different things, some might spend it on the lock gates, but the majority of mine went on the steel piles. We still did almost all the lock gates in my time at Norbury.

'We had the odd problem to deal with as well. The first one of mine, when I hadn't been there all that long, was Lapley slip, in Lapley Cutting above Wheaton Aston. I'd seen it happen before. When Mr Lloyd senior was on at Norbury, he had a slip then which brought all the offside down at Lapley. It was more or less in the same place – the big trees brought it down. I was out on the section with Mr Hyde, the water engineer; we were up at Autherley Junction, and the foreman came, and said, "The water's going over Stretton Aqueduct, onto

The diesel dredger cleared the Lapley Cutting slip of 1970

the A5, we think there's something happened in Lapley or somewhere down there." So we went down to Lapley, and the water was up to the level of the towpath at Stretton. There's a valve on the offside there, so we went and had to lift this valve. There were restrictions at that time of day as to which valves you could lift because there was an injunction to stop us using some of them – but of course this was an emergency, so we ignored it! You see, that injunction started when the British Transport Commission began to take the water from the sewerage works at Wolverhampton; when you used to go down Tyrley locks and Audlem Locks you couldn't see your boat for foam – the boats used to be covered in that foam. Well, they didn't want that water in the Penk so there was a restriction put on. Of course in later years it's been lifted because the water has improved such a lot, and you can use the valves now.

'So anyway we had to lift that valve at Stretton, and then we went to the sewerage works to tell them to shut the water off, and to tell the chap at Autherley Junction to stop the traffic until we had found out what had happened. Anyhow, when we got into Lapley Cutting, we found it had all come down again, trees and all – there were ash trees as you could hardly get your arms around. They had all come from the offside and they were up on the towpath side; they'd all covered up the towpath completely. I said, "Well, what I'm going to do is get the dredger up here." One or two people said to me "You mustn't dredge it, you mustn't dredge it! If you dredge it out you'll have all that bank down from the other side." But I thought that was the only way, it had to come out. So we got the dredger and we dug a way through by pushing some onto the towpath until we got through. Ernie Thomas come down in the meantime, from Hatherton there; he'd had one of the biggest carrying businesses round the Black

Barrow runs were used to clear the previous Lapley slip in the late 1930s, a scene the canal's builders of 120 years before would have recognised instantly

Country, and when the trade started to fall away he set up a marina and club at Hatherton, on the Staffs & Worcs. His hire boats would be waiting. "Ooh," he says, "you'll have a mess!" Anyway, we dug a way through, and I think it was two days from the fall when we let the boats through. We had the dredging boats there, and we dredged it all out, and as it came down the bank we dredged that out, too. But I couldn't see any other way for it. Steve Platt, who was my Area Inspector, came out from Northwich and he says, "You're the bloke here," he says, "you do what you think best. Get on with it." We got the boats through all right, and Ernie Thomas's – some of them tied up there didn't think they'd be through for weeks, you know, but it was about forty-eight hours.

'It was wet that brought that down. There's a lot of water drains down that bank. There's a gutter along at the top and it's sandy, and the water gets through. It's always gone in that one place. As I say, Mr G.T. Lloyd had one there. Of course, it was all hand work then. I had to work on that; they only had the old hand-spoon dredger then. We had the water out then and it had to be wheeled out in barrows up planks put over trestles, and got out like that. Mr Lloyd died at Christmas 1947 so it was before that, but I think it was before I went in the army.

'I had thirty-five men on, including the two foremen, when I went to Norbury. But in later years it dropped down to about twenty-eight or twenty-nine.

'Somebody walked the whole length every week. Certain people had a certain length. They had cards that they had to make up as a record of what they'd seen, that they'd looked up the culverts and any leaks they'd found in the banks or anything. They'd to make sure all the valves were in working order and everything. Then the foreman would go out, with his book, and look at any works that he thought wanted to go onto the programme. He would put them on a card in a rack in the office to whatever priority we thought it was. Of course, a high priority would go towards the top, you see. Then we used to go by boat. I used to go, and the Area Inspector would come, and the Assistant Area Engineer, and we used to walk more than ride on the boat; usually from Gailey to Wheaton Aston the first day, then to Norbury, and from Norbury to Tyrley and Tyrley to Audlem. So we'd check all the paddles, and valves, culverts and all the locks and the workings there.'

Bill is slow to criticise the changing methods applied to the pleasure boat waterway half a century after he learnt the ways of a transport artery. But like many, he is clearly uncertain of the wisdom of looking after a series of 200-year-old structures by travelling from place to place in a transit van. The managers and engineering supervisors who now look after our waterways have many other considerations, namely of budgets, property development and of maximising grant aid from central government and local authorities, and it is often a disappointment to old hands that these appear to take priority over getting the boats through.

Bill and Frances Dean are the rarities amongst those featured in this book in that they live several miles from navigable water, and that they obviously enjoy their quiet retirement bungalow, happy to leave such concerns to others.

GLOSSARY

of selected waterway and boating terms

Barge: an inland, cargo-carrying vessel of more than 14ft beam.
Bowhauling: pulling a boat by manpower. So called because a loop, or bow, was sometimes put in the end of the long line used (not because of the term for the front of a boat).
Butty: related to the modern American word 'buddy'. An unpowered narrowboat, often previously horse-drawn, which is used as a trailer to a steam- or motordriven narrowboat, thus more than doubling the possible cargo capacity.
Bywash: the channel, or culvert, which allows excess water from further up the canal to pass round a lock to the lower pound.
Change boat: a boat kept at the boat repair yard, or dock, for use by crews whose regular craft was under repair.
Cheshire Locks: the twenty-six locks on the Trent & Mersey Canal, most of which are duplicated with two chambers side by side, forming the climb from the Cheshire Plain at Wheelock to the northern portal of Harecastle Tunnel at Kidsgrove.
Company, the: the canal company or navigation authority.
Downgater: a vessel heading downstream, or descending locks; especially in the north-east (hence 'upgate').

'ellum

Down the North: the canals north of Birmingham are always considered to be 'down' by those who have never seen a map, because the locks fall northwards to the Mersey.
Dredger: a boat equipped with machinery, which may be hand-operated, for deepening the navigation channel.
Ebb, the: outgoing, or falling tide; the opposite of 'flood'.
'ellum: the wooden rudder of a horse-drawn narrowboat or butty.
Flat: a regional term for a barge (sailing or horse-drawn) common in the Mersey basin and along the north-west coast of England.
Flood, the: incoming tide, the opposite of 'ebb'.
Flush: a sudden surge of water along the channel of a canal created by emptying a lock.
Grand Unioning: working for the Grand Union Canal Carrying Co's expanding fleet of craft which were built between 1934 and 1937.
Horse marine: a man who offers himself and his horse for hire as a towage contractor to sailing barge owners on north-eastern canals.
Ice boat: a small, strongly built boat used to break a channel through ice.
Inside: the towpath side of the canal.
Keel: bluff, square-sailed, flat-bottomed barge built in many varieties for trade along the east coast and in specific sizes to fit the locks of north-eastern inland waterways. Many later converted to, or built for, motor propulsion.
Outside/offside: the side of the canal opposite the towpath.
Narrowboat: a vessel, usually about 70ft in length which does not exceed 7ft 2in in the beam, common on the Midlands canals.
Neap tides: the lowest tides of the fortnightly sequence, caused by the gravitational pull of

the sun and moon acting in opposition on the water bodies of the earth's surface. The opposite of spring tides. Hence 'neaped': to be stranded or delayed through lack of water in a tidal navigation.

Pound: a level length of canal between two locks.

Puddle clay: noun or verb. To mix clay and water, driving out all the air, in order to form a waterproof lining for a canal.

Round up: to turn a vessel to face bow up into a current or tidal flow, thus allowing better control of her movements.

Semi-diesel: an internal combustion engine burning diesel fuel oil which is started by preheating a part of the cylinder head to almost red-heat. It continues to fire by virtue of the fact that the cylinder-head heat is maintained by the repeated ignitions, as opposed to solely by the compression of fuel/air as in a modern 'full' diesel engine.

shaft

Shaft: a wooden pole, often tipped with a hook, used for moving a boat without power. Hence the verb 'to shaft'.

Spring tide: the highest tides of the fortnightly sequence, caused by the gravitational pull of the sun and moon acting together on the water bodies of the earth's surface. The opposite of 'neap' tides.

Starn: usually of narrowboats, the stern or rear of the boat. The opposite to the **fore end**, which would usually be referred to as the 'bow' on other craft.

Stem, to: to run into, or collide with. To **stem up** is to run aground.

Stoppage: closure to navigation for the duration of repairs or maintenance works.

Stop plank: strong baulk of timber, often with several others, which can be inserted into grooves provided on either side of a water channel to form a temporary dam. Often used to seal off a section of canal or a lock which can then be drained for maintenance purposes. Also used to halt the flow of water into a damaged section of canal from which it would escape.

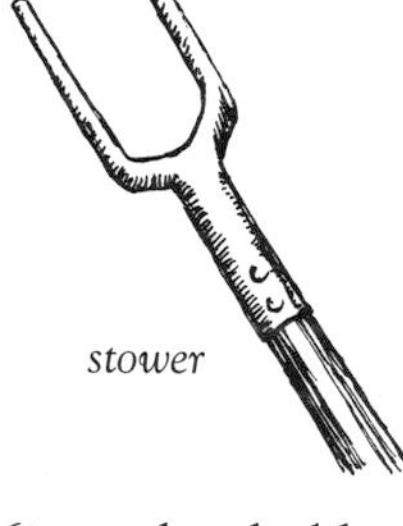

stower

Stower: a long pole with an iron spike (sometimes forked) at one end used to hold a boat in position: the spike is driven into the river bed and the upper part of the shaft is lashed to a bollard on board.

timberhead

Timberhead: a bollard or mooring bit on a boat or barge which is formed from an extension of one of the frames of the vessel.

Trent pan: horse-drawn barges up to 82ft 6in x 14ft 6in with a hold 5ft 3in deep. Slightly smaller 'Nottingham pans' limited to 72ft in length were in use before the construction of the large Trent locks in the 1920s. Those of 72ft x 14ft were able to work on up the Grantham, Nottingham and Trent & Mersey canals or river Soar. Those of 82ft 6in x 14ft 6in, introduced after the river improvements of the 1920s described in Chapter 1, could load 100 tons on 5ft draft but were restricted to the main river and the Nottingham Canal.

Trow: [rhymes with crow] a river and estuary barge of the Severn basin, originally rigged for sailing or towed from the bank by gangs of men.

Upgater: *see* 'downgater'.

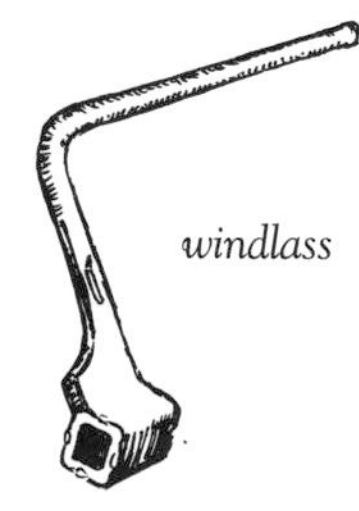

windlass

Winding (hole): verb or (noun) a wide place in the canal where a boat may be turned, so called because horse-drawn boats were turned with the use of the wind to save manual effort.

Windlass: the handle used to turn the drive spindle of the paddle gear on locks and so operate the sluice which allows water to enter or leave the chamber. Usually detachable and carried by the boatman.

ACKNOWLEDGEMENTS

Naturally this book could never have been written without those friends, old and new, whose recollections of life on our inland waterways form the major part of the text. I am most grateful to them for either putting up with the intrusion of a stranger into their homes or retelling stories they have recounted to me in the past. I hope they will enjoy reading their own words as much as I have enjoyed learning of times past on the waters I have only seen during the pleasure boating era. I hope, too, that I have managed to pass on some interesting snippets of history that might otherwise have been lost and that I have told their tales as they would have wished them to be told without introducing mistakes.

Thanks are also due to many people for their help and encouragement particularly Vanessa Wiggins of British Waterways and Tony Conder of the National Waterways Museum at Gloucester who must take some of the blame for getting me down to work on the project in the first place. Several librarians and archivists have cheerfully answered my obscure questions but Roy Jamieson of the British Waterways Archive at Gloucester and Lynn Doylerush at the Boat Museum at Ellesmere Port have been particularly helpful and welcoming. Both resisted my attempts to upset their ordered systems and have every file opened at once with interest and enthusiasm!

Of course such a book could not be produced without the painstaking and accurate work of Richard Dean whose knowledge of the geography of the canal system and ability to set it down on paper is unrivalled. Edward Paget-Tomlinson has managed to illustrate many obscurities which have evaded photographers or would have been impossible to photograph, as well as creating attractive historical scenes in their full colour glory.

I am grateful to Sue Hall and Sue Cleave of David & Charles for keeping me in order, enduring my concept of a schedule and grappling with the many complexities of canal life.

By no means least on the list of my debts is my wife Flip who has not only endured but encouraged the whole proceedings for over two years despite the abandonment of construction work on her kitchen cupboards in mid-stream. She has stepped around my linear living-room floor filing system and cheerfully travelled the country keeping me company and providing constant helpful criticism and encouragement when it was obvious to me that the whole job was quite impossible.

FURTHER READING

Cadbury, George and Dobbs, S.P. *Canals and Inland Waterways* (Pitman, 1929)

de Salis, Henry Rudolph. *Bradshaw's Canals & Navigable Rivers of England and Wales* (Henry Blacklock 1904; David & Charles Reprint 1969)

Faulkner, Alan. *The George and The Mary – A Brief History of the Grand Union Canal Carrying Co Ltd* (Robert Wilson, 1973)

Faulkner, Alan. FMC, *A Short History of Fellows Morton & Clayton Ltd* (Robert Wilson, 1975)

Faulkner, Alan. *Barlows* (Robert Wilson, 1986)

Hadfield, Charles. (series editor), various authors. *The Canals of the British Isles* series (David & Charles)

Hutton, Guthrie. The Crinan Canal – *Puffers & Paddle Steamers* (Richard Stenlake, Ochiltree, Ayrshire)

Langford, J. Ian. *Towpath Guide to the Staffordshire & Worcestershire Canal* (Goose & Son, 1974)

Lewery, Tony. *Flowers Afloat* (David & Charles, 1996)

Mallet, Hugh. *Bridgewater, The Canal Duke, 1736–1803* (Manchester University Press, 1977)

McDonald, Dan. *The Clyde Puffer* (Thomas & Lochar, 1994)

Nicholson's *OS Guides to the Waterways* (Nicholson and Ordnance Survey, 1983–97)

Paget-Tomlinson, Edward. *Britain's Canal & River Craft* (Moorland Publishing Co, 1979).

Paget-Tomlinson, Edward. *The Illustrated History of Canal & River Navigations* (Sheffield Academic Press, 1993).

Schofield, Fred. *Humber Keels & Keelmen* (Terence Dalton Ltd, Lavenham, 1988)

Smith, George. *Our Canal Population* (Houghton 1875, 1878; EP Publishing reprint 1974)

Taylor, Mike. *Memories of the Sheffield & South Yorkshire Navigation* (Yorkshire Waterway Publications, 1988)

Waterways World Magazine (published monthly by Waterways World Ltd, The Well House, High Street, Burton-on-Trent, Staffordshire DE14 1JQ)

Wilson, Robert. *Knobsticks* (Robert Wilson, 1974)

INDEX

Page numbers in *italics* indicate illustrations
Main references are in **bold** type and vessel names in *italic*

INDEX

40-926-1